Great War Modernists

Historicizing Modernism

Series Editors
Matthew Feldman, Professorial Fellow, Norwegian Study Centre, University of York, UK; and Erik Tonning, Professor of British Literature and Culture, University of Bergen, Norway
Associate Editor: Natasha Periyan, Lecturer in Literature, King's College London, UK

Editorial Board
Professor Chris Ackerley, Department of English, University of Otago, New Zealand;
Professor Ron Bush, St. John's College, University of Oxford, UK;
Dr Finn Fordham, Department of English, Royal Holloway, UK;
Professor Steven Matthews, Department of English, University of Reading, UK;
Dr Mark Nixon, Department of English, University of Reading, UK;
Professor Janet Wilson, University of Northampton, UK;
Santanu Das, University of Oxford, UK;
Nan Zhang, The University of Hong Kong, China; and
Kevin Andrew Riordan, Nanyang Technological University, Singapore

Historicizing Modernism challenges traditional literary interpretations by taking an empirical approach to modernist writing: a direct response to new documentary sources made available over the last decade.
Informed by archival research, and working beyond the usual European/American avant-garde 1900–1945 parameters, this series reassesses established readings of modernist writers by developing fresh views of intellectual contexts and working methods.

Series Titles
Arun Kolatkar and Literary Modernism in India, Laetitia Zecchini
British Literature and Classical Music, David Deutsch
Broadcasting in the Modernist Era, Matthew Feldman, Henry Mead and Erik Tonning
Charles Henri Ford, Alexander Howard
Chicago and the Making of American Modernism, Michelle E. Moore
Ezra Pound's Adams Cantos, David Ten Eyck
Ezra Pound and His Classical Sources, Jonathan Ullyot
Ezra Pound's Eriugena, Mark Byron
Ezra Pound's Washington Cantos and the Struggle for Light, Alec Marsh

Great War Modernisms and The New Age *Magazine*, Paul Jackson
Historical Modernisms, Jean-Michel Rabaté and Angeliki Spiropoulou
Historicizing Modernists, Edited by Matthew Feldman,
Anna Svendsen and Erik Tonning
James Joyce and Absolute Music, Michelle Witen
James Joyce and Catholicism, Chrissie Van Mierlo
James Joyce and Cultural Genetics, Wim Van Mierlo
Jean Rhys's Modernist Bearings and Experimental Aesthetics, Sue Thomas
John Kasper and Ezra Pound, Alec Marsh
Judith Wright and Emily Carr, Anne Collett and Dorothy Jones
Katherine Mansfield and Literary Modernism, Edited by Janet Wilson,
Gerri Kimber and Susan Reid
Late Modernism and the English Intelligencer, Alex Latter
The Life and Work of Thomas MacGreevy, Susan Schreibman
Literary Impressionism, Rebecca Bowler
Modern Manuscripts, Dirk Van Hulle
Modernism in Wonderland, Edited by John D. Morgenstern and Michelle Witen
Modernist Lives, Claire Battershill
The Politics of 1930s British Literature, Natasha Periyan
Reading Mina Loy's Autobiographies, Sandeep Parmar
Reframing Yeats, Charles Ivan Armstrong
Samuel Beckett and Arnold Geulincx, David Tucker
Samuel Beckett and the Bible, Iain Bailey
Samuel Beckett and Cinema, Anthony Paraskeva
Samuel Beckett and Experimental Psychology, Joshua Powell
Samuel Beckett's 'More Pricks than Kicks', John Pilling
Samuel Beckett's German Diaries 1936–1937, Mark Nixon
T. E. Hulme and the Ideological Politics of Early Modernism, Henry Mead
Virginia Woolf's Late Cultural Criticism, Alice Wood
Christian Modernism in an Age of Totalitarianism, Jonas Kurlberg
Samuel Beckett and Experimental Psychology, Joshua Powell
Samuel Beckett in Confinement, James Little
Katherine Mansfield: New Directions, Edited by Aimée Gasston,
Gerri Kimber and Janet Wilson
Modernist Wastes, Caroline Knighton
The Many Drafts of D.H. Lawrence, Elliott Morsia
Samuel Beckett and the Second World War, William Davies
Modernist Authorship and Transatlantic Periodical Culture, Amanda Sigler
James Joyce and Photography, Georgina Binnie-Wright

Great War Modernists

D.H. Lawrence, H.D. and Richard Aldington

Lee M. Jenkins

BLOOMSBURY ACADEMIC
LONDON • NEW YORK • OXFORD • NEW DELHI • SYDNEY

BLOOMSBURY ACADEMIC
Bloomsbury Publishing Plc, 50 Bedford Square, London, WC1B 3DP, UK
Bloomsbury Publishing Inc, 1359 Broadway, New York, NY 10018, USA
Bloomsbury Publishing Ireland, 29 Earlsfort Terrace, Dublin 2, D02 AY28, Ireland

BLOOMSBURY, BLOOMSBURY ACADEMIC and the Diana logo are
trademarks of Bloomsbury Publishing Plc

First published in Great Britain 2024
This paperback edition published 2026

Copyright © Lee M. Jenkins, 2024

Lee M. Jenkins has asserted her right under the Copyright, Designs and
Patents Act, 1988, to be identified as Author of this work.

For legal purposes the Acknowledgements on pp. x–xi constitute an
extension of this copyright page.

Cover design: Rebecca Heselton

All rights reserved. No part of this publication may be: i) reproduced or transmitted in any form, electronic or mechanical, including photocopying, recording or by means of any information storage or retrieval system without prior permission in writing from the publishers; or ii) used or reproduced in any way for the training, development or operation of artificial intelligence (AI) technologies, including generative AI technologies. The rights holders expressly reserve this publication from the text and data mining exception as per Article 4(3) of the Digital Single Market Directive (EU) 2019/790.

Bloomsbury Publishing Plc does not have any control over, or responsibility for, any
third-party websites referred to or in this book. All internet addresses given in this
book were correct at the time of going to press. The author and publisher regret
any inconvenience caused if addresses have changed or sites have ceased
to exist, but can accept no responsibility for any such changes.

A catalogue record for this book is available from the British Library.

Library of Congress Cataloging-in-Publication Data
Names: Jenkins, Lee M. (Lee Margaret), author.
Title: Great War modernists : D.H. Lawrence, H.D. and Richard Aldington / Lee M. Jenkins.
Description: London ; New York : Bloomsbury Academic, 2024. |
Series: Historicizing modernism | Includes bibliographical references and index.
Identifiers: LCCN 2023055273 (print) | LCCN 2023055274 (ebook) |
ISBN 9781350285330 (hardback) | ISBN 9781350285378 (paperback) |
ISBN 9781350285347 (pdf) | ISBN 9781350285354 (ebook)
Subjects: LCSH: World War, 1914–1918–Great Britain–Literature and the war. |
Modernism (Literature)–History. | English literature–20th century–History and
criticism. | Lawrence, D. H. (David Herbert), 1885–1930–Criticism and interpretation. |
H. D. (Hilda Doolittle), 1886–1961–Criticism and interpretation. |
Aldington, Richard, 1892–1962–Criticism and interpretation.
Classification: LCC PR478.W65 J46 2024 (print) | LCC PR478.W65 (ebook) |
DDC 820.9358–dc23/eng/20240301
LC record available at https://lccn.loc.gov/2023055273
LC ebook record available at https://lccn.loc.gov/2023055274

ISBN: HB: 978-1-3502-8533-0
PB: 978-1-3502-8537-8
ePDF: 978-1-3502-8534-7
eBook: 978-1-3502-8535-4

Series: Historicizing Modernism

Typeset by Integra Software Services Pvt. Ltd.

For product safety related questions contact productsafety@bloomsbury.com.

To find out more about our authors and books visit www.bloomsbury.com
and sign up for our newsletters.

Contents

List of illustrations	viii
Editorial preface to *Historicizing Modernism*	ix
Acknowledgements	x
List of abbreviations	xii
Introduction: Circling the square	1
1 Life studies: *Women in Love*, word portraits and the war	17
2 The house of fiction: The Mecklenburgh Square novels	45
3 Between the lines: Imagism and the Great War	75
4 Translation, global modernism and the Great War	109
Coda: Squaring the circle	139
Bibliography	148
Index	167

Illustrations

1 Mark Gertler, *The Creation of Eve* (1914)   27
2 Mark Gertler, *The Merry-Go-Round* (1916)   28
3 Mark Gertler, *Gilbert Cannan at His Mill* (1916)   37
4 Jacob Epstein, *Female Figure in Flenite* (1913)   67

Editorial preface to *Historicizing Modernism*

This book series is devoted to the analysis of late nineteenth- to twentieth- century literary modernism within its historical contexts. *Historicizing Modernism* therefore stresses empirical accuracy and the value of primary sources (such as letters, diaries, notes, drafts, marginalia or other archival materials) in developing monographs and edited collections on modernist literature. This may take a number of forms, such as manuscript study and genetic criticism, documenting interrelated historical contexts and ideas, and exploring biographical information. To date, no book series has fully laid claim to this interdisciplinary, source-based territory for modern literature. While the series addresses itself to a range of key authors, it also highlights the importance of non-canonical writers with a view to establishing broader intellectual genealogies of modernism. Furthermore, while the series is weighted towards the English-speaking world, studies of non-Anglophone modernists whose writings are open to fresh historical exploration are also included.

A key aim of the series is to reach beyond the familiar rhetoric of intellectual and artistic 'autonomy' employed by many modernists and their critical commentators. Such rhetorical moves can and should themselves be historically situated and reintegrated into the complex continuum of individual literary practices. It is our intent that the series' emphasis upon the contested self-definitions of modernist writers, thinkers and critics may, in turn, prompt various reconsiderations of the boundaries delimiting the concept 'modernism' itself. Indeed, the concept of 'historicizing' is itself debated across its volumes, and the series by no means discourages more theoretically informed approaches. On the contrary, the editors hope that the historical specificity encouraged by *Historicizing Modernism* may inspire a range of fundamental critiques along the way.

Matthew Feldman
Erik Tonning

Acknowledgements

This book is about creative collaboration, and I could not have completed it without the support of others. My thanks to: my colleagues and students at University College Cork, Lauren Arrington, Michael Bell, Catherine Brown, Lucy Collins, Claire Connolly, Patricia Coughlan, Gráinne Condon, Jane Costin, Santanu Das, Lara Feigel, Terry Gifford, Fiona Green, Annalise Grice, Edel Hanley, Chris Holifield, Donna Krolik Hollenberg, Megan Hultberg, Andrew Harrison, Holly A. Laird, Katy Loffman, Jonathan Long, Joanna Marston, Sean Matthews, Caitríona Ní Dhúill, Nanette Norris, Maureen O'Connor, Clíona Ó Gallchoir, Aisling O'Leary, Ian Patterson, Paul Poplawski, Eve Patten, Jahan Ramazani, Neil Roberts, Joseph Shafer and John Worthen.

I am grateful to the owner for permission to reproduce Mark Gertler's painting *The Creation of Eve* and to Sarah MacDougall at the Ben Uri Gallery for liaising with the owner on my behalf. My thanks to Lisa Cole and Fintan Ryan at the Tate Gallery and to Amy Taylor at the Ashmolean Museum for sourcing the other images reproduced in this book. Thanks, too, to the School of English and Digital Humanities and to the College of Arts, Celtic Studies and Social Sciences at University College Cork for subventions towards the cost of the colour illustrations.

I owe special thanks to Susan Reid, whose consummate skills as editor of the *Journal of D.H. Lawrence Studies* helped me in my first attempts to write about Great War modernism; to Andrew Frayn, for so generously sharing his scholarly expertise on Richard Aldington; to Christopher Pollnitz, for his superb textual scholarship and his consistent support of my own critical efforts; and to Melanie Otto, for her constant encouragement and for her insights into the intermedial modernism discussed in my first chapter.

I owe an immense debt of gratitude to Vivien Whelpton: for her own groundbreaking scholarship as Aldington's biographer, for her practical assistance and advice, and for her acute reading of parts of my book in draft.

My thanks, as always and for everything, to Alex Davis.

At Bloomsbury, I would like to thank my editor, Ben Doyle, for his support of this book from the outset and for his patience with me through the protracted process of writing it. I am grateful to the *Historicizing Modernism* Series Editors for their interest in my project and their advice and to the readers whose informed reports have helped me to shape the final version. Warm thanks, too, to the Bloomsbury team who have so ably assisted me at the various stages of writing and production: assistant editor Laura Cope, Joseph Skingsley, Peter Warren and Mandy Collison.

Extracts from the Cambridge Edition of the *Works of D.H. Lawrence* and *The Letters* are reproduced by kind permission of the Estate of Frieda Lawrence Ravagli and Cambridge University Press.

Extracts from the works of H.D. are reproduced by kind permission of the Literary Estate of H.D. Extracts from *Collected Poems 1912–1944*, *End to Torment*, *Pilate's Wife* and *Hippolytus Temporizes & Ion: Adaptations of Two Plays by Euripides* are reproduced by kind permission of New Directions; extracts from *Bid Me to Live* are reproduced by kind permission of the University Press of Florida; extracts from *Palimpsest* are reproduced by kind permission of Southern Illinois University Press; extracts from *Tribute to Freud* are reproduced by kind permission of Carcanet; extracts from *Asphodel* are reproduced by kind permission of Duke University Press; extracts from *Notes on Thought and Vision and The Wise Sappho* are reproduced by kind permission of City Lights; extracts from *Magic Mirror; Compassionate Friendship; Thorn Thicket: A Tribute to Erich Heydt* are reproduced by kind permission of ELS Editions.

Excerpts from Richard Aldington's prose and poetry are reproduced by kind permission of the Estate of Richard Aldington, c/o Rosica Colin Limited, London.

Abbreviations

D.H. Lawrence: Works

AR	*Aaron's Rod*, ed. Mara Kalnins. Cambridge: Cambridge University Press, 1988.
FWL	*The First 'Women in Love'*, ed. John Worthen and Lindeth Vasey. Cambridge: Cambridge University Press, 1998.
IR	*Introductions and Reviews*, ed. N.H. Reeve and John Worthen. Cambridge: Cambridge University Press, 2005.
K	*Kangaroo*, ed. Bruce Steele. Cambridge: Cambridge University Press, 1994.
LEA	*Late Essays and Articles*, ed. James T. Boulton. Cambridge: Cambridge University Press, 2004.
LP1	*The Poems. Volume I. Poems*, ed. Christopher Pollnitz. Cambridge: Cambridge University Press, 2013.
LP2	*The Poems. Volume II. Notes and Apparatus*, ed. Christopher Pollnitz. Cambridge: Cambridge University Press, 2013.
LP3	*The Poems. Volume III. Uncollected Poems and Early Versions*, ed. Christopher Pollnitz. Cambridge: Cambridge University Press, 2018.
R	*The Rainbow*, ed. Mark Kinkead-Weekes. Cambridge: Cambridge University Press, 1989.
SCAL	*Studies in Classic American Literature*, ed. Ezra Greenspan, Lindeth Vasey and John Worthen. Cambridge: Cambridge University Press, 2003.
STH	*Study of Thomas Hardy and Other Essays*, ed. Bruce Steele. Cambridge: Cambridge University Press, 1985.

WL	*Women in Love*, ed. David Farmer, John Worthen and Lindeth Vasey. Cambridge: Cambridge University Press, 1987.
WWRA	*The Woman Who Rose Away and Other Stories*, ed. Dieter Mehl and Christa Jansohn. Cambridge: Cambridge University Press, 1995.

D.H. Lawrence: Letters

L1	*Letters of D.H. Lawrence. Volume I, September 1901–May 1913*, ed. James T. Boulton. Cambridge: Cambridge University Press, 1979.
L2	*Letters of D.H. Lawrence. Volume II, June 1913–October 1916*, ed. George J. Zytaruk and James T. Boulton. Cambridge: Cambridge University Press, 1981.
L3	*Letters of D.H. Lawrence. Volume III, October 1916–June 1921*, ed. James T. Boulton and Andrew Robertson. Cambridge: Cambridge University Press, 1984.
L4	*Letters of D.H. Lawrence. Volume IV, June 1921–March 1924*, ed. Warren Roberts, James T. Boulton and Elizabeth Mansfield. Cambridge: Cambridge University Press, 1987.
L5	*Letters of D.H. Lawrence. Volume V, March 1924–March 1927*, ed. James T. Boulton and Lindeth Vasey. Cambridge: Cambridge University Press, 1989.
L6	*Letters of D.H. Lawrence. Volume VI, March 1927–November 1928*, ed. James T. Boulton and Margaret Boulton, with Gerald M. Lacy. Cambridge: Cambridge University Press, 1991.
L8	*Letters of D.H. Lawrence. Volume VIII, Previously Uncollected Letters and General Index*, ed. James T. Boulton. Cambridge: Cambridge University Press, 2000.

H.D.: Works

BML	*Bid Me to Live*, ed. Caroline Zilboorg. Gainesville: University Press of Florida, 2011.

CPHD   *Collected Poems 1912–1944*, ed. Louis L. Martz. New York: New Directions, 1983.

Richard Aldington: Works

CPRA   *The Complete Poems of Richard Aldington*. London: Allan Wingate, 1948.

DH   *Death of a Hero*. London: Hogarth Press, 1984.

Introduction

Circling the square

This book is about three modernist writers, D.H. Lawrence, H.D. and Richard Aldington, and their relationships, on and off the page, in the years of the Great War. All three wrote books about the others, each of these novels giving its own version of what went on when their authors came together (with significant others) at 44 Mecklenburgh Square in Bloomsbury in 1917, the year H.D.'s marriage to Aldington fell apart. Together, however, the Mecklenburgh Square novels – Lawrence's *Aaron's Rod*, H.D.'s *Bid Me to Live*, Aldington's *Death of a Hero* (and John Cournos' *Miranda Masters*) – form a closely interrelated cluster of fictions in which the ailing Aldington marriage is a casualty of and a metonym for the wider world-historical trauma of the war.

Lawrence's relationship with the American-born poet H.D. (Hilda Doolittle) and the English poet Aldington was formed in the avant-garde print circuits and friendship circles which fostered the arts in a wartime environment hostile to modernist innovation. H.D. and Aldington had met Lawrence on the eve of the war and his contact with them, individually and as a couple – H.D. and Aldington were married in 1913 – would continue through the war years. Lawrence and 'the Aldingtons' lived at close quarters in London in 1915 and again in 1917; otherwise their connection was carried on, long distance and into the war's long aftermath, in private letters and in the public forum of print. That their association was ad hoc, dictated by wartime contingencies, perhaps explains the curious lapse in collective critical attention – the more surprising since the group biography is now in vogue – to these three writers.[1] This book explores the nexus between Lawrence, H.D. and Aldington, three modernists who, read together, merit more than a combined footnote in literary history. Through their transactions, in print and in person, I argue, we can trace the changing contours of modernism in the years of the Great War and in its aftermath.

In the chapters that follow, on their fiction, poetry, and poetry in translation, Lawrence, H.D. and Aldington – two civilians and a soldier – are read as Great War modernists who write between the lines of modernist and First World War literature. Despite the detente in recent years between these camps and canons, a binary still obtains between modernist experiment and soldierly experience. Aldington, who was both a modernist and a soldier, receives a single, passing, mention in Paul Fussell's still-influential study of 1975, *The Great War and Modern Memory*, and with a few significant exceptions Aldington is as absent a presence in modernist studies as in First World War literary scholarship.[2] A verse revolutionary in the *avant-guerre* and then a war poet, whose first novel, *Death of a Hero*, published in 1929 at the height of the war books boom, had been a bestseller, Aldington has been excluded from modernist and First World War studies, each camp assuming that he writes under the false flag of the other.[3] If there is scant attention to Aldington in *The Great War and Modern Memory*, there is no reference to him at all in Vincent Sherry's 2003 study *The Great War and the Language of Modernism*, a response to Fussell's valorization of combatant literature in which the language of modernism is parsed as a civilian discourse: as a war of words, in which modernism's intellectual culture and aesthetic outflanks that of the canonical war poets, who may have been on the front line but whose verse remains in the late Romantic rearguard.[4] For Sherry the dissident language of modernism incubated in the war years comes to full term in the postwar high modernism of Pound, Eliot and Woolf. Where Sherry's study sidelines modernists such as Aldington who fought in the war, the New Modernist Studies has conscripted the war and all its works, granting no exemptions on formal and stylistic grounds to writing that hardly meets the stricter tests set by older paradigms: as Nanette Norris observes, in the 'expansionist stream of the New Modernist Studies, more and more work purports to be modernist' (Norris 2015c, 1).[5]

Modernism is not now the preserve of 'The Men of 1914', and combatant status is no longer required for entry into a war canon which has opened up to women and civilian writers and is more open-ended in its timeframe: H.D.'s *Trilogy* (1944–6) and Eliot's *Four Quartets* (1936–42) both come under the longer temporal purview of 'World War II' modernism.[6] Aldington, however – whether he is unread because he is, for the most part, out of print or whether he is out of print because he is unread – has been left out of the critical conversation, while Lawrence makes only a cameo appearance as a war poet in standard recent works in the field.[7] At the same time, Lawrence's standing as a modernist is still not secure: as the only poet to publish in the rival Georgian and

Imagist anthologies of the 1910s, Lawrence has long been suspected of having a foot in both these camps.

During the war Lawrence pitched his tent with his wife, Frieda, and, at times, with fellow writers and artists, packing up as and when he fell out with his friends or was ordered to move on by the military authorities. In the summer of 1914 Lawrence and Frieda had come back to England on a visit: with the declaration of war, they were unable to return to Italy, where they had been living in Lerici, and so they took a cottage near Chesham in Buckinghamshire, close to the novelist Gilbert Cannan's little arts colony at Cholesbury. *Women in Love* was conceived there, a novel completed in 1916–17 (in the midst of the period of war) but which, Lawrence explains in his foreword, 'does not concern the war itself' (*WL* 485). If it does not concern the war, *Women in Love* does concern Lawrence's life during wartime and the lives of the writers, artists and intellectuals he encountered in Cannan's Cholesbury circle. The war years, the period of his most profound isolation, also saw Lawrence's closest collaborations with his contemporaries, his affinities and fallings out with avant-garde writers and artists and with Bloomsbury group affiliates who moved in other, if sometimes intersecting, circles feeding into his experiments with a new formula for modern fiction. Lawrence's most radical novel, *Women in Love*, is an experiment in modernist 'life-writing', the mode that Max Saunders (after Stephen Reynolds) calls 'autobiografiction', a coinage which may be 'cumbersome' but does some heavy lifting in amalgamating the mutually allusive modes of autofiction, biofiction, autobiography and biography (Saunders 7).

Lawrence would continue the experiment he had begun in *Women in Love* in *Aaron's Rod*, the first of the Mecklenburgh Square novels. Published in 1922 and set in the immediate postwar period, *Aaron's Rod* nonetheless concerns the war and closely concerns the Aldingtons. 'It is impossible to more than gesture at the tangled lives of Hilda Doolittle, Richard Aldington and D.H. Lawrence (and John Cournos)' in the years of the Great War, Norris warns (2015b, 104). But the tangled lives of their authors are the autobiographical base materials of the Mecklenburgh Square novels, and so I will attempt a potted biography of this tangled mesh of modernists – H.D., Aldington, Lawrence (and Cournos) – before turning to the uses of biography in the Mecklenburgh Square novels themselves.[8]

Lawrence was introduced to H.D. and Aldington on 30 July 1914, five days before war was declared. The occasion was a dinner party hosted at the Berkeley Hotel in London by the American poet Amy Lowell, who was keen to recruit Lawrence to the ranks of the Imagist movement. Spearheaded in 1912 by Ezra

Pound, who had known H.D. in Philadelphia (where the two had been informally engaged), Imagism now had a new leader in Lowell, who had already won over to her side two of the original 'verse revolutionaries', H.D. and Aldington.[9] The connection between Lawrence and H.D. and Aldington, formalized in the annual *Some Imagist Poets* anthologies sponsored by Lowell, would develop when Lawrence and the Aldingtons lived as near neighbours in Hampstead in 1915. H.D. had given birth to a stillborn baby in the spring, a tragedy she attributed to war trauma, and she found a confidante in Lawrence, who would descend into his own wartime underworld that autumn when his novel *The Rainbow* was prosecuted for obscenity.[10] Lawrence retreated to Cornwall at the end of the year, where he would remain until his expulsion from the county in 1917. Lawrence, who had married his 'Hunwife' Frieda (née von Richthofen) in 1914, was now suspected of sleeping with the enemy in more than the biblical sense. On suspicion of signalling to enemy U-boats, the Lawrences were prohibited under the Defence of the Realm Act from entering coastal areas. Lawrence and Frieda came to London, where H.D. gave them temporary sanctuary in her Bloomsbury bedsit.[11]

H.D. and Aldington had taken rooms at 44 Mecklenburgh Square in February 1916 on the recommendation of their mutual friend, the Ukrainian-born Jewish-American writer and translator John Cournos. With Cournos in tow, H.D. and Aldington then decamped to Devon, staying there until June, when Aldington joined up together with his friend and fellow writer Carl Fallas, whose wife – Florence ('Flo') – had become Aldington's lover. Following his first tour of duty Aldington was sent in July 1917 for officer training to Whittington Barracks in Staffordshire. H.D. took lodgings in nearby Lichfield, making occasional visits to the Mecklenburgh Square studio flat she had sublet to Dorothy ('Arabella') Yorke, a young American fashion designer. Yorke, who had been Cournos' sometime fiancée, would become Aldington's lover by the end of the year. When the Lawrences arrived at 44 Mecklenburgh Square that autumn Yorke moved upstairs to Cournos' room in the attic storey he shared with 'munitionettes', young women working in munitions factories: Cournos himself, who had travelled with the Anglo-Soviet Commission to Petrograd, was stranded there amid the turmoil of the October Revolution. On his return to London, Cournos accused H.D. of encouraging Aldington's affair with Yorke. After the stillbirth of her baby daughter in 1915, H.D. had been advised by her doctors to abjure 'marital relations' for the duration of the war; Aldington, conversely, was experiencing a 'yearning of the flesh', which he ascribed to 'the soldier's mood'.[12] Following the surely inevitable breakdown of her marriage, H.D. left London for Cornwall with the musicologist Cecil Gray, a womanizing acquaintance of the Lawrences, with whom – and to Lawrence's evident disapproval – she conceived a child, Frances Perdita, who was born in 1919. As H.D. recalls in *Tribute to Freud*, Lawrence had told her in the 'last letter' she received from him that 'I hope never to see you again' (H.D. 1970, 134). In her sessions with him in Vienna in the 1930s, Freud advised H.D. to return to the novel she had begun in 1918 as a writing cure, a way of coming to terms both with Lawrence and with the traumatic events of the war years. That novel, *Bid Me to Live*, would come out in 1960, a year before H.D.'s death.

Published between 1922 and 1960, the Mecklenburgh Square novels postdate the autographic turn in modernist fiction taken during the war itself. The first chapter of my book locates the origins of 'real-life' fiction or modernist life-writing in fictional form in Lawrence's connection with the makeshift collective of writers and painters which had grown up, in the early months of the war, around Gilbert Cannan's converted windmill and Mill House at Cholesbury.[13] *Women in Love* was conceived there as 'a sequel to the *Rainbow*', which Lawrence was then revising. A sequel insofar as it takes up the generational narrative of *The Rainbow* but 'quite unlike it', *Women in Love* is also, if indirectly, a narrative of the war generation which reflects upon Lawrence's own quest for community in the midst of war (*L2* 606).

At Cholesbury in the Christmas of 1914 Lawrence, in collaboration with the Ukrainian-born translator S.S. Koteliansky, devised a scheme to found a little community or colony of like-minded friends to be called 'Rananim'. A pipe dream, Rananim would sustain Lawrence through the nightmare of the war years and into the postwar decade. Lawrence would co-opt H.D. and Cecil Gray as potential colonists in his 1917 iteration of a Rananim now to be situated, improbably, in the Andes. In 1916, when he was completing *Women in Love*, Lawrence had recruited John Middleton Murry and Katherine Mansfield to what would prove a short-lived experiment in communal living in Cornwall. Murry and Mansfield had been members of Cannan's Cholesbury circle: in 1914 Murry was working there on his autobiographical novel *Still Life* and Cannan on *Mendel*, a *roman à clef* closely based on the life of the painter Mark Gertler, who had set up a studio adjacent to Cannan's windmill. These two books, both published in 1916, provided Lawrence with negative models for the real-life fiction he would attempt in *Women in Love*. In Lawrence's opinion, Murry's literary *nature morte* was deadly dull and self-indulgent, and he dismissed Cannan's artist's book as 'journalism' – journalism of what we would now call the tabloid type: with its transcriptions of private conversations, Cannan's novel is the 1910s equivalent of phone tapping. 'If Gilbert had taken Gertler's story and *recreated* it into art, *good*. But to set down all these statements is a vulgarising of life itself', Lawrence complained (*L3* 35). Lawrence himself would recreate life into art in *Women in Love*, using as his materials both the life of Gertler the artist and Gertler's own artworks (specifically his 1916 painting, *The Merry-Go-Round*). Modernist life-writing, Saunders suggests, is intertextual; the close imbrication of the visual and the verbal arts in *Women in Love* shows that modernist life-writing is also intermedial.[14]

His criticisms of Cannan notwithstanding, Lawrence himself would be charged with violating the privacy of individuals on whom he modelled his fictional characters.[15] Bloomsbury *salonnière* Lady Ottoline Morrell, to whom Lawrence had been introduced at Cholesbury, objected to his portrait of her as Hermione Roddice in *Women in Love*, and Philip Heseltine, a composer and habitué of the bohemian *demi-monde*, threatened a libel suit against Lawrence for the double pen portrait of himself and his mistress – later his wife – Minnie Lucy Channing, nicknamed 'Puma', who was an artist's model. The two appear in *Women in Love* as Julius Halliday and Miss Darrington, aka 'the Pussum': 'Halliday is Heseltine, The Pussum is a model called the Puma, and they are taken from life', Lawrence told Catherine Carswell (*L3* 36). H.D. had read the novel in manuscript in 1917 before passing it on, to Lawrence's dismay, to Lady Ottoline and, despite her reservations about the merits of Lawrence's 'bulky' book, H.D.'s own writing engages *Women in Love* as an often-intimate intertext (*BML* 109). The protagonist of *Asphodel*, written in 1921–2, is Hermione Darrington, a portmanteau name combining Lawrence's Hermione Roddice and Minette Darrington. Like Lawrence's, H.D.'s Mrs Darrington is pregnant: 'Mrs. Darrington was a trench', H.D. tells us, and like H.D. herself, she gives birth to a dead baby in an experience as traumatic and deadly as that of going 'over the top' (H.D. 1992, 141, 192). From the early and unpublished *Asphodel* to her belated '*retour*' to the Great War and to Mecklenburgh Square in *Bid Me to Live*, H.D. weaves *Women in Love* into the 'web', the 'mesh of self', of her own autofictional prose (H.D. 1992, 104).[16]

The second chapter of my book moves, as Lawrence did in 1917, to H.D.'s Bloomsbury bedsit and to the Mecklenburgh Square novels. Francesca Wade's *Square Haunting* – a group study of five remarkable women who lived there in the First World War and between the wars – has marked Mecklenburgh Square as a woman's place on literary maps of the metropolis. Left out of A–Zs of bohemian London in the 1910s, Mecklenburgh Square, as Wade points out, was 'a radical address' in the first decades of the twentieth century (Wade 7).

The square itself (and the adjoining Mecklenburgh Street) was the home or workplace of H.D., Virginia Woolf, classical scholar Jane Harrison, historian Eileen Power and Dorothy L. Sayers, one of the queens of the golden age crime novel, who was embroiled in a non-sexual love affair with John Cournos when she rented H.D.'s old rooms in 1920.[17]

A blue plaque above the door of no. 44 tells us that 'H.D. (HILDA DOOLITTLE) POET AND WRITER LIVED HERE', but H.D. did not have a room of her own there, which is the prerequisite, Woolf insists, for the woman who wants to write. As H.D. puts it in *Bid Me to Live*, what with Aldington's comings and goings, the sudden arrival of internal refugees such as Lawrence and Frieda and the requisition of no. 44 by friends and fellow poets, 'The room was no longer her own' but 'a public highway' (*BML* 50). If there was traffic through no. 44, there is traffic, too, between the Mecklenburgh Square novels. 'You can write a book about us', the H.D. figure, Julia, tells the Lawrence figure, 'Rico', in *Bid Me to Live*: 'I wanted to help too', Julia says, 'only I didn't want a sort of family album. I wanted a book to myself and as things are, the threads are too tangled' (*BML* 105).[18] *Bid Me to Live* is the most successful of her serial attempts to tease out what she described in a postwar letter to Cournos as 'an old tangle', but her novel, to borrow H.D.'s own figures for her autofiction, is itself a thread in the wider web, a layer in the composite palimpsest of the Mecklenburgh Square novels (Hollenberg 147–8).

These books have been read as *romans à clef*, novels with a key to the coterie in which they are set. Sean Latham has commented on the 'viral' qualities of the modern and modernist *roman à clef*, noting that 1920s bestsellers such as Michael Arlen's *The Green Hat* (1924) 'transformed their authors into celebrities who were themselves often then parodied or ridiculed in an ever-expanding web' (Latham 15, 11). Arlen himself duly appears as 'Michaelis' in Lawrence's *Lady Chatterley's Lover* and Lawrence in turn is 'in' very many novels, the most recent of which at the time of writing, Alison MacLeod's *Tenderness* (2021), is described by its author as 'a "dialogue" across time' with *Lady Chatterley's Lover* (MacLeod 595). Like the *roman à clef* but in a more radical adjustment of the relationship of literature to lived experience, the Mecklenburgh Square novels flout the formalist pieties in granting real people entrée into the text, or texts: this is a house of fiction in which people pass through the paper-thin walls of one novel into another.

In *Bid Me to Live* and *Death of a Hero*, H.D. and Aldington are writing back to Lawrence writing them in the satirical sketches of *Aaron's Rod*. But in paying him back in autobiofictional kind, H.D.'s and Aldington's novels remain in debt to Lawrence, even as they contest his influence and example. In *Bid Me to Live*, H.D. refuses the binary of Lawrence's 'man-is-man, woman-is-woman' sexual fix or fixation (*BML* 35), but the close intertextual exchange between her writing and his also underlines Woolf's point in *A Room of One's Own* that 'Some collaboration has to take place in the mind between the woman and the man before the art of creation can be accomplished. Some marriage of opposites has to be consummated' (Woolf 1992a, 136). In the mythology subtending her novel's autobiographical narrative, Lawrence is Dis, the 'husband' to H.D.'s Persephone (*BML* 86). As Maureen McLane suggests, H.D.'s work 'offers its own highly-charged life-writing as mythopoesis' (n. pag.). The mythical 'marriage' between H.D. and Lawrence would not be consummated in the flesh: Janice Robinson's biography of H.D. is a monitory example of how an overdetermined biographical reading yields false positives (Robinson wrongly proposes that Lawrence, not Cecil Gray, was the father of H.D.'s daughter). At the same time, however, a formalist method, according to which any biographical reading is a fallacy, is an ineffectual approach to H.D.'s autofiction, a body of work in which the author interprets her life through her (life-)writing.

Aldington's response to Lawrence and to *Aaron's Rod* is to up the satirical ante: my chapter reads *Death of a Hero* as total satire, a bitter indictment of total war and of the world that brought the war about. Even as he stresses the experiential distance between the home front and the fighting front, Aldington elides the difference between the marital strife of civilian life and soldierly combat:

> How curious are cities, with their intricate trench systems and perpetual warfare, concealed but as deadly as the open warfare of armies! We live in trenches, with flat revetments of house fronts as parapets and parados. The warfare goes on behind the house-fronts – wives with husbands [...].
>
> (*DH* 117)

Saunders, who notes that Aldington's novel 'includes satiric sketches of modernists in its depiction of pre-war bohemian life', points out that 'The novel's satire is much broader, and its pervasive anger is an attempt to expiate the war's blood-guilt, and to recover from his own traumatic experiences' (427). But *Death of a Hero*, like Ford Madox Ford's *Parade's End*, also brings bohemia and the battlefield together, as Aldington, like Ford, takes modernist autobiografiction into the uncharted territory of the war novel.

Death of a Hero puts autofiction under the acute and particular pressure of Aldington's first-hand experience as a veteran, but his novel is also a layer in the Mecklenburgh Square palimpsest. Re-presenting the same series of events – the domestic drama of the Aldington marriage – the Mecklenburgh

Square novels engage each other in an iterative process indicative of the 'compulsion to repeat', which Freud diagnoses as a manifestation of war neurosis (Freud 57): whether the condition in civilians which H.D. identifies as 'delayed shock, the old shell-shock of the first war' or, in Aldington's case, combatant PTSD (H.D. 2012, 24).

Aldington's theme of blood guilt and atonement is 'the theme of the great Greek tragedies of blood': his novel is a dissident reception of the classics in which the Trojan War drags on into the twentieth-century theatre of war (*DH* 245). John Cournos' *Miranda Masters*, by contrast, is read in my chapter as a satyr play of sorts, a comic add-on both to the three-act domestic tragedy played out in the other Mecklenburgh Square novels and to Cournos' own autobiographical trilogy, *The Mask*, *The Wall* and *Babel*. A light satire which sends up H.D. and Aldington for their Hellenophile pretensions (she is 'Aspasia' to his 'Pericles'), *Miranda Masters* is, also, a malicious take down of H.D. for what Cournos saw as her part as pandress in Aldington's affair with Dorothy Yorke. Outdoing Cannan – and Lawrence – in its infringement of personal privacy, *Miranda Masters* reproduces verbatim a number of H.D.'s letters to Cournos, 'Strange epistolary emanations' which Gombarov, Cournos' protagonist, attributes to 'war hysteria'. As Miranda says to Gombarov at the end of the novel 'These war years have played havoc with me, as they have with all of us' (Cournos 1926, 138–39, 267).

The first two chapters of my book, on fiction, are followed by two chapters on poetry and poetry in translation. The authors of the Mecklenburgh Square novels, Lawrence, H.D., Aldington (and Cournos), were all translators and all were also associated with Imagism, the poetic movement which had been at the leading edge of early modernism before the war.[19] Chapter Three of my book considers the repurposing of the Imagist lyric as First World War verse. Lawrence's bona fides as an Imagist have been called in question, but his three most important war poems, 'Resurrection', 'Eloi, Eloi, llama sabachthani?' and 'Errinyes', were all printed on Imagist platforms: in Lowell's anthologies or in little magazines affiliated with Imagism. Uncollected, these three poems would remain under the wire until the recent publication of Christopher Pollnitz's Cambridge Edition of *The Poems*, which exposes the close connectivity between Lawrence's war verse and Imagist print circuits.

The first Imagist poems, by Aldington and H.D., had appeared in the Chicago-based little magazine *Poetry* in 1912 and 1913, placed there by Pound in his self-appointed role as its overseas editor. By the time his anthology, *Des Imagistes*, came out in 1914, Pound was aligning himself with Wyndham Lewis' new movement, Vorticism, of which Imagism was now to be the poetic arm.

H.D.'s 'Oread' is reproduced in Pound's manifesto in the first, 1914, issue of the Vorticist journal *Blast*, the 'whirl' of the sea in H.D.'s poem harnessing the 'fluid force' of Pound's and Lewis' vortex (Pound 1914b, 153–54). Amy Lowell had other ideas, however, and when she introduced Lawrence to H.D. and Aldington in August 1914, she hoped to carry him with them on the second wave of Imagism (or 'Amygism'), which Pound would come to blame for 'the dilution of *vers libre*' into the wishy-washy free verse of the 'new poetry' (Pound 1932, 590). During the Great War, though, Imagism was still strong stuff: Lewis' and Pound's Vortex had imploded with *Blast*'s War Number in 1915, whereas Lowell's *Some Imagist Poets* anthologies mark the longer survival of *avant-guerre* experiment into the war years. H.D.'s 'Oread' is reprinted in the first of the *Some Imagist Poets* anthologies which appeared annually between 1915 and 1917.

As Imagism's new standard bearer, Lowell would proceed on different lines from Pound. The preface to *Some Imagist Poets* (1915) presents the anthology as a 'coöperative volume', its collaborative and collective ethos defined from the outset against Pound's 'arbitrary' and authoritarian editorial policy in *Des Imagistes*. The preface emphasizes the 'mutual artistic sympathy', which has prompted the poets represented in the anthologies Lowell sponsored – Aldington, H.D., John Gould Fletcher, F.S. Flint, Lawrence and Lowell herself – 'to publish our work together' (Lowell 1915, viii). The Imagists put up a united front, but there were divisions in their ranks from the outset, caused by the war and its fallout. Lawrence, for example, had objected to the 'glib irreverence' of Lowell's prose poem 'The Bombardment' (*L2* 232), which is included in *Some Imagists Poets* (1915), while Lowell objected both to the length and the 'farfetched indecency' of Lawrence's 'Eloi, Eloi, lama sabachthani?' when the poem appeared in the same year in an Imagism special issue of the little magazine *The Egoist* (Damon 307–08). By 1916, the mutual sympathy between Aldington and Flint, the two soldier-poets among Lowell's Imagist cohort, was premised on an immediate experience of war which their civilian counterparts could not share. Aldington would dedicate his volume *War and Love* to Flint, telling him in the Foreword that 'among my friends, you will I think be most likely to understand, through similar experiences, the moods it attempts to express' (Aldington 1919b, 5). In Aldington's trench verse in *War and Love* and *Images of War*, the Imagist lyric is put under the unbearable pressure of contemporary history, a pressure that the archaic forms of his early Imagism are unable to withstand. But Imagism is also a compact poetic which fits into the soldier-poet's kit, and in this respect Aldington's war poems meet the Imagist criterion of compression more closely than his looser prewar verse.

When Aldington joined up H.D. took over his role as literary editor of *The Egoist*; she also assumed editorial oversight of the 1917 *Some Imagist Poets* anthology. In both capacities H.D. would restage in the public arena of print the face-off with Aldington and with Lawrence played out in her poem 'Eurydice'. Written in 1916 and published in 1917 in *The Egoist* and in that year's Imagist anthology, 'Eurydice' encodes H.D.'s struggle in her private life and in her poetry with Aldington and Lawrence, who share the mask of Orpheus in the poem. In H.D.'s revisionary mythopoesis Eurydice calls out her faithless husband for abandoning her in a hell of his own making. Her monologue is no less spirited a response to Lawrence who, on reading a draft of an earlier Orpheus-and-Eurydice diptych, had advised H.D. to 'Stick to the woman speaking' (*L8* 23). Taking his advice, H.D. turns on Lawrence and talks back to him through the mask of Eurydice: 'hell must break before I am lost', Eurydice declares, as she refuses to be consigned to the underworld of the feminine unconscious where, Cecil Gray alleged, Lawrence wanted his 'women' to be kept (*CPHD* 55; Gray 1985, 133). The feminist turn in H.D.'s poetics also marks a formal turn, perhaps provoked by Lawrence too, towards longer and more expressive forms. If Lawrence's flouting of Imagist protocols influenced H.D.'s poetic practice, the botanical imaginary of his postwar volume *Birds, Beasts and Flowers* may have its seed in her early Imagism, in the 'flower poems' Lawrence had praised when he met H.D. for the first time in 1914 (*BML* 86).

The fourth chapter of my book considers H.D.'s, Aldington's and Lawrence's wartime verse translations. As Matt Eatough points out, 'modernism was – first and foremost – a translational aesthetic' and my chapter considers H.D.'s early collaborations with Aldington as poet-translators before turning to the Poets' Translation Series, which was launched in 1915 as a 'joint venture' between Aldington and H.D. (Eatough n. pag.). As editors of the series, the two poets followed the Imagist agenda of renovating poetic diction in an attempt 'to create a higher standard for poetry than that which prevails' (Aldington 1915, 7–8). Caroline Zilboorg makes a suggestive further comparison between the Poets' Translation Series and Lowell's Imagist anthologies as contemporaneous enterprises which were also collaborative, both assembling 'a collection of work representing different poets united in principle' (Zilboorg 1991, 70). A working model of 'translation as collaboration', the Poets' Translation Series comprises translations of the classics by Aldington and H.D. and by other hands which were printed in *The Egoist* prior to being issued as pamphlets by the Egoist Press.[20] In contrast to the patriarchal deployment of the classics in patriotic war literature, the Poets' Translation Series prioritized women's voices, from Anyte and Sappho to the women of Chalcis who, in H.D.'s topical translation of *Choruses from the Iphigeneia in Aulis* of Euripides, comment on the predicament of women in time of war.

The series, which was suspended when Aldington entered the army in 1916 and would briefly be revived after the Armistice, effectively bookends his war service. In the field, Aldington would turn to pseudo-translation and other nonstandard forms of classical reception. My chapter draws new attention to neglected works such as his prose poem sequence *The Love of Myrrhine and Konallis* and his sequence of 'Letters to Unknown Women'. Published in *The Dial*, these 'Letters' are addressed, across millennia, to such women of Greek antiquity as Sappho, Helen and Heliodora, the lover of Meleager, the poet who first collected the epigrams gathered in the *Greek Anthology*. A source book for the Imagists, the *Greek Anthology* was the source text too for Aldington's and H.D.'s early collaboration as translators. H.D. returns to that joint venture in translation with Aldington in the title poem of *Heliodora*, the postwar volume in which she also engages with another of Aldington's unknown women: Sappho. Although H.D. may have found in Sappho's fragments an affective and formal analogue for her fractured relationship with Aldington, whose infidelities had left her 'shattered, cut apart, / slashed open', her 'Fragment' poems are not translations but remediations, 'after' Sappho, of H.D.'s own unpublished wartime verse (*CPHD* 182). Aldington had translated a 'new' Sapphic fragment as 'To Atthis' in 1912, but H.D.'s postwar 'Fragment' poems are non-translations in which she speaks through the mask of Sappho – 'a woman, a personality as the most impersonal become when they confront their fellow beings' – to her relationship with Aldington, the unfaithful Atthis who had been her onetime partner in translation (H.D. 1982, 59).[21]

'All of Us', Lawrence's 1916 sequence of verse-translations, is the subject of the second part of my final chapter. Lawrence was not affiliated with the Poets' Translation Series and his translations are not from the classics but, in a complex chain of transmissions, are adapted from German translations of Egyptian folk and work songs. Like the pamphlets issued by the Poets' Translation Series, however, 'All of Us' channels cultural materials distant in space and time to talk to a world at war. H.D. and Aldington are 'bringing the past into the present' in their wartime reception of the classics: in 'All of Us', Lawrence is bringing the Great War into the global orbit in which the war was waged (Zilboorg 1991, 74). The poems in his sequence, located in England, Africa, Mesopotamia and the Western Front, are spoken by women, by workers, by colonial subjects and by people of colour, and my reading draws on translation theory to align

'All of Us' with recent work scholarship on cosmopolitanism and empire in First World War poetry.[22] Lawrence's translations transpose the songs of the Egyptian fellaheen, many of which are ancient in provenance, into topical anti-war poems that speak to the contemporary experience both of the colonized fellaheen themselves (many thousands of whom were conscripted in the war) and of mothers, miners, nurses, soldiers – British subjects who are exploited, too, by their imperial masters of war. Unpublished in its entirety in Lawrence's lifetime, 'All of Us', like the uncollected war poems I discuss in Chapter Three, has recently been restored in the Cambridge Edition of Lawrence's *Poems* and so the sequence may now be read as Lawrence intended: as war poetry for the people. 'All of Us', I argue, deserves new attention as a valuable contribution to global Great War modernism.[23]

The coda to my book comments on Lawrence's afterlife in writing by women who take up the auto/biographical experiment he himself had begun 'in the midst of the period of war' in *Women in Love*. Here I consider critical, creative and biographical receptions of Lawrence in recent works by Lara Feigel, Frances Wilson, Rachel Cusk, Alison MacLeod and Alison Moore before returning, in conclusion, to H.D.'s intertextual engagement with Lawrence, the man who died in 1930 but who comes back, in H.D.'s autofictions and in poetry, throughout her writing life. The first-person speaker of her Second World War poem-sequence, *Trilogy*, goes back to 'your (and my) old town square', a *retour* H.D. would make again in *Bid Me to Live*, the last of the Mecklenburgh Square novels (*CPHD* 507). Circling the Square, H.D. is also squaring the circle, in her belated coming to terms with Lawrence and with 'the Mecklenburg[h] Square days' of the Great War (*L3* 728).

Notes

1 Group studies with remits relevant to but different from that of my book include Delany, Carr 2009 and Kaplan. Recent group studies in which one or more of my Great War modernists appear in different configurations include McDiarmid, Wade and Arrington.

2 See Fussell 220. Of the two references to Aldington in the more recent *Cambridge Companion to the Poetry of the First World War*, one refers to him as a 'combatant-poet', the other as a veteran who was 'H.D.'s husband' (Das 2013a, 119, 60). As a war novelist, Aldington is better served in Frayn's study of First World War prose. As a modernist, however, Aldington remains *persona non grata*: in a recent review in the

Times Literary Supplement, Vivien Whelpton's authoritative two-volume biography was received as an attempt to redeem Aldington's 'failed career' (Girling 12).

3. On the 'war books boom' of the late 1920s see Frayn and Houston.
4. See Sherry 8.
5. Other works which, like Norris' collection, integrate modernist and First World War studies, include Booth, Larabee and Tate.
6. On Second World War modernism, see MacKay.
7. In his introduction to *The Cambridge Companion to the Poetry of the First World War*, Santanu Das says of Lawrence that 'it is a cause of regret that he does not figure in this volume because of pressure of space', although Das does acknowledge that Lawrence's war verse deserves attention insofar as it is 'unlike anything else in First World war poetry' (Das 2013a, 22).
8. See Bonnie Kime Scott's visual image of 'A Tangled Mesh of Modernists' in her anthology *The Gender of Modernism* (10).
9. Aldington uses the phrase 'verse revolutionaries', subsequently borrowed by Carr for the title of her study of the Imagists, in the Introduction to his *Complete Poems* (CPRA 13; see Carr 2009).
10. Lawrence's most recent biographer, Frances Wilson, dates his descent into the 'Inferno' of the First World War to the banning of *The Rainbow* in 1915.
11. In 'The War' chapter of her memoir *Not I, But the Wind* ... Frieda Lawrence recalls her status as 'the Hunwife in a foreign country' (79).
12. Aldington's remarks are made in the Foreword to his *War and Love* (Aldington 1919b, 6).
13. I borrow the suggestive term 'real-life fiction' from Boldrini and Novak, *Experiments in Life-Writing* (145).
14. See Saunders 5 and see the subsection on 'Intermedial Experiments in Life-Writing' in Boldrini and Novak, 166–223.
15. The most egregious violation of personal privacy in Lawrence's fiction is his story 'England, My England', which was prompted by his association with the Meynell family when he and Frieda relocated from Buckinghamshire to a cottage on Wilfred Meynell's estate at Greatham in Sussex in 1915. Percival Lucas, Meynell's son-in-law, who was the original for the character of Egbert, would like his fictional avatar be killed in the war a year after the publication of the story. Although Lawrence's association with the Meynells lies outside the remit of my book, 'England, My England' is noteworthy for its deployment of a biofictional method in a Great War story.
16. H.D. describes *Bid Me to Live* as a '*retour*' to Mecklenburgh Square in 1917 in a 1953 letter to Aldington (Zilboorg 2003, 365).
17. Mecklenburgh Square is not on Peter Brooker's itinerary in his *Bohemia in London*. In his 1932 novel *The Devil Is an English Gentleman*, Cournos would avenge Sayers' (poison) pen portrait of him and their toxic relationship in her 1930 novel, *Strong Poison*.

18 H.D. did keep a family album of kinds in the form of a scrapbook which includes a photo-collage of Lawrence and Aldington. See Collecott (1990).
19 Cournos contributed a prose poem to Pound's inaugural Imagist anthology. 'The Rose', ascribed to 'John Cournos after K. Tetmaier', is adapted from the verse of Polish poet Kazimierz Przerwa-Tetmajer (Pound 1914a, 6).
20 On collaboration between modernist translators and between modernism and translation, see Davison's suggestively titled three-way study of Woolf, Mansfield and Koteliansky, *Translation as Collaboration*.
21 On modernism as non-translation, see Harding and Nash.
22 On cosmopolitanism and empire in First World War poetry, see Ramazani (2020) and Das (2011).
23 For new work on 'All of Us' in First World War literary studies, see McLoughlin.

1

Life studies: *Women in Love*, word portraits and the war

Women in Love, Lawrence's most complex novel, is defined by its antinomies. It is and isn't a sequel to *The Rainbow*; it has a marriage plot and a homosocial bent; it is a quest for *communitas* but is post-human in its imaginary; it marks Lawrence's keenest engagement with modernist aesthetics yet flirts with the conventions of coterie fiction; and it is and isn't a war book. Binaries such as these drive the novel's arguments – with itself, with the inter-arts modernism of the 1910s and with a world at war – over the protracted course of a compositional and textual history which bookends the war years and crosses continents.

Begun in the Tyrol in 1913 and first published in the United States in 1920, *Women in Love* was substantially completed in England in 1916, the year of the Somme. The diegetic temporality or narrative time, however, remains 'unfixed'. In an unpublished Foreword written for the American edition, Lawrence states that while *Women in Love* 'took its final shape in the midst of the period of war' it 'does not concern the war itself': rather, in *Women in Love*, as in Ford Madox Ford's *The Good Soldier* (1915) and Wyndham Lewis' *Tarr* (1918), 'the bitterness of the war may be taken for granted in the characters' (*WL* 485). But unlike Ford's and Lewis' novels, which appeared serially and in book form in the course of the war, a January 1917 report for Constable deemed *Women in Love* unfit to print 'At the present time' due to 'the writer's expressions of antipathy to England and the forms of English civilisation' (*WL* xxxiv).[1]

Women in Love would circulate privately instead among Lawrence's friends and acquaintances. Art critic Clive Bell remarked that the typescript was handed round 'like an Elizabethan sonnet sequence' (MacDougall 2002, 156) among members of Bell's own Bloomsbury set, who recognized in the character of Hermione Roddice – 'a *Kulturträger*, a medium for the culture of ideas' (*WL* 16) – the portrait miniature of one of their own, Bloomsbury *grande dame* Lady Ottoline Morrell: 'Ott. is there to the life', Virginia Woolf declared (Woolf

1976, 475). Morrell herself was appalled by the 'horrible disgusting portrait of me making me out as if filled with cruel devilish *Lust*', finding in the *portrait-parlé* the salacious implication that, as Hermione to his Rupert Birkin, Lady Ottoline wanted Lawrence for her lover (*FWL* xlvi).[2] Morrell and, later, the composer Philip Heseltine (the model for Julius Halliday, in *Women in Love*) complained of character defamation and invasion of privacy, both threatening legal redress against Lawrence's novel for the reputational damage it had done them.[3]

Because it was unpublishable during the Great War, *Women in Love*'s contemporary reception was subtended by a circular logic according to which the novel was read as coterie fiction in the coteries within which it circulated. To members of these closed groups *Women in Love* was an open book, a *roman à clef* the keyholders of which were those in the know. When Catherine Carswell, whose affiliation was to Lawrence and not to any clique, read his novel in typescript she asked him 'why must he write of people who were so far removed from the general run, people so sophisticated and "artistic"'. Defending his representation of creative types over normal people, Lawrence told Carswell that 'There, at the uttermost tips of the flower of an epoch's achievement, one could already see the beginning of the flower of putrefaction which must take place before the seed of the new was ready to fall clear'. Her response was that whatever value these *fleurs du mal* – whether upper-crust Bloomsberries such as Lady Ottoline or bohemians such as Heseltine – may have for him 'as a writer', Lawrence would not find them 'much use either as friends or in the formation of a group for the furthering of new life' (Carswell 38–9). So it would prove, and in *Women in Love* 'artistic' people present the symptoms of a degenerating civilization and not, as Lawrence had once hoped, its cure. But if his pen portraits are case studies of modern malaise, they are also life studies, drawn from Lawrence's interpersonal interactions with their subjects in an early experiment in the hybridized genre we today term 'biofiction'.

Where his sometime friends alleged libel and identity theft, for literary critics *Women in Love*'s biofictionality is a red herring: Lawrence's apocalyptic novel has bigger fish to fry. Even Lawrence's biographers avoid the biographical fallacy via-à-vis *Women in Love*. Frances Wilson's premise, in *Burning Man*, that 'no writer before Lawrence had made so permeable the border between life and literature' (Wilson 2021a, 1), is a recent exception to the biographical rule proved by *The Cambridge Biography of D.H. Lawrence*, in the second volume of which Mark Kinkead-Weekes warns against 'crude ideas about "sources", or simple extrapolations of literature to life' (Kinkead-Weekes 172). Conceding that 'Lawrence often wrote best when his imagination took off from real people and settings', Kinkead-Weekes nonetheless insists that the novel's characters are 'transformed well beyond "life" by the power of Lawrence's imagination' (Kinkead-Weekes 172, 331). Placed as it is here in quibble marks '"life"' in the lowercase is of lesser significance than the phenomenon which Lawrence himself, in his essay 'Why the Novel Matters', calls 'Life with a capital L' (*STH* 194). Why Lawrence matters to the novel, however, may have as much to do with 'life' as with 'Life', at least according to Martin Amis, who points out that 'writing fiction about real men and women is an extraordinary thing to go and do'. 'D.H.L. started it', Amis says, and he identifies Lawrence as 'the first serious life writer' (Amis 83). In Lawrence's novels, that is, 'real men and women' amount to more than biographical raw material but flesh out a new genre in which 'life' and writing combine.

Women in Love's biofictional pen portraits merit reappraisal in the light of Lawrence's recalibration of the relation of 'life' to writing since it is from 'experiments in literary portraiture', Max Saunders suggests, that generic categories of 'autobiography, biography, fiction, and criticism begin to interact, combining and disrupting each other in new ways' (Saunders 1). Its near synonymy with literary portraiture puts the *roman à clef*, too, into Saunders' generic mix. Indeed, as Sean Latham has shown in *The Art of Scandal*, the *roman à clef*, like other modernist modes of life-writing, is in more than one sense a 'vital genre': in meshing life with art the modernist *roman à clef* 'played a generative albeit unexamined role in the twentieth-century renovation of the novel' (Latham 12, 7).

That renovation of the novel is predicated at least in equal measure on the revolution of the word brought about by what Laura Marcus describes as modernism's 'visual turn' and *Women in Love*, again like Lewis' *Tarr*, reveals the close imbrication of the modernist *roman à clef* with contemporary innovations in the visual arts (Marcus 242). As Marcus points out, 'The staging of a radical transition in representational modes, from Impressionism to what would be termed Post-Impressionism in the early 1910s, with artists including Cézanne, Matisse, Picasso, Van Gogh and Gauguin central to it, was of profound importance for a number of modernist writers', among them Lawrence and Virginia Woolf (Marcus 251). Woolf herself connects the verbal to the visual arts in her famous statement in 'Character in Fiction' (1924) – also issued as 'Mr Bennett and Mrs Brown' in a Hogarth Press pamphlet – that 'on or about December 1910 human character changed', a change which Woolf implicitly and Marcus explicitly attributes to the First Post-Impressionist Exhibition, mounted by Roger Fry at the Grafton Galleries in London (Woolf 1988, 421).[4]

Like Woolf's, Lawrence's conception of human character and of character in fiction is premised on a changing of the old guard for an avant-garde. In a letter to Edward Garnett of June 1914 defending the 'futuristic' quality of 'The Wedding Ring' – an early composite of *The Rainbow* and *Women in Love* – Lawrence rejects 'the moral scheme into which all the characters fit' in the fiction of Turgenev, Tolstoy and Dostoevsky, the Russian opposite numbers, in Lawrence's letter, of Arnold Bennett and the Edwardian novelists in Woolf's essay (*L2* 182). Lawrence, who had read F.T. Marinetti's Futurist 'Manifesto tecnico' (1912) during his sojourn in Italy in 1913, tells Garnett that 'it is the inhuman will, call it physiology, or like Marinetti – physiology of matter, that fascinates me':

> You mustn't look in my novel for the old stable ego of the character. There is another ego, according to whose action the individual is unrecognisable, and passes through, as it were, allotropic states [which] are states of the same single radically-unchanged element […] as diamond and coal are the same pure single element of carbon.
>
> (*L2* 183)

The son of a miner, Lawrence exploits the familiar idiom of carbon and of coal to explain the defamiliarizing concept of character in fiction, formed under the experimental pressure of Marinetti's Futurism, on which his new novel is premised. 'I have been interested in the futurists', Lawrence told Arthur McLeod in June 1914. 'I got a book of their poetry […] and a book of pictures – and I read Marinetti's and Paolo Buzzi's manifestations and essays – and Sofficis [sic] essays on cubism and futurism. It interests me very much' (*L2* 180). The letters to Garnett and McLeod prove the important point Andrew Harrison makes in his study of Lawrence and Italian Futurism that we need 'correctives to a version of Lawrence which would alienate him from the major English and mainland European movements of his time' (Harrison 2003, xviii).

Futurist aesthetics inform Lawrence's theory of character in fiction and inflect the visual semiotics of both *The Rainbow* and *Women in Love*. Lawrence draws these elements together in *Women in Love*'s pen portrait of Heseltine as 'Halliday', in whose London flat, we are told, hang 'one or two new pictures' in 'the Futurist manner' (*WL* 74).[5] In this scene, as in the bigger picture of the theory of image-text relations, the verbal portrait and the visual arts are co-extensive – as W.J.T. Mitchell suggests, the 'speaking picture', while it may seem indicative of 'figurative extensions of the pictorial into regions where pictures have no real business', is more than 'merely a figure for certain effects in the arts, but lies at the common origin of writing and painting' (Mitchell 31, 28). In a Cubist word portrait such as Gertrude Stein's 'Pablo Picasso' (1909), for example, the pretext for which is Picasso's painting *Portrait of Gertrude Stein* (1906), the printed page assumes the spatial properties of the picture plane. Lawrence's only dealings with Stein's word paintings were practical – in 1927, he arranged for copies of her *Portrait of Mabel Dodge at the Villa Curonia* (1911) to be shipped from Florence to Mabel Dodge (Luhan) herself, at her hacienda in New Mexico – and the relationship between the verbal portrait and visual art in *Women in Love* is of a different order than that suggested by Stein's prototypical mixed-media 'combines'.[6] *Women in Love*'s dialogue with the visual arts is conducted instead in set piece scenes featuring art objects – Futurist pictures, West African carvings, a bas-relief factory frieze, a bronze statuette – which galvanize heated exchanges over ideologies of the aesthetic and the relationship of art to life.[7] In the 'Crême de Menthe' and 'Fetish' chapters, the artworks in Halliday's flat – Futurist paintings juxtaposed with 'negro statues, wood-carvings from West Africa', one representing a woman in the throes of childbirth – form a modernist-primitivist dyad which carries the symbolic charge of the Arctic-African polarity projected in the novel (*WL* 74). Futurist paintings and 'fetishes' mark the dissolution of transhistorical, European and African, civilizational cycles in which the mind is supervenient on the body (as in the modern machine age) or the body on the mind (as in 'primitive' cultures).

The art-talk generated by paintings, carvings and sculptures in *Women in Love* is carried on by characters who are themselves 'speaking likenesses' of writers and artists, including 'social artist[s]' such as Ottoline Morrell, or of writers who are represented as visual artists in Lawrence's word portraits of them (*WL* 300). For the character of Gudrun Brangwen, who is a sculptor, Lawrence draws on the writer Katherine Mansfield, making Gudrun's 'little carvings' of birds and animals – which themselves may be modelled on Vorticist Henri Gaudier-Brzeska's miniature duck and dog sculptures – plastic-art proxies for Mansfield's own art of the short story (*WL* 39).[8] In this example, as in that of Halliday and his Futurist wall art, Lawrence's literary portraiture and his novel's intermediality become mutually constitutive. Like the novel's pen portraits, moreover, the art works 'curated' in *Women in Love* have a dual ontology, in that their originals – 'real men and women' and real art objects – exist outside the world of the text, tangible proofs of Nelson Goodman's point, in *Ways of Worldmaking*, that 'the so-called possible worlds of fiction lie within actual worlds' (Goodman 104).

Lawrence and the Little Cholesbury Vortex

The actual world within which the possible world of *Women in Love* was conceived – an ad hoc little arts colony of writers and painters – provided Lawrence with raw materials for his novel's interrelated experiments in biofiction and intermediality. When the outbreak of war in August 1914 made it impossible for Lawrence and Frieda to return to Italy, they took a cottage called The Triangle near Chesham in Buckinghamshire, close to Gilbert and Mary Cannan's house and converted windmill at Cholesbury. The Cannans' Mill cottage, decorated with frescoes by Vladimir Polunin, chief scene painter for Sergei Diaghilev's Ballets Russes, was a show house of cutting-edge interior design, while the Mill itself, with its winding stairs leading up to Cannan's circular writing room at the apex, was studiedly a writer's tower. Compton Mackenzie's verbal sketch of Cannan at his mill in *The South Wind of Love* (1937) is given a pop of avant-garde colour in the form of 'the first number of a publication called *Blast* bound in crude pink'. As the editor of *Blast*, Wyndham Lewis, would recall, the 'immense puce cover' of the 1914 issue 'was the standing joke in the fashionable drawing-room' (Lewis 46–7), and the Vorticist review is likewise a joke in Mackenzie's novel when the protagonist, John Ogilvie, asks the Cannan figure, Frederick Rodney, 'You take this stuff seriously?'. 'On the whole, yes', Rodney replies. 'It's a bit noisy. But we have to blow up the old world' (Mackenzie 1942, 268–69). In Mackenzie's lampoon, Cannan's Cholesbury Mill, situated some thirty miles northwest of the capital, is a Greater London Vortex.

Mackenzie's mockery aside, Cannan's Cholesbury shows that 'the situated sociality of modernist art' in the 1910s extended beyond the metropolitan precincts of the Bloomsbury district and of bohemian haunts such as the Café Royal and the Cave of the Golden Calf to provincial outposts (Brooker 2007, 131). As Cannan's biographer observes, Cholesbury 'became for a time a poor man's Garsington': like Ottoline Morrell's Garsington Manor in Oxfordshire – the rural enclave for the Bloomsbury group from 1915 – the Cannans' place served as 'a focal point and a refuge' for writers and artists in the early months and years of the war (Farr 108). The painter Mark Gertler set up studios there, first in an adjacent farm cottage and then in Cannan's motor shed, making the Mill House almost 'a second home' – a home from his family's home in London's East End – until Garsington became 'a sort of home' for him instead (Farr 111; MacDougall 2002, 118). Lawrence would visit Garsington on several occasions in 1915, but he had been introduced to Morrell by Cannan in 1914. Through Cannan, Lawrence also met Martin Secker, later to become his English publisher, and Compton Mackenzie, who was then Secker's best-selling author. In October 1914 Katherine Mansfield and John Middleton Murry moved to the nearby village of The Lee, renewing their earlier associations with Lawrence and Cannan, both of whom had contributed before the war to Murry's and Mansfield's modernist little magazine, *Rhythm* (1911–13).[9]

The wartime reunion at Cholesbury of members of the *Rhythm* group was hardly joyful but something of the inter-arts dynamic of the prewar avant-garde was revived there, nonetheless. The 'Rhythmists' were now without J.D. Fergusson, the Scottish Fauvist, who had supplied *Rhythm*'s cover art (a naked and insouciant Eve, apple in her hand) and who appears as 'Ramsay' in the autobiographical novel on which Murry was then working, the turgid *Still Life* (1916). Lawrence, Murry and Mansfield were joined at Cholesbury instead by another painter, Gertler, whose patron, the art collector Sir Michael Sadler, was the father of Michael Sadler (later Sadleir), who had cofounded *Rhythm* with Murry. *Rhythm* has until recently been relatively neglected among the little magazines of early English modernism, muted by its noisier successor, *Blast* (1914–15). Both were inter-arts reviews which in their intercalated text-and-image formats dithered 'the boundaries between painting and text', putting verbal and visual art forms in 'spatial dialogue with each other' (Gasiorek 20). *Rhythm*, however, had been conceived in the vitalist spirit of Bergson (one of the 'blasted' in Lewis' review).[10] Subtitled 'Art Music Literature', *Rhythm* sponsored 'a shared "Bergsonian modernism" thought to apply across the arts' (Brooker 2009, 326), thereby fostering what Daniel Albright calls 'concord between artistic media' (Albright 6). Showcasing the 'mixed arts' modernism of the prewar period, the August 1912 issue features artist Anne Estelle Rice's illustrated article on 'Les Ballets Russes' and – spliced into the text of the first act of Cannan's play, *Miles Dixon* – her line drawing of Nijinsky and Karsavina performing in *Le spectre de la rose*. In the same number, Rice's block print of a scene from Diaghilev's production of Mallarmé's *L'Après-midi d'un faune* forms the footer for the final page of Mansfield's story 'Tales of a Courtyard' (Albright 6).[11] 'For one stream of Modernism, the arts seem endlessly interpermeable', Albright suggests, and he cites the 'multiplanar coordinations of diverse arts' in *Women in Love* as a case in point (Albright 6). In the 'Water-Party' chapter, for example, Gudrun Brangwen performs eurythmic 'Dalcroze movements' while her sister, Ursula, sings the German folk songs and American blackface minstrel tunes beloved of Frieda Lawrence and Katherine Mansfield, respectively. In the 'Breadalby' chapter, the Brangwen sisters take part with other house guests in 'a little ballet, in the style of the Russian Ballet of Pavlova and Nijinsky' (*WL* 166, 91). In bringing the sister arts of dance and music and of painting and sculpture into the ambit of the modernist novel, *Women in Love* reprises the interartistic register of *Rhythm*, if not its prewar *elan vital*.

Lawrence's novel would be shaped in significant ways by his contact with Cannan's Cholesbury circle and its Bloomsbury tangent. At Cholesbury, on the evening of Christmas Day in 1914, the Lawrences and Cannans, together with Mansfield and Murry, Gertler and the Ukrainian Jewish émigré and translator S.S. Koteliansky ('Kot'), performed three interlinked little plays at the Mill House. Cannan reported to Ottoline Morrell that 'After a merry dinner we began to act little impromptu plays and those went on and on, growing one out of the other & absurdly & sometimes almost terribly into life.' 'The mill is still very queer with it', he told her (Farr 115). The last of these playlets dramatized the rising sexual tension which would, for a time, turn the Murry-Mansfield partnership into a love triangle: in February 1915, Mansfield left Murry to travel behind the front lines to join her French lover, the writer Francis Carco. Murry had conceived this 'play within a play' to catch the conscience of Mansfield and so scupper her affair with Carco, but his plan backfired when Mansfield and her stage lover, played by Gertler, went off script. Instead of returning to her husband, as per Murry's scenario, Mansfield remained with Gertler, the stand-in for Carco, at the play's denouement. The evening's entertainment ended in disarray, with Mansfield and Gertler kissing and cuddling.[12]

Gertler described Murry's play that goes wrong in a letter to Dora Carrington: 'No one knew whether to take it as a joke or scandal. Fortunately, the next day everybody decided to take it as a joke. The Lawrences were the last to come to this decision, as they were most anxious to weave a real romance out of it' (Carrington 79). But if life was imitating art in the play, art was also imitating art, given that, as Keith Sagar has pointed out, 'the Murrys and Gertler seemed to be casting themselves in the roles Lawrence had already created for Gerald, Gudrun and Loerke' in 'The Sisters', the novel he was currently writing (Sagar 169). It may not quite be the case, then, that Lawrence 'transferred the dynamic of the triangular relationship' of the play 'to his next novel, *Women in Love*', as Gertler's biographer suggests, but Lawrence did take a page out of the Christmas playbook in remodelling the character of Loerke, in part, on Gertler, the Loerke-Gudrun-Crich triangle in the novel now replicating that between the three Cholesbury players: Gertler, Mansfield and Murry (MacDougall 2002, 106). Recalling the events of Christmas 1914 in a letter to Lytton Strachey, Gertler notes that 'all the writers of Cholesbury [felt] inspired to use it in their work', Mansfield in her short stories 'Brave Love' (1915) and 'Je ne parle pas français'

(1918), while Cannan's and Murry's novels *Mendel* and *Still Life*, both published in 1916, feature love triangles (Carrington 77).¹³ In the writing it prompted, by several hands, we might see the Christmas skit as a dress rehearsal for the Mecklenburgh Square novels I discuss in Chapter Two – Lawrence's *Aaron's Rod*, Richard Aldington's *Death of a Hero*, H.D.'s *Bid Me to Live* and John Cournos' *Miranda Masters* – which are premised on another love triangle formed in another circle of Lawrence's friends later in the war years.

Back at The Triangle, in January 1915 Lawrence took the decision to divide the novel he had begun in 1913 as 'The Sisters' – continued under the working title 'The Wedding Ring' – into two books: *The Rainbow*, which was published in September 1915 and prosecuted for obscenity in November, and *Women in Love*, which would appear in Secker's English edition in 1921, a year after the novel's first American publication.¹⁴ Lawrence described *Women in Love* as 'a sequel to the *Rainbow*, though quite unlike it' and his complex and evolving relationship to European and English modernisms of the 1910s may be traced in the continuities and differences between the two novels (*L2* 606). Tony Pinkney, for example, analogizes the 'Gothic modernism' of *The Rainbow* to the expressionism of the Dresden-based *Die Brücke* group (1905–13). As their name suggests, the *Die Brücke* artists – Fritz Bleyl, Erich Heckel and Ernst Ludwig Kirchner – sought to 'bridge' past and present through, for instance, the revival of the woodcut print.¹⁵ The open attitude to sexuality also promoted by this bohemian collective is flagged in the female nude featured on Bleyl's poster for the first *Die Brücke* exhibition in 1906; deemed pornographic under Germany's penal code, the poster was prohibited from public display. *The Rainbow*, likewise suppressed for its alleged obscenity, also sponsors an artisanal and 'feminine' aesthetic, represented in Will Brangwen's wood-carving of the creation of Eve.

Pinkney finds a further Anglo-German affinity between the architectonics of *The Rainbow* – embodied in the womb-like Gothic arch of Lincoln Cathedral and culminating in 'the earth's new architecture' created by the curve of the rainbow itself – and the architectural expressionism sponsored by Walter Gropius (*R* 459).¹⁶ As Pinkney explains, 'the trauma of the Great War' caused Gropius to renege on the 'austere modernist style' of his model factory for the 1914 Cologne *Deutscher Werkbund* exhibition. Instead, in the first, 'handicraft', manifesto of the Bauhaus (1919) – which carried as its cover art Lyonel Feininger's woodcut titled *Cathedral* – Gropius would call for a 'return to crafts', identifying a model for modernist schools in late medieval craft guilds (Pinkney 76–7). Pinkney tracks an inverse trajectory in Lawrence's aesthetics according to which his engagement with an organic and expressionist mode of 'Northern modernism' in *The Rainbow* is thrown over, in *Women in Love*, for a dangerous dalliance with the abstractions of the metropolitan avant-garde; in consequence, the latter novel turns into a reflection of the 'high' modernist ethos it ostensibly critiques.[17] But in pointing up what he sees as Lawrence's inadvertent collusion with high modernism, Pinkney plays down the active quality of Lawrence's involvement with the avant-garde. At Cholesbury, Lawrence had participated in what Brooker identifies as the 'collective life of modernist experiment' in the 1910s, and the 'three-way conversation' begun there between Lawrence, Gertler and Cannan would inform and interanimate the literary and artistic practice of all three men (Brooker 2007, 9).[18]

'A violent maelström': Lawrence and Gertler

The remediations of Gertler's paintings in Lawrence's novels – *The Creation of Eve* (1914) in *The Rainbow* and *The Merry-Go-Round* (1916) in *Women in Love* – suggest that Lawrence's relationship to modernism evolved in close synergy with Gertler's in the war years: the culture shift between Lawrence's books is mirrored by that between Gertler's pictures. Lawrence, who visited his studio abutting the Mill House in Cholesbury in the autumn of 1914 when Gertler was working there on *The Creation of Eve* (Figure 1), would repurpose the painting in *The Rainbow* as Will Brangwen's 'wood-carving':

> He was carving, as he had always wanted, the Creation of Eve. It was a panel in low relief, for a church. Adam lay asleep as if suffering, and God, a dim, large figure, stooped towards him, stretching forward His unveiled hand; an Eve, a small, vivid, naked female shape, was issuing like a flame towards the hand of God, from the torn side of Adam. [...] There was a bird on a bough overhead, lifting its wings for flight, and a serpent wreathing up to it.
>
> (R 112–13)[19]

Will's panel, like Gertler's painting, is animated by a 'creaturely' expressionism: the votive deer in Gertler's picture is not reproduced in the carving, but the bird on the bough appears in both (Pinkney 65). The 'serpent wreathing up to it' which Lawrence has inserted into his 'Creation-panel' replicates in visual imagery his novel's revisionary retelling of the book of Genesis, the interpolation of the serpent seemingly conflating the creation with the temptation of Eve (R 113, 138).[20] According to Stuart Sillars, however, the presence of the snake 'defines the moral polarities of the carving' not in terms of the theological opposition of

Figure 1 Mark Gertler, *The Creation of Eve* (1914).
Private Collection. Photo: Courtesy of Ben Uri Museum and Gallery.

good and evil but as 'something far more akin to the Blakeian contrarieties which generate human emotional progression' (Sillars 194). In this reading, Lawrence's re-creation draws out the Blake-like quality of Gertler's *Creation of Eve*, which was itself inspired by the Blake exhibition held at the Tate Gallery in 1913–14.[21]

When Gertler's own picture was exhibited at the London Group show in December 1915 the *Pall Mall Gazette* charged it with 'blasphemy': but as his biographer points out, the controversy the painting provoked was really 'fuelled by a suspicious and increasingly jingoistic press which linked experimental modernism to a subversive, foreign culture', a link embodied in Gertler's suspect identity as the son of first-generation Jewish immigrants from Austria-Poland (MacDougall 2012, 32). The *Morning Post* denounced the painting as 'hunnishly indecent' and in a letter to Carrington, Gertler complained that 'Some people in a rage [had] stuck a label on the belly of my poor little "Eve" with "Made in Germany" written on it!' (MacDougall 2012, 32). The hostile reception of

Gertler's picture closely replays that of *The Rainbow* a couple of months earlier, which, with its dedication in German to a German dedicatee (Frieda's sister, Else Jaffe) was deemed by reviewers to be a pro-German 'orgie of sexiness' – hunnishly indecent, like Gertler's painting (Shorter 96).

In February 1915 Gertler moved his London studio from Whitechapel to Hampstead, where the Easter fun fair on the Heath would inspire his 1916 masterpiece, *The Merry-Go-Round* (Figure 2). In contrast to the creaturely organicism of *The Creation of Eve*, the carousel horses of Gertler's new painting indicate a new 'interest in mechanized forms' which Sarah MacDougall attributes to the influence of London Group members David Bomberg, a fellow-traveller of the Vorticists, and C.R.W. Nevinson, the sole 'English Futurist', both former classmates of Gertler's at the Slade School of Fine Art (MacDougall 2012, 36).[22] Gertler's initial impression of the colourful fun fair was that 'The effect was like a rainbow!!!' but as MacDougall notes 'this first joyous vision was soon infected by the hysteria of war' (MacDougall 2012, 38). Gertler's growing opposition to the war may have been fuelled by Frieda Lawrence: in 1915 Gertler would

Figure 2 Mark Gertler, *The Merry-Go-Round* (1916).
Tate Gallery, London. Photo: Tate.

break with his patron, Edward ('Eddie') Marsh, who was private secretary to Winston Churchill in his capacity as First Lord of the Admiralty, reminding Marsh in a letter that 'Mrs Lawrence has written to you about your attitude towards the war' (Carrington 101–02).

Lytton Strachey, Gertler's Bloomsbury group friend and a pacifist, admired *The Merry-Go-Round* but told Ottoline Morrell that 'if I were to look at it for any length of time, I should be carried away suffering from shell-shock'. '[A]s for liking it one may as well think of liking a machine gun', Strachey said, his analogy aligning Gertler's painting with a work such as *War-Engine* by another Slade contemporary, Edward Wadsworth (Woodeson 226, 171). *War-Engine* is reproduced in *Blast* 2 (1915), the war number of their magazine in which the Vorticists were fighting a war on two fronts, forging an artistic alliance with the national war effort against Germany while continuing to prosecute what Paul Peppis describes as their 'avant-gardist war against established social, political, and artistic institutions, in which they tried to maintain their pre-war effort to revolutionize English art and life' (Peppis 41). Gertler's whirligig of rotating, mechanical forms harnesses the dynamism of the Vortex but does so to dissident ends: *The Merry-Go-Round* is an indictment of the war machine and of war hysteria, which is no less powerful because it is implicit. *The Merry-Go-Round*, like *Women in Love*, is an artwork in which 'the bitterness of the war may be taken for granted' (*WL* 485).[23]

In the autumn of 1916 Gertler sent Lawrence, who was now living in Cornwall, a black-and-white photograph of *The Merry-Go-Round*. Lawrence's response was that Gertler's 'terrible and dreadful picture' is the 'best *modern* picture I have seen' (*L2* 660). Lawrence, like Strachey, saw *The Merry-Go-Round* as a war machine but in his keener observation of its moving parts – its 'violent mechanical rotation and complex involution' – Lawrence discerned the entropy or accelerated decline of the cycle of modern civilization itself. Through the open mouths of its carousel riders, *The Merry-Go-Round* utters, Lawrence says, the 'great-death-cry of this epoch'. Riveted together at the head, these riders embody an 'utterly mindless human intensity of sensational extremity' as they pleasure themselves on toy horses which, like the Victorian 'horse-action saddle', operate as sex gadgets. The carousel ponies are also weaponized war horses, manifestations, like their male riders in military uniform, of the mechanized 'obscenity' of the war (*L2* 660–61).[24] Even the clouds above the carousel are 'curving like white missile-tracks through the sky' (Cork 137).

The cyclical rotation of the roundabout, his biographer suggests, is also 'a highly personal expression of Gertler's discontent at his circular relationship with Carrington' (MacDougall 2002, 128).[25] Male and female, the riders on the carousel are positioned in trios and in its suggestion of troilism the picture presents a distorted, fairground mirror, reflection of the improbable love triangle which had formed in 1916 between Gertler, Carrington and the flamboyantly gay Strachey. For his part, Lawrence must have recognized in *The Merry-Go-Round*'s 'threesies' a painterly equivalent of the triangular relationships of *Women in Love*, the Birkin-Hermione-Ursula, Birkin-Gerald-Ursula, Gudrun-Gerald-Loerke triangles which form and break apart under the pressures of the primary drives named as 'Death and Love' in the title of chapter twenty-four (*WL* 321). 'I realise *how* superficial your human relationships must be', Lawrence tells Gertler in his letter, and 'what a violent maelström of destruction and horror your inner soul must be'. Gertler's 'outer life means nothing', Lawrence says, in comparison to 'the violent and lurid processes of inner decomposition' revealed in his painting (*L2* 660): if it is superficially a *peinture à clef*, *The Merry-Go-Round* is also subtended by a more profound symbolic meaning. The double – 'outer' and 'inner' – vision of Gertler's painting reflects that of the novel Lawrence was then completing, the likeness between the two artworks underwritten by the shared vocabulary of 'dissolution' and 'decomposition' in Lawrence's letter to Gertler and in *Women in Love* (*WL* 253; *L2* 660). In the 'Gudrun in the Pompadour' chapter of *Women in Love*, for example, Julius Halliday reads aloud for the amusement of his friends 'choice bits' from a letter he has received from Rupert Birkin to do with 'destruction', 'reduction' and the 'Flux of Corruption' (*WL* 383). Gudrun intervenes: '"I walked away with Birkin's letter," she said', the purloined letter substituting, in the novel, for Lawrence's volume of poems, *Amores*, published in 1916 and dedicated to Ottoline Morrell, a copy of which Katherine Mansfield – egged on by Gertler – had filched from friends of Philip Heseltine in the Café Royal (*WL* 385).

In his letter to Gertler Lawrence asserts that *The Merry-Go-Round* is a national treasure which should be 'bought *by the nation*': 'I'd buy it if I had any money' (*L2* 661). Gertler's picture, which 'was found rolled up in his studio after his death' in 1939, would not be bought for the nation until the Tate acquired it in 1984 (MacDougall 2012, 40). Although he didn't have the money to buy it himself, *The Merry-Go-Round* would be placed on permanent literary loan to Lawrence when he wrote Gertler's new picture into his new novel. The 'Snow' chapter of *Women in Love* makes *The Merry-Go-Round* part of the German sculptor Loerke's design for a 'great granite frieze for a great granite factory in Cologne':

It was a representation of a fair, with peasants and artizans in an orgy of enjoyment, drunk and absurd in their modern dress, whirling ridiculously in roundabouts, gaping at shows, kissing and staggering and rolling in knots, swinging in swing-boats and firing down shooting alleys, a frenzy of chaotic motion.

(WL 423)[26]

This exercise in ekphrasis indicates that Lawrence had overcome the anxiety expressed in his letter to Gertler as to the capacity of the verbal arts to apprehend the visual arts: 'language is no medium between us', Lawrence had said in the letter. While he can 'understand' *The Merry-Go-Round*, Lawrence tells Gertler that 'I don't want to translate you into ideas'. In signing off, he says that 'I feel I write stupidly and stiltedly': where Gertler's art is 'articulate', his letter 'reads awkward', as Lawrence, awkwardly enough, puts it (*L2* 660–61). Lawrence also warns of what would be lost in translation if Gertler remade *The Merry-Go-Round* as a sculpture: to translate the visual into the plastic arts would be to forfeit eloquence for 'a form of incoherent, less poignant shouting' (*L2* 661). Gertler began a wood carving of *The Merry-Go-Round* (now lost) nonetheless and it would be Lawrence himself who would recast Gertler's painting into its sister art of sculpture – via the ekphrastic 'art-speech' of *Women in Love* – when he incorporated *The Merry-Go-Round* into Loerke's architectural frieze (*SCAL* 13). 'Sculpture, it seems to me, is truly a part of architecture', Lawrence told Gertler in a later letter, thinking perhaps of Jacob Epstein, whose own early sculpture is a part of architecture in, for example, his controversial caryatids for the British Medical Association building in the Strand (*L3* 46).[27] The architectural provenance for Loerke's frieze, however, is in reliefs for model factories of the kind designed by Gropius and Gerhard Marcks: indeed Loerke's representation of the mechanical toys of workers' playtime celebrates the *Werkbund* ethos – 'let us make our places of industry our art', Loerke proposes, and 'our factory-area our Parthenon' (*WL* 424).[28] In interpolating Gertler's *The Merry-Go-Round* into Loerke's factory frieze, then, Lawrence is building a powerful critique of the military-industrial complex into its ideological superstructure. The 'swirling' 'roundabouts' in Loerke's design are reproductions of Gertler's whirligig, the symbol, for Lawrence, of the 'violent maelström of destruction and horror' of machine-age modernity and of the mechanized carnage of the First World War (*L2* 660).

Together with *The Merry-Go-Round*, Loerke's blueprint may have another visual arts pretext in another Vorticist scene of a (Flemish) fair, Wyndham Lewis' *Design for a Programme Cover – Kermesse*, which was reproduced in the war number of *Blast*.²⁹ The design for Loerke's frieze may be a composite, in the same way that Loerke himself is a composite character: 'part Jewish', Loerke is modelled both on Gertler, whose family's origins in 'Polish Austria' he shares, and on German sculptor Josef Moest, whom Loerke resembles in his unprepossessing physical appearance and abrasive personality (*WL* 428, 425).³⁰ J.B. Bullen speculates that Lawrence likely encountered Moest in person in Italy in 1913, when he was beginning the first version of *Women in Love* at Gargnano on Lake Garda (Bullen 845). Bullen also points out that the detailed description in *Women in Love* of Moest's *Godiva* statuette (1906) means that Lawrence 'must at least have possessed a photograph' of it and indeed, in the novel, Loerke shows the Brangwen sisters a 'photogravure reproduction' of the piece (Bullen 845). Loerke's *Godiva* figurine, in contrast to the Anglo-German amalgamation of Vorticist painting and Die Form architecktur in his carved relief, is a direct steal from the original, an exact replica of the Moest bronze of the same name:

> The statuette was of a naked girl, small, finely made, sitting on a great naked horse. The girl was young and tender, a mere bud. She was sitting sideways on the horse, her face in her hands, as if in shame and grief, in a little abandon. Her hair, which was short and must be flaxen, fell forward, divided, half covering her hands.
>
> (*WL* 429)

His *Godiva*, Loerke insists, is '*not* mechanical', but Ursula Brangwen spurns it nonetheless as a 'stock and stupid and brutal' image, one which brings to her mind, perhaps, another horse and rider: Gerald Crich, the industrial magnate, who subdues his startled Arab mare with 'mechanical relentlessness' in the 'Coal-Dust' chapter (*WL* 429–30, 111).

In his defence of the *Godiva* figurine, Loerke is not now the mouthpiece for the *Werkbund* philosophy of form following function but for the formalist aesthetic of the autonomous artwork:

> [It] is a Kunstwerk, a work of art. It is a work of art, it is a picture of nothing, of absolutely nothing. It has nothing to do with anything but itself, it has no relation with the everyday world of this and the other, there is no connection between them, absolutely none, they are two different and distinct planes of existence, and to translate one into the other is worse than foolish, it is a darkening of all counsel, a making confusion everywhere. Do you see, you *must not* confuse the relative world of action, with the absolute world of art. That you *must not* do.
>
> (*WL* 430–31)

Where Gudrun agrees, asserting that '*I* and my art, they have *nothing* to do with each other', Ursula is impatient with Loerke's pretence of aesthetic autonomy. Insisting that his sculpture 'is a picture of himself, really', she tells Loerke that 'The horse is a picture of your own stock stupid brutality, and the girl was a girl you loved and tortured and then ignored' (*WL* 430–31).

The dispute between Ursula and Loerke in *Women in Love* rehearses Lawrence's own quarrel with the Bloomsbury doctrine of Significant Form. First postulated by Roger Fry in the 1900s, the concept would be adumbrated in Clive Bell's influential thesis in *Art* (1914) that the 'significance' of the artwork 'is unrelated to the significance of life. In this world the emotions of life find no place' (Bell 10). In his own essay in art criticism, 'Introduction to These Paintings' (1929), Lawrence takes up the argument in the Alps between Ursula and Loerke when he travesties Bell's '"white peaks of artistic inspiration"' and sends up Bell's sermonizing on the secular religion of art: 'Purify yourselves of all base hankering for a tale that is told, and of all low lust for likenesses. Purify yourselves, and know the one supreme way, the way of Significant Form' (*LEA* 199).[31] Lawrence's heretical credo of 'Art for Life's Sake' flouts the formalist commandments of the Bloomsbury aestheticians, albeit that his understanding of the relationship between art and life is more nuanced than Ursula's blunt assertion that 'The world of art is only the truth about the real world, that's all' (*WL* 431).[32]

'A little colony'

However crude, Ursula's insistence on the 'real world' referentiality of art – as evinced in her greater interest in the young female art student who was the model for Loerke's *Godiva* than in the statuette as an autotelic *objet d'art* – is an implicit commentary on the function and status of Lawrence's own (pen) portraits and his harsh treatment of their real-world subjects. Ursula's humanism offsets the misanthropy of her other half, Rupert Birkin, who – in a radically disaffected restatement of Lawrence's own 'carbon' theory of character – explains that he is 'not very much interested any more in personalities and in people' because people are 'all essentially alike, the differences were only variations on a theme' (*L2* 183; *WL* 305).[33] But Birkin's post-anthropocentric vision of 'a world empty of people, just uninterrupted grass, and a hare sitting up' (*WL* 127) is set against his no less profound desire for *communitas*:

> There's somewhere we can be free—somewhere where one needn't wear much clothes—none even——where one meets a few people who have gone through enough, and can take things for granted—where you be yourself, without bothering. There is somewhere—there are one or two people—
>
> (*WL* 316)

The proliferating dashes in this passage underscore the desperation of Birkin's quest for a little community or colony of the kind that Lawrence himself and his Cholesbury friends had first imagined in 1914. Its name, 'Rananim', was adapted from the Hebrew version of Psalm 33:1 ('Ranani Sadekim Badanoi'), sung by Kot at a Christmas Eve party hosted by the Lawrences at The Triangle. In January 1915, Lawrence sent Kot a draft 'constitution' for Rananim, together with a sketch of the 'badge' of the 'Order of the Knights of Rananim': a phoenix rising from its nest of flames (*L2* 252).

Lawrence had come across the 'strange, vital emblem' of the phoenix in Kitty Lee Jenner's book *Christian Symbolism* and henceforth he would adopt it as his personal symbol (*R* 109).[34] A phoenix would be embossed on Heinemann's Phoenix Edition of D.H. Lawrence in the 1950s, but before it became a book stamp the phoenix device had appeared *in* a book by Lawrence – on the butter stamper, which is the 'first thing' Will Brangwen makes for Anna in *The Rainbow*: 'In it he carved a mythological bird, a phoenix, something like an eagle, rising on symmetrical wings, from a circle of very beautiful flickering flames that rose upwards from the rim of the cup' (*R* 108).[35] As a symbol of regeneration, Will's phoenix is connected to his carved church panel, *The Creation of Eve*, which he chops up and burns when Anna objects that his Eve – like the doll-like Eve in Gertler's painting – 'is like a little marionette'. But, we are told, a 'new, fragile flame of love came out of the ashes', and Anna duly discovers that she is 'with child' (*R* 162).

In Lawrence's letter to Kot, however, the phoenix is the symbol of collective regeneration: it is the blazon of a new 'Order' of artists and writers rising out of the conflagration of the First World War. Lawrence elaborated on his 'pet scheme' in a letter to his old Eastwood friend, Willie Hopkin, in January 1915: 'I want to gather together about twenty souls and sail away from this world of war and squalor and found a little colony' (*L2* 259). By the following month, Lawrence had decided that 'the island shall be England' and 'that we shall start our new community in the midst of this old one' (*L2* 277). Prevented from sailing away elsewhere by wartime travel restrictions, Lawrence now determined to embark instead, in collaboration with philosopher Bertrand Russell, on a programme of public lectures. Lawrence explained the scheme to Russell's then lover, Ottoline

Morrell: 'We think to have a lecture hall in London in the autumn, and give lectures: he on Ethics, I on Immortality: also to have meetings, to establish a little society or body around a *religious belief which leads to action*.' 'You must preside over our meetings. You must be the centre-pin that hold us together', Lawrence told Morrell: 'Garsington must be the retreat where we come together.' A third party to Lawrence's and Russell's *folie à deux*, Morrell was to 'form the nucleus of a new community which shall start a new life amongst us' (*L2* 359, 271).

When Lawrence fell out first with Russell and then with Morrell his plan for a social revolution to be headquartered at Garsington fell apart. Russell's lectures went ahead, solo, at Caxton Hall while Lawrence switched his allegiance to Murry, now placing his hopes in *The Signature*, an anti-war journal advertised to potential subscribers as 'a series of six papers on social and personal freedom by D.H. Lawrence and J.M. Murry'. *The Signature* folded after its third issue. Morrell, meanwhile, had ended her friendship with Lawrence after reading *Women in Love* in typescript. Life followed art here, in that the chapter set at 'Breadalby', a fictional reconstruction of Garsington Manor, stages a dress rehearsal of their rift in the scene in which Hermione Roddice, the Morrell figure, hits Birkin on the head with a lapis lazuli paperweight. In the aftermath, a concussed Birkin imagines that 'If he were on an island, like Alexander Selkirk, with only the creatures and the trees, he would be free and glad' (*WL* 108).

Prior to its mooted – and now moot – relocation to Garsington, Rananim had been an 'Island idea' although of a communal kind (*L2* 277), and even the androphobic Birkin comes to reimagine inhabiting his island not as a solitary castaway but in the company of one or two likeminded friends.[36] As Andrew Harrison notes, the 'original shared fantasy of Rananim and the plan to inhabit an island to which it gave rise' was the collective conception of Cannan's circle at Cholesbury (Harrison 2018, 954): Cannan himself, indeed, claimed to have created an anterior island fantasy in his *Windmills: A Book of Fables*, which would be published by Secker in 1915 and is dedicated 'to my friend D.H. Lawrence' (Cannan 1920, n. pag.). *Windmills* is the story of a floating island, Samways Island, which brings to a halt a war between Fatland (England) and the Fatterland (Germany). In the preface to the 1920 American edition, Cannan calls his book a 'Prophecy', claiming that he had completed his fables 'a few months before the outbreak of war' in August 1914 (Cannan 1920, xvi, xiii). If we take Cannan at his word then *Windmills* is indeed a prophetic book in its presentation of an aerial view of continental trench warfare *avant la lettre* (Cannan also predicts the formation of the League of Nations and even that of the European Union: one of the promises made in the Manifesto of Samways

Island is the creation a 'United States of Europe') (Cannan 1920, 100, 104). Whether or not his book predicted the Great War, Harrison is surely right to suggest that Cannan's concept of an island with its own manifesto informs the 'Island idea' of Rananim.

Cannan's *Windmills* is a satire on militarism which takes its epigraph from the allegory, in Swift's *Tale of a Tub*, of the war between the wind-worshipping Aeolians and the 'huge terrible monster called Moulinavent, who, with four strong arms, waged eternal battle with all their divinities, dexterously turning to avoid their blows, and repay them with interest' (Cannan 1920, n. pag.). Moulinavent turns their divine afflatus back against the Aeolians (Bedlamites) and in the same way, the epigraph implies, Cannan himself – who sometimes wrote under the pseudonym 'Moulin à Vent' – harnesses the wind of war to the production of the anti-war satires, such as *Windmills*, which he turned out at Cholesbury Mill (Farr 123).[37]

Portraits and artists: Cannan, Gertler, Lawrence

Cannan himself is the object of satire in Compton Mackenzie's novel *The South Wind of Love* where, as the quixotic Frederick Rodney, he tilts against windmills in what Mackenzie, who was a veteran of the conflict, sees as his muddle-headed opposition to the First World War (Rodney avoids active service on pacifist principle, yet serves as a special constable on the home front). 'The windmill was Freddie's curiously appropriate workshop', Mackenzie comments, in what may be an allusion to Cannan's *Windmills*: in the urgent narrative present of 1914, however, the more obvious implication of the remark is that, like Rodney, Cannan is fighting imaginary giants while his friends are facing actual enemies (Mackenzie 1942, 268). Mackenzie's protagonist, Ogilvie, also detects in Rodney's 'self-conscious modernity and susceptibility to books instead of mankind' the early onset of the schizophrenia which in 1923 would cause Cannan to be institutionalized for the rest of his life (he died in 1955) (Mackenzie 1942, 268). In a novel which appeared over two decades after the events it describes, Mackenzie implies a causal connection between Cannan's incipient bipolarity and his contradictory stance on the war.[38]

Where Mackenzie is writing with the benefit of hindsight, Gertler – who shared Cannan's pacifist principles – painted his disturbingly prescient portrait of Cannan, *Gilbert Cannan at His Mill* (Figure 3), in the summer of 1915 (the painting, which is dated 1916, was shown at the London Group exhibition in

June 1916). As his biographer notes, Cannan saw himself both as great, and as 'Tiny man!' (Farr 45): both as an embodiment of Swift's 'huge' Moulinavent and as a mannikin or homunculus (the title of Cannan's autobiographical debut novel is *Peter Homunculus* (1909)). Gertler gives us the 'Tiny man' in his painting, in which Cannan's foreshortened figure, guarded by two enormous dogs, is overshadowed by the conical mass of the mill looming up behind him.[39] In an op. ed. piece for *Rhythm* in 1912, Cannan had raged against a modernity 'dominated by machines' while conceding that 'my only means of circulating my call to arms is by machinery': even radical writing, that is, is grist to the mill of modern print culture (Cannan 1912, 111). Mackenzie believed that his repeated ascent of the spiral staircase winding up to his circular study at the top of Cholesbury Mill had driven Cannan mad, but Gertler's picture, as Ruth Hoberman astutely observes, 'echoes Lawrence's view of Cannan' as 'trapped within the very machinery he had hoped to transcend' (Hoberman 41–2). Confined in a prison of his own making, Cannan is trapped in a 'form of life' which, like his windmill, can only 'turn round, turn in upon itself' (*L2* 285).[40]

Figure 3 Mark Gertler, *Gilbert Cannan at His Mill* (1916).
Ashmolean Museum, Oxford. Photo: Ashmolean Museum.

Gilbert Cannan at His Mill is Gertler's portrait of a writer: Gilbert Cannan's *Mendel: A Story of Youth*, published in 1916, is a verbal portrait of the artist, Mark Gertler, as a young man. *Mendel* is located both in the East End and, like the London chapters of *Women in Love*, in bohemian hotspots such as the Café Royal (the 'Paris Café' in Cannan's novel and the 'Pompadour Café' in Lawrence's). Cannan also takes his reader to 'Merlin's Cave', modelled on the Cave of the Golden Calf, Frida Strindberg's famous nightclub off Regent Street. Among the artworks commissioned for the entrance was Lewis' mural, *Kermesse*, which may have suggested the figures who are 'kissing and staggering and rolling in knots' in the design for Loerke's frieze in *Women in Love*. In Cannan's description, Lewis' four dancers are 'so locked together that they were like one creature, a strange, grotesque quadruped', a mirror image of the couples – modelled on Gertler and Carrington and their fellow painter John Currie and his model and mistress Dolly Henry – whose interlocked stories are told in *Mendel* (Cannan 1916, 250). Like Lewis', Gertler's (or 'Mendel's') is 'metropolitan art', the art of the Great London Vortex, or what Cannan, in an oblique allusion to *The Merry-Go-Round*, calls the 'whirligig of London' (Cannan 1916, 220, 208).

Mendel is party to the three-way conversation between Cannan, Gertler and Lawrence begun at Cholesbury in the autumn and winter of 1914, but the novel's contents were taken, often verbatim, from prior conversations between Gertler and Gilbert and Mary Cannan at their Mill House that January. Gertler, like the eponymous Mendel, 'had absolutely no reserve' in telling his friends about his life: writing to Carrington on his first visit to Cholesbury, Gertler admits that 'I told [the Cannans] all about myself. They were so interested in my life, I told them all about where I came from and all about my people' (Cannan 1916, 91; Carrington 63). The subsequent breach of what Gertler had considered a confidence would cause him to break with Cannan. A modernist *Künstlerroman à clef* in three 'Books', *Mendel* traces the triangular relationship – prior to the attachment Carrington formed to Strachey – between Gertler (Mendel Kühler in the novel), Carrington (Morrison) and their contemporary at the Slade School of Fine Art, C.W.R. Nevinson (Mitchell).[41] The novel also tells the lurid tale of the murder-suicide, in October 1914, of artist John Currie (James Logan) and Dolly Henry (Nelly Oliver).[42] These two, with Mendel as 'an unnecessary third', form another triangle: 'There had been himself', Mendel thinks, and 'Logan and Oliver, three people' (Cannan 1916, 296, 427).

Lawrence and Frieda make the first of what would be their many biofictional appearances in *Mendel*. Cannan's representation of Lawrence in the composite character of Logan is a pen portrait of the writer as an artist which both complements Lawrence's own biofictional practice and prefigures later fictional Lawrences, from Mark Rampion in Aldous Huxley's *Point Counter Point* (1928), who is both a painter and a writer, to the 'L' figure in Rachel Cusk's *Second Place* (2021), who is a visual artist. The characters of Logan and Oliver are a mash-up of Currie and Henry and the Lawrences, who themselves had a reputation for (lower-level) domestic violence: Logan sounds very much like Lawrence when he 'cheerfully' says to Mendel, after a fight with Oliver, that 'a row's a row! [...] And one is all the better for it' (Cannan 1916, 329). Logan also has Lawrence's 'extraordinary gift of mimicry' and, like Lawrence, Logan is a master of invective: 'These clods, these hods, these glue-faced ticks have no more sap in them than a withered tree' (Cannan 1916, 165, 219). Again like Lawrence, Logan preaches a doctrine of male supremacy which he bathetically fails to practice: Logan advises Mendel 'to take a woman and keep her in her place' but the minute Nelly 'bawled for her tea [...] Logan hastened to make it, and disappeared into the bedroom'. The henpecked Logan is presented as a closet homosexual who seeks a 'David and Jonathan' bond with another man (Cannan 1916, 259, 282). In what may be a case of Cannan's 'Tiny Man' syndrome by proxy, Mendel sees himself as 'a pigmy by the side of the gigantic Logan', who is 'like a figure of Blake, immense, looming prophetic' (Cannan 1916, 176–77).

Frieda Lawrence claimed not to recognize herself in the character of Nelly Oliver, perhaps because Cannan's demeaning representation strips Frieda of her aristocratic von Richthofen birthright, giving her the barer lineaments of Dolly Henry's – and Lawrence's – working-class background instead; Nelly is a Northern shop girl turned artist's model. Frieda would compare Cannan's pen portrait unfavourably with Lawrence's characterization of her as Ursula in *Women in Love*. Writing to Kot in December 1916, after reading Gertler's copy of *Mendel*, Frieda told him 'I never recognised myself! Except some of L's speeches I recognised – I was sorry that Gilbert made me quite so horrid – so vulgar – But there ... I want you to read L's new novel – It is so *good* and to my satisfaction I am a nicer person there than Gilbert made me' (*L3* 52). Like Frieda although for a different reason, both Gertler and Lawrence disparaged *Mendel*, Lawrence telling their mutual friend, Kot, that 'It is, as Gertler says, journalism: statement, without creation ... very sickening. If Gilbert had taken Gertler's story and *re-created* it into art, *good*. But to set down all these statements is a vulgarising of life itself' (*L3* 35). Cannan's novel seems to preempt Lawrence's criticism in the scene in which Logan explains to Mendel that 'Accurate imitation is not necessarily an expression': 'A picture must be a created thing. It must have a life of its own' (Cannan 1916, 232).

The young Mendel, whose creed is 'where life is, there is art' and who has an uncanny ability to reproduce objects in paint, must learn – as Gertler, the so-called 'Yiddish Cézanne', had to learn – to 'translate the object on to the canvas' (Cannan 1916, 144, 53).[43] But the different praxis of the novel, Cannan suggests, is to transliterate, rather than to 'translate', life into art. 'A picture's a picture and a book's a book', Logan insists. To 'read' his portrait of Nelly (the likely original of which is Currie's portrait of Dolly Henry, exhibited as *Reminiscence of Venus* in 1913) is to ruin it, Logan insists, his objection to turning 'art' into 'literature' seconding that of Clive Bell, who maintains, in *Art*, that 'literature is a misleading guide to the history of art' (Cannan 1916, 260; Bell 56). Lawrence's own misgivings about translation between mediums notwithstanding, *Women in Love*, in a far cry from *Mendel*'s 'journalism', puts the relationship of art to life under the experimental pressure of a 'mixed arts' modernism in which the visual and verbal arts engage one another.

The difference between Lawrence's aesthetic and Cannan's is measured as physical distance in Mackenzie's *The South Wind of Love*, in which the Lawrence figure, Daniel Rayner's, cottage is located some twenty miles away from Frederick Rodney's converted windmill (The Triangle was in fact less than two miles from Cholesbury Mill). Rayner, like Rodney, 'was one of several young novelists who had impressed upon literary opinion during the last three or four years the fact that for better or for worse a new generation was coming along' (Mackenzie 1942, 267). The literary opinion referenced here is that of Henry James, whose article 'The Younger Generation', a group assessment of Cannan, Lawrence, Hugh Walpole and Mackenzie himself, had appeared in the *Times Literary Supplement* in March 1914. Cannan's fiction 'belongs to the order of *constations*, pure and simple', James finds, and in categorizing Cannan's *Round the Corner: Being the Life and Death of Francis Christopher Folyat, Bachelor of Divinity, and Father of a Large Family* (1913) accordingly, as a 'document', he closely anticipates Lawrence's definition of Cannan's fiction as 'statement' (James 1914, 134). James elects the Mackenzie of *Sinister Street* (1913–14) the leading writer of 'this selected cluster of interesting juniors' while the Lawrence of *Sons and Lovers* (1913) 'hang[s] in the dusty rear' (James 1914, 134). Mackenzie himself takes a different view in *The South Wind of Love*, where he sends up Rodney's (Cannan's) addle-brained avant-gardism and sees Rayner (Lawrence) as the best mind of the younger generation. '[M]ore truly a poet than the others, and with the added advantage of belonging to the people, the real people', Rayner has 'an original voice'. Ogilvie, Mackenzie's autobiographical protagonist, turns his back on Rodney and his windmill but he offers Rayner his own 'Torre Saracena' in

'Citrano' – the fictional surrogate for Mackenzie's Villa Solitaria on the isle of Capri – 'as a refuge' (Mackenzie 1942, 268, 279).[44]

Lawrence would visit Mackenzie in Capri in 1919–20 but he remained in England for the duration of the war, finding pro tempore 'refuge' in little communities of like-minded people in Cholesbury, Greatham, Garsington and at Higher Tregerthen in Cornwall where, in 1916, the Lawrences, with Murry and Mansfield, tried and failed to found a little colony of four – or five, if, as Lawrence hoped, Heseltine agreed to join them there. He didn't: Lawrence told a doubtful Murry that 'we can all be friends together' on the same day – 8 March 1916 – that Heseltine said of Lawrence in a letter to the composer Frederick Delius that 'personal relationship with him is impossible' (*L2* 569; Gray 1934, 118). Lawrence had promised Murry and Mansfield that 'our Rananim' would be 'like a little monastery' (*L2* 564), but it was more like *Wuthering Heights*, Murry told Ottoline Morrell (Kinkead-Weekes 326). Six weeks later Murry and Mansfield beat their retreat, after which Lawrence completed *Women in Love* in 'Katharine's [*sic*] Tower', a turret abutting Murry's and Mansfield's former cottage (*L2* 569). Whatever '*wuthering*' went on at Higher Tregerthen, Murry would recall with some pathos Lawrence saying, of this prospective Cornish Rananim, 'that when we four were together he felt that the new conditions, the new vitality, really *were*, and that if we had not met down in Bucks, he would never have believed that it might be' (Murry 1935, 336).

Notes

1   *The Good Soldier* was part-serialized in Wyndham Lewis' modernist magazine *Blast* in 1914–15; *Tarr* appeared in *The Egoist* in 1916–17.
2   Kate Millett, who describes Hermione Roddice as a 'caricature' of Ottoline Morrell and who takes Birkin for Lawrence, fallaciously claims that Morrell had been 'Lawrence's mistress for a time'. Millett imputes a motive of 'class revenge' to the caricature (Millett 263 n.92).
3   In February 1917, Ottoline's husband Philip Morrell wrote to Lawrence's agent, J.B. Pinker, stating that a libel suit would follow should the novel be published (see *FWL* xlvii; *L3* 95). Heseltine threatened legal action on the publication of the first English edition of *Women in Love*, prompting publisher Martin Secker to ask Lawrence to make changes to the second impression and to pay Heseltine and his former mistress – now his estranged wife – damages and costs. See B. Smith 192–93.
4   Fry's exhibition at London's Grafton Galleries, 'Manet and the Post-Impressionists', ran from 8 November 1910 to 15 January 1911.

5 Describing his 'tiny studio attic' in Chelsea in a 1916 letter to Delius Heseltine told him that it has 'for decoration two Allinsons, a Tibetan devil, a West African carving, and rows of books' (quoted in Gray 1934, 117). London Group member Adrian Paul Allinson, a friend of Gertler and of John Currie, painted scenes from the Ballets Russes and in *The Café Royal* (1915–16) of the bohemian haunt frequented by Heseltine and by the Halliday of *Women in Love*.
6 Notwithstanding his statement that 'I think nothing of Gertrude Stein' (*L5* 642), Lawrence's defence in the Foreword to *Women in Love* of his style of 'continual, slightly modified repetition' bears suggestive comparison with Stein's discussion, in 'Portraits and Repetition', of her method of serial composition (*L6* 191; *WL* 486). Lawrence had heard about Mabel Dodge Luhan's arts colony at Taos, to which he would travel in 1922, from Stein's brother and fellow art collector, Leo, when they met in Florence; Leo Stein would become the subject of one of Lawrence's own word portraits in *Aaron's Rod*. Writing to S.S. Koteliansky in 1926, Lawrence told him 'I have never met Gertrude Stein, but if you remember the deaf fellow in *Aaron's Rod*, that is her brother' (*L5* 419).
7 On *Women in Love* and the avant-garde see Katz-Roy.
8 See Costin 349.
9 *Rhythm* was issued by Secker in its final year of production.
10 See *Blast* I (1914), 22.
11 For *Rhythm*, see Binckes.
12 See Kinkead-Weekes 171.
13 For Katherine Mansfield's use of the events, see MacDougall (2002, 105).
14 See Ross (1979).
15 The *Brücke* group took its name from Nietzsche's view of man in *Thus Spake Zarathustra* as 'a rope, fastened between animal and Superman – a rope over an abyss. A dangerous going-across' (Cork 24).
16 See Pinkney 67, 76.
17 See Pinkney 70. Jack Stewart takes issue with Pinkney, who reads *Women in Love* 'against itself, as part of a deconstructionist project of unmaking the ideological assumptions of modernist aesthetics – a method that leads him to devalue the experimental, visionary form of Lawrence's most complex novel, seeing it as a reflection of the high modernist ethos it attacks' (Stewart 4).
18 For an informed assessment of the Lawrence-Cannan-Gertler relationship, see Hoberman.
19 See MacDougall (2012, 30).
20 For Lawrence's writing as a 'counter-Bible', see Wright 87. The deer in Gertler's painting resembles that in Lucas Cranach's *Adam and Eve* (1526), which depicts the temptation, not the creation, of Eve.
21 See MacDougall (2012, 30).

22   Bomberg's affinity in 1914 was with Vorticist art although he was unaffiliated to the Vorticists and did not contribute to *Blast* magazine. Nevinson was the coauthor with F.T. Marinetti of the manifesto 'Vital English Art' but after his first-hand experience of the front line in 1915 he would repudiate the Futurist glorification of war. See Cork 74.
23   Like *The Merry-Go-Round*, *Women in Love* 'indirectly reflects the bitterness of the war in the fiercely aggressive, even murderous interpersonal actions of its characters' (Ross 1991, 7).
24   Lawrence's 1926 story 'The Rocking-Horse Winner' suggests the masturbatory action of rocking on a wooden horse.
25   MacDougall suggests that *The Merry-Go-Round* is a vision of cultural disintegration which simultaneously expresses Gertler's despair over his relationship with Carrington, a circular relationship that Gertler described as having 'neither beginning nor end' and which turned into a triangle when Carrington fell in love with Strachey (MacDougall 2002, 129).
26   Lawrence told Gertler that he had made *The Merry-Go-Round* 'part' of Loerke's 'fair' (*L3* 46).
27   See Woodeson 234. Lawrence was interested to hear Epstein's opinion of *The Merry-Go-Round qua* painting (see *L2* 661); of Gertler's carving of *The Merry-Go-Round*, Epstein says only that Gertler abandoned it *in media res*. See Epstein.
28   See Bullen 844. According to Bullen, Loerke's frieze is 'based on Gerhard Marcks' decoration of Gropius' model factory in the Werkbund exhibition in Cologne' (Bullen 846).
29   Lisa Tickner suggests that Lewis' design 'appears to figure a sexual assault' (Tickner 87). For Lawrence's possible allusion to Lewis' *Kermesse*, see Costin 343.
30   Lawrence told Gertler 'there is a man – not you, I reassure you – who does a great granite frieze for the top of a factory, and the frieze is a fair, of which your whirligig, for example, is part. – (We knew a man, a German, who did these big reliefs for great, fine factories in Cologne)' (*L3* 46).
31   Bell, in *Art*, invokes 'the austere and thrilling raptures of those who have climbed the cold, white peaks of art' (Bell 12).
32   See the title of Sagar's study of Lawrence: '*Art for Life's Sake*'.
33   According to Lawrence's 'carbon' theory of character 'the individual is unrecognisable' but 'passes through […] states of the same single radically-unchanged element' (*L2* 183).
34   For Lawrence's phoenix emblem, see *R* 506 and *L2* 250, 252.
35   The phoenix device first appeared on one of Lawrences' major publications on the front panel of the first privately printed edition of *Lady Chatterley's Lover* (1928) and is featured on the front board of the Secker edition of *The Man Who Died* (1931). In 1960, the phoenix would push Penguin's signature bird off the front

cover of the first unexpurgated English edition of *Lady Chatterley's Lover* following the Regina V. Penguin Books trial at the Old Bailey. I am grateful to Jonathan Long and to Paul Poplawski for this information.

36 See Turner and Worthen, who differentiate between Lawrence's ideas of 'Rananim' and 'The Island'.
37 For the identification of the Aeolians with Bedlamites, see Larsen 204.
38 A committed pacifist and conscientious objector, Cannan was, with Bertrand Russell, closely involved with the No-Conscription Fellowship.
39 One of the dogs, Luath, is the model for Nana in J.M. Barrie's *Peter Pan* (1904). Mary Cannan's first marriage was to Barrie, for whom Cannan worked as secretary.
40 See MacDougall (2002, 93). In the painting Cannan is 'trapped in a world dominated by the huge, conical mill and the stark vertical lines of trees and fence'; his study, at the apex of the tower, is 'overhung with the windmill's blades […] evoking with their meaningless repetition Cannan's own entrapment' (Hoberman 41–2).
41 'Mendel' was the Yiddish name by which Mark Gertler's family called him.
42 'I have read parts of my diary and the beginning of my "Currie" chapter to Gilbert', Gertler told Dora Carrington in a letter of August 1916 (Carrington 123).
43 Art critic Richard Shone called Gertler a 'Yiddish Cézanne'. See Hussey iii.
44 The Lawrences rented an apartment in the Palazzo Ferraro in Capri, since Mackenzie was himself in residence at his Villa Solitaria.

2

The house of fiction:
The Mecklenburgh Square novels

In October 1917, when Lawrence and Frieda were expelled from Cornwall, H.D. offered them the use of her 'cold studio living-room' in Mecklenburgh Square on the fringe of London's Bloomsbury district (*BML* 8). Lawrence would acknowledge the kindness of an anonymous 'American girl' in 'The Nightmare' chapter of *Kangaroo*:

> The American wife of an English friend, a poet serving in the army, offered her rooms in Mecklenburgh Square, and the third day after their arrival in London Somers and Harriett moved there: very grateful indeed to the American girl. They had no money. But the young woman tossed the rooms to them, and food and fuel, with a wild free hand.
>
> (*K* 248)

The Lawrences stayed at 44 Mecklenburgh Square from 20 October until 30 November. H.D. was lodging in Lichfield, close to the barracks where her husband, Richard Aldington (the 'poet serving in the army'), had been reassigned for officer training, but on her return visits to London, H.D. formed, with Lawrence and Frieda, what she describes as 'a perfect triangle' (*BML* 46). Other triangles would form and fall apart in 'the Mecklenburg[h] Square days' (*L3* 728): between H.D., Aldington and Dorothy ('Arabella') Yorke, the sometime fiancée of Ukrainian-born, Jewish-American writer and translator John Cournos; between Cournos, Yorke and H.D.; between H.D., Aldington and the composer Cecil Gray, who had been a neighbour of the Lawrences in Cornwall; and, tentatively at least, between Lawrence, Frieda and Gray. All these people, with the exception of Cournos – who was in Petrograd in the autumn and winter of 1917 – appear in fictionalized form in the early chapters of Lawrence's novel *Aaron's Rod*.

Published in 1922 but begun in 1917–18, *Aaron's Rod*, according to Mark Kinkead-Weekes, registers Lawrence's 'impatience with heterosexual jealousies and intensities' (Kinkead-Weekes 457). Indeed, in the chapter titled 'The Dark Square Garden', Aaron tells Josephine Ford, who is modelled on Dorothy Yorke, 'I'm damned if I want to be a lover any more' (*AR* 66), an assertion that seemingly signals the turn to the homosocial relationships that dominate *Kangaroo* and *The Plumed Serpent* (1926), novels in which 'Lawrence took on and rescripted the post-war reckoning with male community and male love' (Cole 186). Yet relationships of that order had preoccupied Lawrence in the war years too: in the motif of 'bromance' in the first version of *Studies in Classic American Literature*, for example, and in the bond between Birkin and Crich in *Women in Love*, the cancelled prologue to which is candidly homosexual. *Aaron's Rod*, then, may be read as 'the end of *The Rainbow, Women in Love* line' (*L4* 92): as the final volume of Lawrence's English trilogy of the 1910s as well as the first book in the later 'Leadership' trilogy continued in *Kangaroo* and completed in *The Plumed Serpent*. In its early chapters, moreover, *Aaron's Rod* supplements *Women in Love*'s satire at the expense of Café Royal society and Bloomsberries such as Ottoline Morrell with pen portraits of members of 'another Bloomsbury set' (Schaffner 185): the 'Half Bohemians', as Lawrence calls them in *Aaron's Rod* (*AR* 45), who drifted in and out of 44 Mecklenburgh Square, among them H.D. and Aldington (Julia and Robert Cunningham in the novel), Yorke (Josephine Ford), and Gray (Cyril Scott).

Aaron's Rod moves on from the Mecklenburgh Square milieu at midpoint, when the novel discards the mythico-symbolic form of *Women in Love* for the mobility of a picaresque plot which enacts Lawrence's own postwar flight out of England. A second set of word portraits – of the expatriate writer Norman Douglas and members of his male circle – bookend the novel, the closing chapters of which are set in Italy in the Anglo-Florentine literary scene. But if *Aaron's Rod* dramatizes Lawrence's postwar disaffection with and departure from what H.D. would describe as 'that particularly Bloomsbury scene and those people', his novel is itself, at least in part, the product of the 'scene' of London modernism in the war years (Zilboorg 2003, 304). And as the product, in particular, of the Mecklenburgh Square days *Aaron's Rod* is the precipitant of the other Mecklenburgh Square novels: Aldington's *Death of a Hero*, H.D.'s *Bid Me to Live* and Cournos' *Miranda Masters*. These closely interrelated fictions overwrite Lawrence's version of the events of 1917 – 'the worst year of the war' for civilians – but do so in Lawrence's own autobiofictional idiom, thereby replicating the nexus in *Aaron's Rod* itself between the modernist novel and life-writing in time of war (Carr 2009, 850).

Collectively, these Mecklenburgh Square novels have received little sustained attention. Peter Firchow, one of a handful of critics to have commented on the remarkable recursiveness of the texts in question, observes in a 1980 article that

> [h]ere is a situation which, if not unique, is certainly highly unusual: four novels – one by a major writer, two by writers of considerable importance, the last by a writer of some talent and reputation – dealing with parts of the same series of events, events in which they were all in crucial ways participants.
>
> (Firchow 55)

By contrast, in an article from 1987, Fred Crawford finds in the same four novels 'a confusing welter of contradictory accounts [of the breakdown of the Aldington marriage], replete with unmitigated lies' (Crawford 49). Crawford's judgement is that Aldington alone emerges from this battle of the books with any honour, insofar as *Death of a Hero* maintains an objective distance from the events described. By contrast, the other three novels – *Aaron's Rod*, *Miranda Masters* and *Bid Me to Live* – all 'demonstrate a trait of their authors that we must deplore' in that 'these novelists perverted their art and cheapened their talent by making their fiction serve selfish and even base ends'. Crawford takes Lawrence, Cournos and H.D. to task for shirking 'the service to general truth that distinguishes fiction from mere lying' and thus reneging on the novelist's responsibility 'to present the truth of life' (Crawford 64–5). There is a more intricate interweaving of life with fiction in and between all four texts than Crawford's cruder binary between truth and lies allows, however, which calls into question the generic as much as the ethical integrity of the novel.

The claim that the Mecklenburgh Square novels serve only the selfish ends of their individual authors is countered by Firchow's more acute point that '*Bid Me to Live* is heavily indebted to both *Aaron's Rod* and *Death of a Hero*, just as the latter novel is heavily indebted to the former', to the extent that 'these three novels can only be read and interpreted fully and satisfactorily when taken together as a kind of "trilogy"' (Firchow 72). Taken as the first volume in a three-handed trilogy, *Aaron's Rod*'s full meaning is contingent on its reception in the two further volumes of that trilogy, *Death of a Hero* and *Bid Me to Live*. Read together, the three novels form a composite text which mirrors, in its trilogical structure, the triangular relationships with which all three novels are concerned, underpinning the analogies with the triform genre of Attic tragedy posited in two of them. In *Bid Me to Live*, H.D.'s fictional surrogate, Julia, describes herself, in her Bloomsbury bedsit with its 'Three long French windows', as living 'in the middle of a trilogy' (*BML* 3), while in Aldington's *Death of a Hero* lived experience, which is 'cut sharply into three sections – pre-war, war, and post-war', is likened to a 'House of Atrides tragedy' (*DH* 199, 24).[1]

If *Aaron's Rod*, *Death of a Hero* and *Bid Me to Live* are taken together as a tragic trilogy, then Cournos' *Miranda Masters* is the satyr play to that trilogy, a comic appendage which travesties the Hellenophile pretensions of the Aldingtons in the characters of Miranda and Arnold Masters. *Miranda Masters* also supplies a ludic coda to Cournos' own autofictional novel-trilogy, *The Mask* (1919), *The Wall* (1921) and *Babel* (1922). But when Gombarov – Cournos' close fictional alter ego in *Miranda Masters* and in his trilogy – learns of the love affair between Arnold (Aldington) and Winifred (Dorothy Yorke), the narrator tells us that 'Life appeared to be a comic nightmare, a burlesque tragedy', oxymorons which show that, despite its comic aspects, *Miranda Masters*, too, is a tragedy of kinds: as Cournos says in the novel, 'tragedy [...] is but comedy in inversion' (Cournos 1926, 250, 98). Its self-reflexive meditations on the relationship between life and art and between literature and lived experience, moreover, make *Miranda Masters* as much a novel of ideas – or a novel of ideas about the novel – as it is thinly veiled revenge porn.

Lawrence, in the character of Richard Ramsden, only appears offstage in *Miranda Masters*, a ghosting which may be Cournos' quid pro quo for his own absence from *Aaron's Rod*. Gombarov cautions Miranda against Ramsden, telling her that 'Everything he touches falls to ashes in the contact' (Cournos 1926, 176), a warning H.D. would recall in *Bid Me to Live*, where the aptly named Julia Ashton, as Diana Collecott observes, 'appropriates Lawrence's icon of a phoenix rising from the ashes' (Collecott 1999, 96). Despite his caveat against Ramsden, however, Gombarov himself subscribes uncritically to the Lawrentian credo that 'art should not be less vital than life', although he is less sure of how to put that philosophy into literary practice: 'how was one to write a modern novel, yet retain the sense of art merging with life which the Greeks more than any other people expressed in their drama?' (Cournos 1926, 110, 119). Like Cournos, Aldington believed that 'the Greeks alone of European nations, succeeded in solving the great problem – they coincided life & art' (Zilboorg 2003, 78). Of the moderns, Aldington affirms in his biography, Lawrence came closest to the Greek example in writing novels which are less '"works of art"' than '"life-experiences"' (Aldington 1950b, 145). Aldington identifies what Paul Delany would later define as Lawrence's 'characteristic style of transforming life into art', a style adopted and adapted by Aldington, H.D. and Cournos in their receptions of Lawrence's fiction (Delany 226). Collectively, the Mecklenburgh

Square novels, with their 'memories strung along the frail spider-web' (*BML* 12), prove Virginia Woolf's point that 'Fiction is like a spider's web, attached ever so lightly perhaps, but still attached to life at all four corners' (Woolf 1992a, 53).

'The War Again': *Aaron's Rod*

The first chapters of *Aaron's Rod* are set not in the Mecklenburgh Square days of 1917 but in the immediate postwar period. 'We were dispersed and scattered after War 1', H.D. says of her circle (H.D. 1986, 184), and yet in Lawrence's novel 'here they were, in the old setting exactly, the old bohemian routine' (*AR* 57). Lawrence had taken a less jaded view in October 1917, when he wrote to Gray from 44 Mecklenburgh Square that '[o]ne seems to be, in some queer way, vitally active here. And then people, one or two, seem to give a strange new response' (*L3* 174). Of these 'people', he had identified H.D., Yorke and Gray himself as new recruits for Rananim, a little colony now to be located in Colombia on estates owned by relatives of Lawrence's friend, David Eder. 'The Andes become real and near', Lawrence told Gray, assuring him that the colonists would 'sail off' there in the spring (*L3* 174). In his autobiography, however, Gray confesses that 'the idea of spending the rest of my life in the Andes in the company of Lawrence and Frieda, filled me with horror – the combination of the mountain heights and the psychological depths was more than I could sanely contemplate' (Gray 1985, 132). For his part, Eder, a pioneering English psychologist, was also a Zionist whose greater commitment was to the exodus of European Jewry to Palestine, where Eder himself would travel in 1918.[2] '[L]ike the Israelites in the desert, we shall come to some Canaan', Lawrence had opined (*L2* 466), but in the spring of 1918 he was still in England: he would remain there until November 1919, when at long last he would sail off, not to South America, but on the boat to France, en route to Italy.

Unlike *The Rainbow*, which had been suppressed, and the then unpublishable *Women in Love*, the first 150 pages of *Aaron's Rod* were 'as blameless as *Cranford*', Lawrence assured Cynthia Asquith in a March 1918 letter (*L3* 227). These opening pages, Aldington explains, 'are improvised variations on Lawrence's own experiences', including his interactions with Aldington himself, H.D. and other members of their Mecklenburgh Square set. H.D. had taken the Lawrences in, but 'to do Lawrence a good turn', Aldington remarks, 'was to arouse bitter resentment at having to be under an obligation, and provoked his satirical malice'. Provoked himself perhaps by injured pride Aldington insists that the verbal sketches of himself, H.D. and others lower these early chapters of *Aaron's Rod* to 'the level of spiteful gossip', whereas the scenes set in Florence at the end of the novel are 'much more lively and amusing', albeit that 'some of the portraits of English people in Italy, being easily identified from salient traits which were exaggerated into caricature, gave much offence' (Aldington 1976, 7–10).

Lawrence's portraits of Norman Douglas' expatriate circle – 'They all snapped and rattled at one another, and were rather spiteful but rather amusing' – gave particular offence to Douglas himself, whom Lawrence had first met in London when Douglas was working at the *English Review* (*AR* 215).[3] Douglas is James Argyle in *Aaron's Rod*, where he presides, in Florence, over a party 'all of men', among them Algy Constable (Reginald 'Reggie' Turner, who had been a close associate of Oscar Wilde) (*AR* 214). Other members of Argyle's circle appear in the novel, including Walter Rosen; a pen portrait of Gertrude Stein's brother, art collector Leo Stein; and Louis Mee, who is modelled on Maurice Magnus, formerly business manager to modernist theatre practitioner Gordon Craig and now Douglas' factotum. A 'modern rogue', Magnus would subsequently draw Lawrence into his 'shady affairs', one consequence of which would be Lawrence's sole exercise in 'straight' biography: his 'Memoir of Maurice Magnus', which was written as a preface to Magnus' own *Memoirs of the Foreign Legion*, posthumously published in 1924 (*IR* 46–7).

Douglas' objection to Lawrence's habit of 'putting people' into his books is highly disingenuous, given that Douglas was aware in advance that Lawrence 'might be so amused at certain aspects of Florentine life as to use it for "copy" in some book' (Aldington 1950a, 19 *AR* 325). Douglas' own literary reputation, moreover, rested on a *roman à clef* – *South Wind* – a satirical exposé of expatriate society on the island of Capri. Following his sojourn in Florence, Lawrence had travelled with Frieda to Capri in December 1919, leasing an apartment at the top of the Palazzo Ferraro until early March 1920, when the Lawrences relocated to Taormina in Sicily. Capri, Jamie James observes, was 'a haven for an international community of writers and artists': a 'Futurist beachhead' had been established there in 1917 by the painter Fortunato Depero and one of the first exhibitions of Futurist art had been put on in the cosmopolitan Caffe Morgano, the island's equivalent of the Café Royal (J. James 6, 124). The year 1917 also saw the publication of Douglas' *South Wind*, in which Capri is fictionalized as Nepenthe, the name – an allusion to the narcotic which banishes memory and grief in Homer's *Odyssey* – perhaps explaining the novel's 'thundering silence about the cataclysm of blood that was engulfing Europe' in that year (J. James 42). 'Coming back on leave to London in 1917', Aldington recalls, he had found in *South Wind* 'so complete and welcome a contrast to the scenes and dismal ethics from which I had temporarily escaped' (Aldington 1954, 2). Novelist Compton Mackenzie had come to Capri before the war, lured there in 1913 by Douglas' seductive travel narrative, *Siren Land* (1911). Ten years after the appearance of *South Wind* – which Mackenzie's first wife, Faith, had typed up for Douglas on a typewriter later loaned to Lawrence – Mackenzie published the first of his own Caprese *romans à clef*, *Vestal Fire* (1927). In the following year Mackenzie's *Extraordinary Women* came out, a comedy about Capri's lesbian community which includes a pen portrait of Radclyffe Hall (Aurora 'Rory' Freemantle), whose own more serious and significant sapphic novel, *The Well of Loneliness*, also published in 1928, was prosecuted for obscenity.

Capri (Sirene) is presented in *Vestal Fire* as a 'microcosm of European culture', the Mediterranean destination of choice for Marinetti and for '*Pesce, cani, tedeschi, americani, automobile, lesbiane, nazionalisti*, and finally *fascisti* [who] all land in turn upon that fantastic rock' (Mackenzie 1985, 410–11). From this motley crew Mackenzie singles out as his protagonist the gay French aristocrat Count Jacques d'Adelswärd-Fersen (Count Marsac, in the novel), a poet, novelist and drug addict who settled on Capri and oversaw the construction of the lavish Villa Lysis (Villa Hylas) there, the specifications for which included a built-in opium den. In temporary exile from Sirene, Marsac writes his own novel about the islanders: 'Everybody was walking about the Piazza reading to one another the insulting descriptions of his neighbour' (Mackenzie 1985, 243). Mackenzie's *mise en abyme* – a *roman à clef* enclosed within a *roman à clef* – makes his novel more than merely a period piece, perhaps, but a self-reflexive meditation on its own biofictional praxis. But at the same time, the island gossip – the 'catspaw of rumour', 'the miaows' of scandal – stirred up by Marsac's book is so much grist to Mackenzie's own novel's rumour mill (Mackenzie 1985, 141, 235, 242). *Romans à clef* spin an 'ever-expanding web', but *romans à clef*, Capri-style, weave a cat's cradle (Latham 11).

The cattiness of Capri society was Lawrence's reason for leaving the island. Characteristically, he had had hopes of the place, writing from the Palazzo Ferraro in January 1920 that 'Life opens itself in little new circles. Here we struggle along in Italian and German and French and English, on this island which is a little Babel' (*L3* 453). However, unintentionally his simile conveys a warning and indeed, a few days beforehand, Lawrence had disparaged Capri as 'overcosmopolitanised' to another correspondent (*L3* 452). By February, Lawrence would be complaining to Catherine Carswell that Mackenzie's Capri is a 'Cat-Cranford': in 1922, Marinetti would proclaim Capri a 'Futurist island', but for Lawrence it was 'a stewpot of semi-literary cats' which, riddled with small town talk, harked back to Elizabeth Gaskell's *Cranford* (J. James 124; *L3* 469). 'I like Compton Mackenzie as a man', Lawrence told Carswell, 'but not as an influence. I can't stand his island' (J. James 124; *L3* 469). In conflating Mackenzie with 'his island' – with his 'Cat-Cranford' Capri – Lawrence implies that it is Mackenzie who is behind the times. Both Mackenzie and Lawrence are practitioners of the 'New Novel', according to Henry James, but Lawrence's fiction diverges from that of his contemporaries in 'The Younger Generation' in part at least because of his recoil from Mackenzie's insular 'influence' (H. James 1914, 133).

Mackenzie's *Vestal Fire* 'contains a series of wicked portraits of monomania', Sally Beauman observes: 'Egotists stalk its pages' (Beauman 1985, n. pag.). Mackenzie himself stalks the pages of Lawrence's story 'The Man Who Loved Islands'. First printed in *The Dial* in July 1927, the year in which *Vestal Fire* – a novel about the isle of Capri, written on another island, Jethou, in the English Channel – appeared, Lawrence's story is a psychologically acute portrait of mono- or islomania. The 'Man', Cathcart, who inhabits island after smaller island in a quest for his 'Happy Isle', his 'Hesperides', is clearly modelled on the Mackenzie who lived on a succession of islands and would be buried on Barra, an islet in the Outer Hebrides (*WWRA* 153). In a 1920 letter to Mackenzie, who had recently become tenant of Herm and Jethou, Lawrence asked him, 'What is this I hear about Channel Isles? The Lord of the Isles. I shall write a skit on you one day' (*L3* 594). 'He wanted an island all of his own' in order 'to make it a world of his own', Lawrence says of the 'Man': 'this story will show how tiny it [an island] has to be, before you can presume to fill it with your own personality' (*WWRA* 151). Offended by Lawrence's 'skit', Mackenzie threatened legal action should 'The Man Who Loved Islands' be reprinted in Martin Secker's English edition of *The Woman Who Rode Away and Other Stories* (1928). 'I'm disgusted at Compton Mackenzie taking upon himself to feel injured', Lawrence complained to Secker: '"People are sure to recognise him – " And what if they do? Will it hurt him?' In a further letter to Secker on the subject, Lawrence insists that 'The Man who loved islands has a philosophy behind him, and a real significance. I consider myself I have done Mr Monty [Edward Montague Compton Mackenzie] a great deal of honour. If he can't see it, it shows what a cheapjack he is' (*L6* 205, 218).

With 'The Man Who Loved Islands', Mackenzie must have felt, Lawrence was adding insult to the injury he had already done to Compton and Faith Mackenzie in another short story, 'Two Blue Birds', which had appeared in *The Dial* in April 1927. This tale, about 'a woman who loved her husband, but […] could not live with him', draws on a conversation Faith had had with

Lawrence on his return visit to Capri in 1926, when Mackenzie was living on Jethou (*WWRA* 5). Despite Lawrence's assurance to Secker to the contrary, Faith Mackenzie did 'object to her portrait-sketch' in 'Two Blue Birds', as well as to the story's 'malicious caricature of Monty' and its 'monstrous perversion of [the] facts' of the Mackenzie marriage (*L6* 68).⁴ Cameron, the husband in the story, is a writer who dictates to his secretary in 'ten hours a day intercourse, à deux, with nothing but a pencil between them: and a flow of words' (*WWRA* 7). His wife, by contrast, 'didn't want to take him down in shorthand' and he can't read her: her eyes 'seemed to speak many inexplicable dark volumes' (*WWRA* 10, 15). The wife asks her husband, who is 'doing an article on the Future of the Novel', why he doesn't do 'something lively in the life of the novelist' instead – in other words, why he doesn't have sexual 'intercourse' with his secretary – but Cameron continues his dictation regardless: '"Just where we were, Miss Wrexall?" came the sound of his voice' (*WWRA* 14–15). Notwithstanding his secretary's ominous name, Cameron's article on the future of the novel, taken down in her competent shorthand, is in safe hands: the future of the novel itself, however, is not. Lawrence's own essay on 'The Future of the Novel' – printed with the incendiary title 'Surgery for the Novel – Or a Bomb' on its publication in the *Literary Digest International Book Review* in 1923 – insists that the new novel has 'got to have the courage to tackle new propositions' and 'to present us with new, really new feelings, a whole new line of emotion, which will get us out of the old emotional rut' (*STH* 155).

A decade after Lawrence's death, Mackenzie would pay him back in biofictional kind in *The West Wind of Love*, the third volume in his *Four Winds of Love* novel-saga. The generous pen portrait of Lawrence as Daniel Rayner in *The South Wind of Love*, discussed in my first chapter, is now replaced by a less sympathetic cameo. Rayner sends the protagonist, Ogilvie, a postcard from 'a private hotel in Bloomsbury', reminding him of their meeting in 1914 and asking him 'to find rooms for Hildegarde and me in Citrano [Capri]' (Mackenzie 1941, 248). The 'weary years of the war' had been 'a period of continuous mental torment' for Rayner who, now that the war has ended, is showing signs of an 'incipient messianic megalomania'. When Raynor leaves Citrano en route via Monte Cassino – where Lawrence had visited Maurice Magnus, who was hiding from his creditors there – for the South Seas, Ogilvie wonders 'Was he a portent, a phenomenon, or merely a freak? Were the circumstances of modern life exasperating to egomania the consciousness of his own vital personality?' What Rayner sees as potential remedies for 'the sickness of Western civilisation' – 'Back to the land … back to the noble savage … back to simplicity … nudism … negro sculpture … primitive rhythms … atonal music' – amount, in Ogilvie's judgement, to 'a vain attempt to escape from the results of mechanization' (Mackenzie 1941, 253). Yet going to the South Seas had been Mackenzie's own idea, and in 1920 – the narrative present of the Rayner episode in *The West Wind of Love* – Mackenzie was actively encouraging Lawrence to sail off there with him (see *L3* 462).[5]

In a 1950 interview with Lawrence's biographer Harry T. Moore, Mackenzie would complain that 'Lawrence's fiction often gives a distorted view of his acquaintances because "he had a trick of describing a person's setting or background vividly, and then putting into the setting an ectoplasm entirely of his own creation"' (Moore 187). Mackenzie's own fiction, he would explain in a 1953 letter to Edward Nehls, is the truthful inverse of Lawrence's 'trick'. Notwithstanding his disclaimer in *The South Wind of Love* that 'it will be a waste of time for people to try to identify characters' with their real-life originals, Mackenzie told Nehls that 'I called Lawrence Daniel Rayner': 'You will find an impression of Lawrence in my novel *The Four Winds of Love*. Apart from names and places most of it is factually and conversationally exact' (Mackenzie 1942, n. pag.; Nehls 455). It was precisely this exactitude – what Henry James identifies as the 'documented aspect' of the early twentieth-century New Novel – which had led Lawrence, when he left Capri for Sicily, to put clear water between his own fiction and Mackenzie's in the same way that in 1916 Lawrence had distanced his own biofictional practice from that of Cannan, who had resorted in *Mendel* to 'journalism' and to 'statement' (*L3* 35). Like Cannan, Lawrence in 'Two Blue Birds' transposes private conversation into the public medium of print, but the imbrication of life and art in Lawrence's story has a 'real significance', for the future of the *roman à clef* and for the future of the novel.

Commenting on *Aaron's Rod* in *Looking Back: An Autobiographical Excursion*, Norman Douglas, like Aldington, remarks on Lawrence's 'love of scoring off people to whom he is under an obligation'. Douglas finds in Lawrence's pen portraits of himself and his circle of friends the same quality of 'cattishness' to which Lawrence had objected in Mackenzie's – and Douglas' – 'Cat-Cranford' Capri, although Douglas also concedes that Lawrence's 'work is in the nature of a beneficent, tabu-shattering bomb' (Nehls 12–14). As Lawrence himself insists in 'Surgery for the Novel – Or a Bomb', if fiction has a future, 'it's got to break a way through, like a hole in a wall', letting in a 'cold stream of fresh air' to dispel the 'stuffiness' of the 'house of fiction'.[6] 'Suppose a bomb were put under this whole scheme of things, what would we be after?', Lawrence asks (*STH* 154–55). A bomb is put into Argyle's café-bar in the penultimate chapter of *Aaron's Rod*. Attributed to Italian anarchists, the bomb is a proxy device planted by Lawrence to blow up Douglas' effete café-society clique and, with it, the conventions of (coterie) fiction:

> CRASH!
>
> There intervened one awful minute of pure shock, when the soul was in darkness.
>
> Out of this shock Aaron felt himself issuing amid a mass of terrible sensations: the fearful blow of the explosion, the noise of glass, the hoarse howl of people, the rushing of men, the sudden gulf, the awful gulping whirlpool of horror in the social life.
>
> (*AR* 282)

The café bomb plot also operates as a plot device in that in its aftermath Aaron finally submits himself, man to 'greater man', to an authentic 'leader': to Rawdon Lilly, the novel's surrogate for Lawrence himself (*AR* 299). In its conclusion, then, *Aaron's Rod* is in lockstep with Lawrence's other 'Leadership' novels, *Kangaroo* and *The Plumed Serpent*, in which resurgent masculinities are again performed against a postwar backdrop of political insurgency.

The febrile atmosphere of the Armistice, with 'the violence of the nightmare released now into the general air', is registered in *Aaron's Rod* from the outset:

> The hollow dark countryside re-echoed like a shell with shouts and calls and excited voices. Restlessness and nervous excitement, nervous hilarity were in the air. There was a sense of electric surcharge everywhere, frictional, a neurasthenic haste for excitement.
>
> (*AR* 15)

In transposing the Mecklenburgh Square days of 1917 to the postwar period Lawrence is recoding war neurosis – the continuous traumatic stress of life during wartime – as the post-traumatic stress which is manifested again in 'The Nightmare' chapter of *Kangaroo* (*AR* 5). In *Aaron's Rod*, PTSD is personified in the minor character of Captain Herbertson, who is introduced in the chapter aptly titled 'The War Again'. Belying his 'appearance of bright diffidence' the captain 'had the war at the back of his mind, like an obsession' (*AR* 113–14) and in the same way, Steven Vine notes in his introduction to the 1995 Penguin edition, the Great War 'haunts and harries' *Aaron's Rod* itself 'with the force of trauma' (Vine xix).[7]

'Double nightmare': *Death of a Hero*

Richard Aldington's introduction to the 1950 Penguin edition of *Aaron's Rod* is the more personal paratext of a player in events restaged in the novel who also took part in the Big Show that was the Great War. Although his introduction dismisses Lawrence's satirical sketches of the Mecklenburgh Square set as malicious gossip, Aldington's own – savagely satirical – war book, *Death of a Hero*, is nonetheless woven into the Mecklenburgh Square novels' autobiofictional 'spider-web' (*BML* 12). Like Lawrence, Aldington takes the modernist *roman à clef* out of the confines of coterie fiction, but like Ford Madox Ford's *Parade's End* tetralogy, which also involves a home front love triangle, *Death of a Hero* takes the *roman à clef* into the uncharted territory of the full-blown war novel. 'There are two kinds of men, those who have been to the front and those who haven't', Aldington told Lawrence in a wartime letter, and *Death of a Hero* underscores that existential difference (Aldington 1968, 197). For example, *Death of a Hero* takes up the musical motif of *Aaron's Rod* in the music notations which accompany its three parts, but the different tempo of Aldington's 'jazz novel' is 'appropriate' to 'its theme' in that the soundtrack of the postwar decade – the Jazz Age – had been rehearsed on the battlefields of the First World War: 'CRASH! Like an orchestra at the signal of a baton the thousands of guns north and south opened up'. If the uppercase 'C R A S H !' of the exploding café bomb in *Aaron's Rod* is echoed here, it is also outgunned by the 'super-jazz' of artillery bombardment (*DH* 371, 321). Where Lawrence's postwar plan was to put a bomb under the whole scheme of the novel, Aldington implies that the Great War itself has blown the generic conventions apart to the extent that, according to its author, *Death of a Hero* is 'not a novel at all' (*DH* n. pag.).

Commenting on the composition of *Death of a Hero* in his autobiography, *Life for Life's Sake*, Aldington says 'I wrote and destroyed part of such a book in 1919; and in 1925 and 1927 I made other abortive starts […] time was needed for the assimilation and arrangement of these experiences' (Aldington 1968, 301). Aldington acknowledged in a 1919 letter to Amy Lowell that he was suffering from 'a sort of deferred shell-shock', and for Aldington and other survivors the war would tick away on a time fuse triggered a decade later with the war books boom. Published in 1929, *Death of a Hero* 'came out as the boom in war books was in full swing' (Aldington 1968, 301). Aldington had completed his novel in 1928 in the south of France, at La Vigie on Port Cros in the Îles d'Hyères. Lawrence, now terminally ill, visited him there that October and November, when he read Aldous Huxley's newly published novel *Point*

Counter Point and recognized himself in the character of writer and painter Mark Rampion. 'I am in a novel – ', Lawrence announces in his *Pansies* poem of that title: 'I read a novel by a friend of mine / in which one of the characters was me' (*LP1* 423). Lawrence is 'in' Aldington's novel, too; appearing in *Death of a Hero* as a character – Comrade Bobbe, who is one of a trio of litterateurs with Shobbe (Ford Madox Ford) and Tubbe (T.S. Eliot) – he is also invoked in propria persona in Aldington's narrator's (qualified) tribute to 'D.H. Lawrence', who is 'probably the greatest living English novelist' (*DH* 224).

Aldington duly defers in his own war novel to Lawrence's definitive account of the repercussions of the Great War on the home front. 'I shan't attempt to describe the sinister degradation of English life in the last two years of the war', the narrator of *Death of a Hero* explains, because 'Lawrence has done it once and for all in the chapter called "The Nightmare" in his book *Kangaroo*' (*DH* 224) – a chapter in which Aldington himself is present in absentia as the 'poet serving in the army'. In contrast to 'D.H. Lawrence' the great novelist, however, the character who is modelled on Lawrence in *Death of a Hero* is a 'queer-Dick' in more than one sense. Comrade Bobbe, whose activities are 'subsidized by a demented eugenist and a vegetarian Theosophist', is 'obviously a homosexual type', despite his talk of the 'genuine out-reaching of the inward unconscious Male-life to the dark Womb-life in Woman' (*DH* 110, 125, 127). A 'sandy-haired, narrow-chested little man with spiteful blue eyes and a malevolent class-hatred' Comrade Bobbe 'exercised his malevolence with comparative impunity by trading upon his working-class origin and his indigestion, of which he had been dying for twenty years' (*DH* 124–25). The greater malevolence here is in the fictional treatment of the Lawrence who was in fact dying – not of dyspepsia but of tuberculosis – almost as Aldington finished his book. Lawrence may have been on his way to a sanitorium after leaving Port Cros, but his parting shot to the author of *Death of a Hero* was that 'If you publish this, you'll lose what reputation you have – you're plainly on the way to an insane asylum' (Ridgway n. pag.).

The cruelty of Aldington's caricature (Bobbe, unlike Lawrence, is a conscientious objector but, like him, has an 'excellent faculty of imitation') may be payback in kind, if also in excess, for Lawrence's thumbnail sketch of Aldington as the generic soldier (as a 'stoutish young Englishman in khaki' who is 'about to be demobilised') in *Aaron's Rod* (*DH* 125; *AR* 28). The scene in Lawrence's novel in which the Aldington figure, Robert Cunningham, is introduced is set in the 'drawing-room' of Shottle House in the Nottinghamshire mining country and is played as drawing-room comedy (*AR* 26). Aldington's novel, alternatively, deploys a mode of total satire to travesty a world which has sanctioned total war. As Gérard Genette states in *Palimpsests* 'satire is born from tragedy' (Genette 14), but Aldington proposes a reverse genealogy in *Death of a Hero* in which tragedy is born from satire: 'The death of a hero! What mockery, what bloody cant! What sickening putrid cant!', Aldington's narrator protests, but he also acknowledges that 'Somehow or other we have to make these dead acceptable, we have to atone for them, we have to appease them'.[8] 'Atonement – how can we atone?', the narrator asks, and he adduces Greek tragedy as a medium for effecting the catharsis his own narrative seeks: 'The whole world is blood-guilty, cursed like Orestes, and mad, and destroying itself, as if pursued by an infinite legion of Eumenides' and so 'Somehow we must atone, somehow we must free ourselves from the curse – the blood-guiltiness'. Aldington's theme, in *Death of a Hero*, is 'the theme of the great Greek tragedies of blood' (*DH* 35, 245).

A 'House of Atrides' tragedy, *Death of a Hero*, like the *Oresteia*, is a 'drama of the double'.[9] In Aeschylus' trilogy, Orestes is an archetype of the divided self, cursed for an act of matricide which also amounts to a murder committed 'against a part of the self' (Burkman 92). In his autofictional novel, Aldington's identity is likewise split between his unnamed narrator, who is a Great War veteran, and the fallen 'hero', George Winterbourne, who probably 'committed suicide in that last battle of the war' (*DH* 23). Like Aldington, the narrator is a poet (now turned biographer) who had been the friend of Yeats and Marinetti before the war, while Winterbourne, who had been a painter in civilian life (Robert Cunningham in *Aaron's Rod* is a sculptor) is, like Aldington himself, involved in a wartime love 'triangle of husband, wife, lover' (*DH* 57). The narrator, who is harried by the survivor's guilt which is the modern manifestation of those ancient avengers the Eumenides or Furies, regards himself as Winterbourne's 'executor' in more than the legal definition and so is 'writing the life' of Winterbourne as 'an atonement, a desperate effort to wipe off the blood-guiltiness' of the war (*DH* 23, 36). For his part, Winterbourne is a reluctant actor both in the theatre of war and in the domestic drama of his private life: he is 'living in a sort of double nightmare – the nightmare of the War and the nightmare of his own life. Each seemed inextricably interwoven' (*DH* 226).

Elizabeth and Fanny, his wife and lover, are the double source of Winterbourne's trouble on the domestic front; loosely modelled on H.D. and Dorothy Yorke, the two women are transposed by Aldington, who gives his wife his mistress' looks. 'So very Egyptian' with her 'straight black hair', Elizabeth resembles H.D. only in her 'nervous manner' (*DH* 178, 132). It is Elizabeth Paston and not Fanny

Welford who is a dead ringer for the nearly synonymous Josephine Ford, the Dorothy Yorke figure in *Aaron's Rod*, although it is Fanny who, like Yorke, 'contrived to look stunningly fashionable' (*DH* 179).[10] The narrator tells us that 'each was not so much the antithesis as the complement to the other' and the two women are at one in their common indifference to Winterbourne's fate (*DH* 177–78). As H.D. puts it in *Bid Me to Live*, to Rafe, the Aldington figure in her novel, Julia (H.D. herself) and Bella (Dorothy Yorke) 'were simply abstractions, were women of the period, were WOMAN of the period, the same one' (*BML* 62). What Rafe's wife and mistress *do* have in common, H.D. points out, is that far from being immune to their soldier-husband-lover's war neurosis, both women are themselves psychological casualties of the conflict: where Winterbourne's 'nerves' are 'all to pieces', Julia is 'shot to bits', and 'Bella is shot to pieces' (*DH* 24; *BML* 41, 62). Elizabeth and Fanny in *Death of a Hero* are presented not as civilian victims of the war's fallout but as adepts in the allied arts of war and love in 'veiling the ancient predatory and possessive instincts of the sex under a skilful smoke-barrage of Freudian and Havelock Ellis theories' (*DH* 24).

'I am recording facts', the narrator of *Death of a Hero* insists, but Aldington's novel is a fictionalized biography which, in substituting fictions for 'facts', is hardly faithful to the biographical record (*DH* 171). The stillbirth of H.D.'s and Aldington's baby daughter in 1915 is replaced in the novel by Elizabeth's false alarm pregnancy scare while in another counterfactual fiction 'George had not set foot on the boat which took him to the Boulogne Base-Camp for the first time, before both Elizabeth and Fanny had become absorbed in other "affairs"' (*DH* 27). As Christopher Ridgway observes in his introduction to the 1984 Hogarth Press edition '*Death of a Hero* is a grossly unjust representation of Aldington's life with H.D., since the disintegration of the marriage might more justly be blamed on him' (Ridgway n. pag).

Aldington may insist in his own preface that 'all we claim is that we try to say what appears to be the truth' but although *Death of a Hero* speaks truth to power in calling out 'cant' – the old lie told to justify the Great War – the novel doesn't necessarily corroborate what Fred Crawford deems 'the truth of life' in other aspects (*DH* n. pag.). Rather, in *Death of a Hero*, as in Siegfried Sassoon's semi-autobiographical 'Sherston' trilogy, first-hand experience – including, in Aldington's case and in Sassoon's the author's hands-on experience of the war – is mediated via a second-hand, because fictionalized, mode of life-writing. Like Aldington, Sassoon was pursued by his 'nerve-furies', but *Death of a Hero* is more radically disaffected than the Sherston trilogy in its 'tripartite survey of English society' before, during and after the war (Sassoon 1988, 212; *DH*

n. pag.). Aldington's novel, a topical take on ancient tragedy in its three-part structure and theme of 'blood-guiltiness', also forms the middle part of a trilogy with *Aaron's Rod* and *Bid Me to Live*: a trilogy in which all three novels, like the three stories which make up H.D.'s *Palimpsest* (1926), dramatize, in different versions, the same set of events.

'The war will never be over': *Bid Me to Live*

Palimpsest, an early precursor to *Bid Me to Live*, is the first of what H.D. described in a letter to Cournos as her 'attempted "novels"', autographic prose experiments in which 'writing and life' are not 'diametric opposites' but where 'life and letters' meet (Hollenberg 150; H.D. 1992, 76, 4). In a *Newsweek* interview printed to coincide with the publication of *Bid Me to Live* in 1960, however, H.D. defined her novel in more conventional terms: 'it is a *roman à clef*, and the keys are easy enough to find. I am Julia. And all the others are real people' (Durand 92–3). When one of those real people, Aldington, read *Bid Me to Live* in manuscript in 1953 he told H.D. in a letter that it is 'better than the equivalent chapters in *Aaron's Rod* where Lorenzo was in one of his fits and guying us all' (Zilboorg 2003, 362). Susan Stanford Friedman's similar if sharper point is that in *Bid Me to Live* H.D. 'rescripts a series of contemporary male texts', including *Aaron's Rod*, 'some of which were written for or about her'. Julia Ashton, for example, H.D.'s fictional avatar in the novel, 'is an answer to Lawrence's Julia Cunningham' in *Aaron's Rod*, 'a self-portrait that is closer to the biographical record and that implicitly critiques Lawrence' (Friedman 1990a, 144, 153).

Among the fictional liberties which *Aaron's Rod* – like *Death of a Hero* – takes with the biographical record, it is Julia and not Robert Cunningham (Aldington) who is the first of the pair to commit adultery, justifying in fiction if not in fact Lawrence's disapproval of H.D.'s liaison with the womanizing Cecil Gray. 'After all, one doesn't leave one's husband every day, to go and live with another man': so Tanny, the Frieda Lawrence figure in *Aaron's Rod*, declares, although this is exactly what Frieda herself had done in 1912 in leaving her then husband, Ernest Weekley, to go and live with Lawrence (*AR* 50). In *Bid Me to Live*, H.D. is writing back to Lawrence writing her in *Aaron's Rod*: his Julia is 'like a witch' (*AR* 27), but H.D.'s Julia is 'a witch with power', a 'wise-woman with her witch-ball' who feminizes Lawrence's intuition that 'Cornwall is a country that makes a man psychic' when she goes and lives there with Cyril Vane (Cecil Gray) (*BML* 89; *K* 226).

Bid Me to Live is rewriting as feminist revision, but in correcting the biographical through the bibliographical record the novel also reveals the close interleaving of H.D.'s interpersonal and intertextual relationships with the male writers in her circle. Her novel is a critique of *Aaron's Rod*, *Death of a Hero* and *Miranda Masters*, but it is also a collaboration of kinds with Lawrence, Aldington and Cournos on a composite text: the Mecklenburgh Square novel-palimpsest, of which *Bid Me to Live* supplies the final layer. The gloss on the title page of H.D.'s *Palimpsest* explains that a palimpsest is 'a parchment from which one writing has been erased to make room for another' (n. pag.) but as Sarah Dillon points out in her discussion of 'Murex', the second story layer in *Palimpsest*, H.D.'s definition omits the most compelling feature of the palimpsest: the 'trace' of original or earlier writing which is not wholly 'erased' but remains at least partly legible through or under later inscriptions. As Dillon points out, a palimpsest is made up of multiple texts, 'involved and entangled, intricately interwoven, interrupting and inhabiting one another' (Dillon 2018, 29). Although Dillon's is a more capacious definition it is confined to H.D.'s own 'palimpsestuous' (or intratextual) praxis in *Palimpsest*, closing off consideration of the palimpsestic (or intertextual) relationship between H.D.'s writing and that of her contemporaries.[11] That relationship is played out, in *Bid Me to Live*, in *mise-en-scènes* of writing, like the letter Julia writes to the Lawrence figure, Rico, in the final chapter where writing back to Lawrence is figured as a palimpsestic form of over-writing:

> I will go on scribbling. This very notebook is from the Zennor post-office-stationery-cum-what-not corner shop. You know it. This notebook is a replica of the one you were writing in that day.

Rico, we are told, 'had spread the note-book open on his knee and was scribbling away' – on the early chapters of *Aaron's Rod*, perhaps, which Lawrence had begun in the Mecklenburgh Square days (*BML* 105, 46).[12]

Aaron's Rod is the first layer in the Mecklenburgh Square palimpsest, and so it is, in the terminology of Genette's *Palimpsests*, the 'hypotext' from which *Bid Me to Live*, *Death of a Hero* and *Miranda Masters*, as 'hypertexts', derive. Each of these last three, then, is 'a text in the second degree', 'i.e., a text derived from another preexistent text' (Genette 5).[13] That *Bid Me to Live* is a text in the second degree is all but acknowledged in the novel itself, when Julia tells Rico, in her letter to him, that 'You can write a book about us'. 'I wanted to help too', Julia goes on to say, 'only I didn't want a sort of family album. I wanted a book to myself and as things are, the threads are too tangled' (*BML* 105). H.D. would not have a book to herself and nor in the Mecklenburgh Square days did she have a bedsitting room of her own: the arrival of Rico and Elsa (Frieda Lawrence) means that for Julia 'The room was no longer her home, her own'. 'Elsa's workbag was lying on the floor by one of the table-legs', the spilled contents of the sewing bag material proof of Sydney Janet Kaplan's point, in her composite study of Lawrence, John Middleton Murry and Katherine Mansfield, that 'The filaments of intertextuality' are 'tangled' (*BML* 50; Kaplan 7).

The tangled intertextuality of the Mecklenburgh Square novels is tied up with 'the tangled lives' of their authors and significant others 'during the First World War years' (Norris 2015b, 104). In *Bid Me to Live*, the Lawrence figure, Rico, comes on to Julia (H.D.) only to recoil from her touch with his '*noli me tangere* (his own expression)' – an expression borrowed by Lawrence from Saint John's Gospel for the title of his 1929 *Pansies* poem in which the speaker says 'don't confuse / the body into it, let us stay apart' (*BML* 48; *LP1* 406). Rico, in casting Julia off with his *noli me tangere* line, is casting her as Mary Magdalene to his risen Christ, just as Lawrence had done in acting, or so Cecil Gray alleged, as a 'Jesus Christ to a regiment of Mary Magdalenes', H.D. among them (Gray 1985, 133). Rico – like Lawrence – also directs the Garden of Eden charade at 44 Mecklenburgh Square, in which Julia plays the part of 'the tree of life' while Rico takes the starring role of 'Gawd-a'-mighty'. Rico, who is researching the novel he is writing, asks Julia, indirectly, if she and Vanio (Gray) are sleeping together, but she refuses to answer: 'Rico, your puppets do not always dance to your pipe. Why? Because there is another show'. Lawrence may be pulling the strings in *Aaron's Rod* but H.D. puts on another version of what went on in the Mecklenburgh Square days. 'I am aware of your spider-feelers' Julia says to Rico, but 'I am not walking into your net' (*BML* 67, 100). In *Bid Me to Live*, H.D. herself is the spider-artist who weaves Lawrence into her autofictional web.

The intertextuality of H.D.'s novel is pointed up from the outset in its full title, now restored in Caroline Zilboorg's new edition: *Bid Me to Live (A Madrigal)*. A madrigal is a part song scored for a number of performers in a pattern of contrapuntal imitation.[14] 'An echo, a slightly-varying repetition, is fundamental to the madrigal form' (Tylee 238) and in the parenthetical title of H.D.'s novel there is an echo of Aldington's poem 'Madrigal' – an 'ironic echo', according to Alice Kelly, in that H.D. is 'evoking in the midst of war the image of a lyric form associated with Elizabethan love songs' (Kelly 2020, 185).[15] As Friedman suggests, 'the term "Madrigal" resonated for H.D. with the issues of war and love (love-and-war)' and H.D.'s subtitle resonates more specifically with Aldington's *War and Love*, his 1919 poem sequence which I discuss in the following chapter (Friedman 1990b, 249).[16] The main title of *Bid Me to Live (A Madrigal)* is itself taken from a madrigal, Robert Herrick's 'To Anthea, who may Command him Anything'. The opening words of Herrick's 'To Anthea' are also spoken or sung in *Death of a Hero*: on the evening he meets his wife to be, Elizabeth Paston, at a literary party, George Winterbourne 'began to sing "Bid me to live"' (*DH* 152). Herrick's madrigal is sung again by the Aldington figure, Rafe Ashton, in *Bid Me to Live* and the phrase 'Bid me to live' returns as a refrain – an 'echo of an echo' – throughout H.D.'s novel (*BML* 6).

Herrick's words form an ironic comment on the story of love and war in H.D.'s novel and in Aldington's, whose 'hero' sings 'Bid me to live' but dies on the battlefield. While Rafe, in *Bid Me to Live*, comes through the 1914–18 war, H.D. warns that 'the war will never be over' (*BML* 4), an ominous refrain which in its iterative quality becomes a self-fulfilling prophecy, explaining her novel's belated '*retour*' to the war years more than forty years after the Armistice (Zilboorg 2003, 365). 'The war will never be over': that returning phrase is a textual symptom, perhaps, of the repetition-compulsion identified by Freud as a manifestation of war trauma: 'The terrible war which has just ended gave rise to a great number of illnesses' which may be categorized as 'traumatic neurosis', Freud suggested in 1920, including the 'compulsion to repeat' (Freud 50, 57). H.D. had consulted Freud in Vienna in the early 1930s in order 'to free myself of repetitive thoughts and experiences – my own and those of many of my contemporaries' (H.D. 1970, 13). But in her subsequent sessions with Erich Heydt in Zurich in the 1950s H.D. would find herself back in 'the room', back in the moment, in 1917, when she had walked in on Aldington and Dorothy Yorke in bed together in the room at 44 Mecklenburgh Square: a primal scene of adultery, her memory of which had been erased by traumatic amnesia (*BML* 2).[17]

'Kick over your tiresome house of life' Lawrence advised H.D. when her marriage to Aldington began to fall apart (*BML* 35). But H.D., like Lawrence himself, and Aldington and Cournos, would reconstruct that house of life as a house of fiction: a house cohabited in each of these novels by the same characters. Things from adjacent texts also rematerialize in the Mecklenburgh Square novels, like the 'lump of lapis-lazuli' in *Bid Me to Live* which Rico gives to Julia, leaving it 'on the table, where Julia had been sitting, writing' (*BML* 84). Positioned there, the piece of lapis is, like Julia's Zennor notebook, a 'replica', a re-presentation of the 'blue, beautiful ball of lapis lazuli that stood on [Hermione Roddice's] desk for a paper-weight' in the 'Breadalby' chapter of *Women in Love*, underpinning the likeness between H.D.'s Julia and Ottoline Morrell, the model for Lawrence's Hermione (*WL* 105).[18] The paperweight is a blunt instrument in Lawrence's novel, Latham suggests, in that the scene in which Hermione hits

Rupert Birkin on the head with the ball of lapis lazuli 'brings the book's critique of coterie culture to an appallingly violent climax' (Latham 144). But as an *objet retrouvé* the paperweight has a subtler function, sitting on the fine line in *Bid Me to Live* between life and writing and between H.D.'s writing and Lawrence's. A textual artefact, the lump of lapis-lazuli also has the ontological heft of what Christopher Bollus terms 'objects in the real' (Bollus 59): 'There WAS a blob of lapis', H.D. insisted in a letter to Aldington. 'L. gave it to me that time they stayed at M. Square. He said or F [Frieda] said that the "Ott" had hit him with it. I unfortunately had the lapis cut, gave half away and lost the other half. Symbolical?' (Zilboorg 2003, 358). However, 'Symbolical', as a material object the paperweight cannot be fully absorbed into the symbolic order of H.D.'s novel.[19]

Whether or not Ottoline Morrell gave Lawrence a lapis-lazuli paperweight which he may or may not have given in turn to H.D., another of his women friends, Mary Cannan, *did* give Lawrence a 'lapis seal' or letter stamp (*L4* 190). Lawrence's letters were of greater value, in H.D.'s estimation, than his poetry or his fiction: 'Why, in your interminable novels, do you not write – to someone, anyone – as you write to me in your letters?', Julia asks Rico in *Bid Me to Live*. To Julia, 'Rico's flaming letters had been no ordinary love-letters' but a lifeline: 'this cerebral contact had renewed her'. Julia hides Rico's letters from Rafe, locking them away in her 'jewel-box' (*BML* 100, 33). Lawrence's 'flaming' letters would be burned after the war when Aldington took away the trunk containing his own correspondence with H.D. and Lawrence's letters to her which H.D. had stored in the basement of 44 Mecklenburgh Square when she went to Cornwall with Gray in 1918. 'I left your letters with everything else in London' Julia tells Rico in *Bid Me to Live*. 'I did not have to bring them. I know them by heart' (*BML* 100).[20] These letters or letter fragments, transcribed from memory in *Bid Me to Live*, are reproduced verbatim from H.D.'s novel in the Cambridge Edition of *The Letters of D.H. Lawrence*. The letters to H.D. are ascribed to Lawrence but, as Kinkead-Weekes says, 'sound like Lawrence made over into her own voice' (Kinkead-Weekes 419), suggesting that the 'doublejointed' genre of life-writing to which letter-writing belongs extends to joint authorship (Saunders 7).[21]

In *Bid Me to Live* Julia writes Rico a letter which she never means to send: as the Lawrence figure in *Aaron's Rod*, Rawdon Lily, remarks, 'When a man writes a letter to himself, it is a pity to post it to someone else. Perhaps the same is true of a book' (*AR* 264). Julia's is, in any case, a dead letter since it is addressed, c/o Rico, to the Lawrence who had died thirty years before H.D.'s novel was published. Lawrence's own letters, however, posthumously published in Aldous Huxley's 1932 edition, had brought him back to life for his friends and contemporaries.

Writing to her partner, Bryher, in 1933, H.D. told her that 'I have been soaking in D.H.L. letters, not too good for me, but Freud seems to agree with me for once. Evidently, I blocked the whole of the "period" and if I can skeleton-in a vol. about it, it will break the clutch' (Friedman 1981, 30). That 'vol.' – *Bid Me to Live* – is, according to H.D.'s daughter, Perdita Schaffner, 'straight autobiography, a word-for-word transcript' (Schaffner 186). A transcription of lived experience or feminist reinscription: *Bid Me to Live* supports both interpretations. In the letter to Lawrence with which the novel concludes, H.D. collapses the false binary of his 'sex-fixations, his man-is-man, woman-is-woman' in an assertion of artistic equity and of creative androgyny in which the '*gloire*' – a loan word from Lawrence and from Virginia Woolf, which for H.D. connotes aesthetic vision itself – is 'both' (*BML* 35, 107).²² 'Perhaps I caught the *gloire* from you', Julia suggests to Rico, but the affective or viral quality of that *gloire*, she tells him, 'isn't in your books, it was in your letters, sometimes' (*BML* 107). The *gloire* is in 'both' in *Bid Me to Live*, a book in which life and letters meet.

Life and letters: *Miranda Masters*

In the 1922 letter to John Cournos in which she discusses her own 'attempted "novels"', H.D. also tells him that she is 'most eager to read "Babel"', the final volume in his autofictional trilogy charting the Ukrainian-born Cournos' remarkable journey from the Philadelphia ghetto to the avant-garde circles of 1910s London (Hollenberg 150–51). In chapter six of *Babel*, Cournos' protagonist and alter ego, John Gombarov, attends a salon at 'a large Georgian house' in London:

> A little statuette, hewed out of granite, which stood on a writing desk [...] attracted his attention. It was the figure of a pregnant negress, and she stood in an attitude of torment, curved almost into a question mark, her two hands on her stomach. It bore the inscription, *The Fecund Earth* [...]. There was an extraordinary potency in it for so small a piece of stone. Hardly more than fifteen inches high, it yet gave an illusion of bigness; decorative, it was yet deliberately crude; a thing fraught with elemental forces, wrought by them from within and without; it was as a mountain in travail giving birth to new life.
>
> (Cournos 1922, 251, 255)

As its title tells us, *Babel* speaks in more than one tongue, and the language of this passage is that of the 'Crème de Menthe' chapter of Lawrence's *Women in Love*. Cournos' *salonnière*, Mrs Rodd, isn't modelled on Philip Heseltine (Julius

Halliday, in *Women in Love*) but she is nearly synonymous with Lawrence's Hermione Roddice, while Mrs Rodd's house at 44 Soho Square is a forwarding address for 44 Bedford Square, the townhouse in which Ottoline Morrell held her celebrated Thursday soirées. For the salon scene in *Babel*, Cournos – like H.D., in *Bid Me to Live* – borrows a prop from *Women in Love*. The 'African' figurine is carved of granite, not of wood, but as a textual artefact, the statuette is a 'curio' out of Lawrence's 'modernist cabinet' (Pinkney 96) in the close resemblance it bears to the West African 'fetish' which so fascinates Gerald Crich when he visits Halliday's Soho flat:

> there were several negro statues, wood-carvings from West Africa, strange and disturbing, the carved negroes looked almost like the foetus of a human being. One was of a woman sitting naked in a strange posture, and looking tortured, her abdomen stuck out [...] she was sitting in childbirth, clutching the ends of the band that hung from her neck, one in each hand, so that she could bear down, and help labour. The strange, transfixed, rudimentary face of the woman again reminded Gerald of a foetus, it was also rather wonderful, conveying the suggestion of the extreme of physical sensation, beyond the limits of mental consciousness.
>
> (*WL* 74)[23]

Is the likeness between these passages merely coincidental, given that African carvings were common primitivist property in the 1910s?[24] Or is Cournos fetishizing Lawrence's representation of the 'fetish', cashing in, with his replica statuette, on the symbolic capital of *Women in Love*'s original? Should we parse the passage from *Babel* as pastiche or parody or plagiarism? Or is Cournos experimenting with a more radical form of recursion, feeding a scene from Lawrence's novel into his own in an intertextual playback loop? These interpretations need not be mutually exclusive if we accept Genette's classification of parody – together with caricature and forgery – as 'hypertextual' genres. Hypertextuality per se, in Genette's definition, is an intentional form of the '*transtextuality*' which creates 'a relationship of copresence between texts or among several texts' (Genette 1).

A verbal simulacrum of Halliday's 'fetish', Mrs Rodd's statuette is also modelled on Jacob Epstein's *Female Figure in Flenite* (1913), a sculpture carved from serpentine stone, or 'flenite' in Epstein's coinage (Figure 4). The piece was owned not by Lady Ottoline but by the Imagist poet and aesthetician T.E. Hulme; when Hulme was killed in the trenches in 1917, Epstein reacquired the piece.[25] Cournos comments on Epstein's flenite series in his 1917 article 'New Tendencies in English Sculpture and Painting':

Figure 4 Jacob Epstein, *Female Figure in Flenite* (1913).
Tate Gallery, London. © the Estate of Sir Jacob Epstein. Photo: Tate.

> His little figures, in hard green flenite, of women tortured with pregnancy, are, in spite of their subject – revolting to many, masterpieces of workmanship. It is extraordinary how statues so small, and massed so serenely, could suggest such hugeness and such intense torture, like mountains in travail.
>
> (Cournos 1917b, 774)

Epstein, Alan Munton notes, had become 'familiar with the "primitivism" of the Parisian avant-garde' in 1912 when he was working in Paris on his Oscar Wilde monument and began to collect African and Oceanic sculpture, buying from Paul Guillaume, the dealer who 'turned the fetish into a commodity' (Munton 79). If as a collector Epstein was complicit in the commodity fetishism that marketed non-Western religious artefacts as artworks, then as a sculptor in his own right Epstein would be charged with producing a modernist imitation of 'tribal' or 'primitive' art: of practicing primitivism in what Genette would term 'the second degree'. In 'Mr Epstein and the Critics', published in *The New Age* in December 1913, Hulme had countered the criticism levelled at Epstein's flenite carvings that 'an artist has no business to use formulae taken from another civilisation'. Such formulae, Hulme insisted – preempting the Lawrence of *Women in Love* – are apposite 'in the peculiar conditions in which we find ourselves, which are really the breaking up of an era' (Hulme 251–52). Epstein himself subsequently rebutted the charge that his sculpture was 'largely influenced' by 'African work', insisting as Brancusi had also done that 'my work is not African'. Rather, Epstein affirmed, his 'green flenite woman expresses all the tragedy and enigma of the germinal universe', a statement which contradicts the symbolic meaning – the degeneration of a civilizational cycle – which Lawrence intuited from his 'pregnant negress' but comports with the inscription, *The Fecund Earth*, appended to the flenite figure in *Babel* (Epstein n. pag.).

The charges of imitativeness and even plagiarism made against Epstein in his 'archaic' period could also be levelled at Cournos for reproducing the 'fetish' episode of *Women in Love*, down to the avant-garde interior design connecting Halliday's flat and Mrs Rodd's drawing room in which an 'African' sculpture is set off by Futurist paintings.[26] As Cournos was aware, Lawrence's novel had itself been charged with identity theft due to its libellous pen portraits of Philip Heseltine (as Julius Halliday) and Ottoline Morrell (as Hermione Roddice). The subjects of Cournos' own pen portraiture in *Babel* include H.D. and Aldington, introduced in chapter six as 'a young couple' who, like Gombarov, admire the 'little statuette' in Mrs Rodd's drawing room. They are Mr and Mrs Hector Cowley, 'otherwise known as Heracles and Hylas, because of the Greekishness of their poetry', Mr. Rodd explains to Gombarov – not, he hastens to add, 'that there is anything pseudo-classic about their work' (Cournos 1922, 256). Their surname makes the couple the legitimate heirs of seventeenth-century poet-translator Abraham Cowley, yet the inference is that with their Hellenistic pretensions these decadent moderns are the end of Abraham's line. Like H.D. and Aldington, Cournos was associated with Imagism – a 'pseudo-classic' poetics more than nominally influenced by the visual culture of modernism – in its Poundian period, and both Gombarov and the Cowleys admire the flenite figurine, which is positioned, like the lapis paperweight on Julia's writing table in *Bid Me to Live*, on Mr Rodd's 'writing desk' (Cournos 1922, 255).[27] The sculpture, or Cournos' verbal copy of it, is associated with the written word and with the visual and plastic arts, media which meet in Mr Rodd himself, who is a verbal portrait not of Lady Ottoline's politician husband, Philip Morrell, but of Bloomsbury art critic Clive Bell.

Babel takes Gombarov on a whistlestop tour of the bohemian milieux of a London 'tottering' on the brink of war (Cournos 1922, 328). Cournos locates the avant-garde in the *avant-guerre*, as Peter Brooker points out, but at the same time – or in a modernist experiment *with* narrative time – *Babel* restages a set piece from *Women in Love*, a novel written 'in the midst of the period of war' (*WL* 485).²⁸ Although he changes the cast of characters and installs Epstein's sculpture in his salon chapter in lieu of Lawrence's African carving, Cournos showcases the transmedial circulation and interchange of the verbal and visual arts between *Women in Love* and *Babel* itself and the Mecklenburgh Square novels.

Cournos, who is ghosted by Lawrence in *Aaron's Rod*, gaslights H.D. in *Miranda Masters*: following her walk-on part as Mrs Cowley in *Babel*, H.D. now features as the eponymous villainess of the piece. Miranda, aka 'Aspasia', is a modern hetaira who carries her 'Greek torch', the 'symbol of old life, now dying', through the darkness of wartime London (Cournos 1926, 1–4). A 'neurotic', Miranda is also, in the judgement of her husband, Arnold Masters, 'a woman of genius – the greatest poetess, to his way of thinking, since Sappho'. Arnold 'did not, as others would have done, regard her condition as hysteria attributable to the war', but attributes her disturbed state of mind instead to postpartum grief for their 'infant', the daughter 'born dead' who had been 'as beautiful, if hearsay is to be believed, as the most beautiful of her chiselled poems' (Cournos 1926, 12, 4). Her sexual abstinence following the stillbirth means that Miranda and Arnold sleep in their bed with a 'sword' between them like medieval tomb effigies. When Arnold is sent away for officer training, Miranda, on Gombarov's recommendation, sublets her room in 'one of the most charming of the numerous Bloomsbury squares' to Gombarov's erstwhile fiancée Winifred Gwynne (Dorothy Yorke) (Cournos 1926, 33, 18). On Arnold's return to London and in the absence of Gombarov, who has gone off to Russia, a sexual relationship begins between Arnold and Winifred. Gombarov blames Miranda for actively encouraging the affair, just as he had blamed her for leading him on and then turning him down as a lover when Arnold had first enlisted; in his frustration, Gombarov had taken Miranda's advice to 'Go into the street', to a prostitute, worrying afterwards that he has contracted a sexually transmitted disease, for which he blames Miranda too. 'When I said I could love you', Miranda subsequently explains in a letter to Gombarov, 'I meant if it would help Arnold' (Cournos 1926, 178, 158). Gombarov, then, twice plays 'second fiddle to Arnold', but it is Miranda, he claims, who is 'the direct author of his misfortunes'. Miranda channels Arnold's infidelities into her poetry – 'The hurt I suffered has freed my song', she tells Gombarov. Likewise, Gombarov attempts to reclaim a 'vestige of himself' by turning to 'his book, into which he had poured all his suffering' (Cournos 1926, 156, 181–2). His book is *The Mask*, which was begun at 44 Mecklenburgh Square and is the first volume in the autobiographical trilogy which Cournos would call his 'life-work' (Cournos 1935, 287). *Miranda Masters*, as the coda to that trilogy, is a 'page from the book of his life' which proves the adage that revenge is a dish best served cold (Cournos 1926, 160).

H.D. read *Miranda Masters* on its publication in 1926 and she would continue to correspond with Cournos for several years afterwards: surprisingly, perhaps, given that his novel reproduces verbatim several of her letters to him.[29] Life and letters meet – with a vengeance – in Cournos' novel. Although H.D. herself would reproduce from memory parts of Lawrence's letters to her in *Bid Me to Live*, blurring the lines between genres and between public and private domains in her experimental life-writing, in *Miranda Masters* Cournos pushes at the envelope of acceptable taste as much as of literary convention. Lawrence is a dominant presence in the letters from H.D. which are directly transcribed, but rendered as direct speech – 'intensely uttered, nervous, almost hysterical speech' – in *Miranda Masters*:

> There is a yellow flame – bright, hard, clear, terrible, cruel! There is the yellow that sees in me its exact complement. There is a power in this person to kill me! I mean literally. [...] You no doubt know of whom I speak as a cruel fire. I do not want that person to die. He has a great gift! But I must be protected! I know you will protect me from him ....
>
> (Cournos 1926, 175)[30]

Miranda's verbal iteration of the visual theory of personality posited by H.D. in her own letter shows Cournos' neurotic protagonist in her true colours: 'I now seem to see clearly colours in relation to people', Miranda says. Arnold is 'wine-red', like the Aldington figure in *Aaron's Rod*, who 'drank red wine in large throatfuls' (*AR* 28), while Gombarov himself, perhaps as a touchstone of their friendship, is 'lapis-lazuli blue!' (Cournos 1926, 174–5).

Miranda's Bloomsbury 'rooms' have 'told many tales', Cournos says, his own novel among them (Cournos 1926, 38). Closely intertwined with the other Mecklenburgh Square novels, *Miranda Masters*' metaphors of threading and weaving – 'like a thread in a pattern', Cournos writes, 'Arnold wove his words into the woof of [Miranda's] thought' – are worked into and reworked in the Penelope's web of H.D.'s autofiction (Cournos 1926, 58). In *Bid Me to Live*, 'the thread binding past and present was not broken' but is a 'thin living web' (*BML* 23). 'We have held together as artists', Gombarov says of himself and Miranda, and he identifies artists as the 'chosen' few whose task it is 'to carry on the creative thread', while of the interpersonal tangle between Miranda, Arnold and himself, Gombarov remarks that 'your fate and his and mine are irrevocably interwoven' (Cournos 1926, 197, 174). Another metaphor in *Miranda Masters*, that of 'the experiment', is repeated in *Bid in Live* but with a different result (Cournos 1926, 154). Where the experiment in *Miranda Masters* consists of Miranda's meddling in other people's love affairs, in *Bid Me to Live*, the experiment conducted by Rico, the Lawrence figure, in 'a test-tube, this room', is an experiment with the autographic novel itself and its human subjects: 'there they were, separate elements in a test-tube. The experiment was under way' (*BML* 57, 52).

'I am not one of those who holds art more important than life', Gombarov opines in *Miranda Masters*. 'Indeed I think the great thing is to have both in equal measure, to strike a balance somewhere between the two. Life should be an art, and art should not be less vital than life' (Cournos 1926, 110). *Miranda Masters* is nonetheless a *roman à clef*, a novel with a key to a house of life: the authors of the other Mecklenburgh Square novels – Lawrence, Aldington and H.D. – throw away the key and tear down the dividing wall between the house of fiction and the house of life.

Notes

1   In his autobiography Aldington says of *Death of a Hero* that 'I wanted the construction to follow the main lines of a Greek tragedy' (Aldington 1968, 302).
2   The David Eder Farm in Kent was established in the 1930s to prepare prospective Jewish emigrants to set up self-sufficient little colonies – *kibbutzim* – in what would become the state of Israel. See Eder's *Memoirs of a Modern Pioneer*.
3   For Douglas' sexual proclivities, see Cleaves' critical biography, *Unspeakable*. '[T]he facts about Douglas no man would dare to print', Lawrence remarked in a 1925 letter (*L5* 231).
4   See Mackenzie (1967, 84–5).
5   In June 1926 Mackenzie invited Lawrence to accompany him on a trip to the Outer Hebrides, an invitation Lawrence declined (see *WWRA* xxxvii). In the 1930s Mackenzie built the house on Barra where *The Four Winds of Love* was written.
6   Henry James describes the novel as the 'house of fiction' in his 1909 preface to *The Portrait of a Lady* (H. James 1986, 45).
7   On Lawrence, Eliot and war trauma, see Krockel.
8   Genette is citing Renaissance scholar Julius Caesar Scaliger.
9   For Orestes and the 'double', see Burkman 18.

10 According to Aldington the characters of Elizabeth and Fanny were drawn from two of his postwar lovers, Valentine Dobrée and Nancy Cunard, perhaps suggesting that in his novel Aldington is exercising the same discretion – not to kiss and tell – with which he treats H.D. and Yorke in his autobiography. Cunard is a sitter for one of the 'satirical portrait-biographies' in Aldington's 1932 collection, *Soft Answers*. Constance, in 'Now She Lies There', is a 'symbolical figure, an embodiment of the post-war plutocracy and its jazz Dance of Death', of 'the bored revellers who had caroused so drearily over the graves of the war dead' and who had 'got drunk once too often and lost their money – the blood money of the dead legions' (Aldington 1949, 18, 105).

11 Dillon discusses both Lawrence and H.D. in her monograph *The Palimpsest* but she does so in discrete chapters. The focus of her Lawrence chapter is on the figure of the palimpsest in his poetry.

12 On H.D.'s 'metafiction of intertextual play', see Friedman (1990a, 151).

13 The palimpsest for Genette is a figure for textuality per se, whilst hypertextuality, a subset, denotes 'any relationship uniting a text B' – 'the *hypertext*' – and 'an earlier text A' – 'the *hypotext*' (Genette 1).

14 For the madrigal as musical form, see Corneilson 229.

15 Kelly is quoting from Friedman (1990b, 233–34). Aldington's poem 'Madrigal' appears in his volume *Exile and Other Poems* (1923).

16 See Monteverdi, *Madrigals of Love and War* (1638).

17 On her analysis with Heydt, see H.D. (2012). For traumatic amnesia, see Pederson 334.

18 Firchow posits that 'Julia Cunningham [in *Aaron's Rod*] may be an intentional reworking of aspects of Hermione Roddice's character' (Firchow 73). The subject of H.D.'s autographic novel *HERmione*, written in 1927 and published in 1981, is her early relationship with Frances Gregg.

19 Frances Wilson states in her biography of Lawrence that when *Women in Love* was published 'Ottoline noted that she had given Lawrence a present of a similar lump of lapis lazuli', but the only provenance Wilson provides for its extratextual existence is another text: H.D.'s *Bid Me to Live* (Wilson 2021a, 111).

20 Aldington took the trunk to Hermitage in Berkshire where he rented the cottage in which the Lawrences had lived. He asked his neighbour there to burn the letters (see Whelpton 2021).

21 On the status of these letter fragments, see Worthen.

22 Lawrence's poem 'Gloire de Dijon' is included in his 1917 volume *Look! We Have Come Through!* For 'gloire', see Wade 91. Woolf plays with the word 'gloire' in her own experimental autobiofiction, *Orlando* (1928) (Woolf 1992b, 85).

23 Lawrence had written to Ottoline Morrell in January 1916 asking that she bring with her on her visit to him in Cornwall 'one or two books … anything really

African, Fetish Worship or the customs of primitive tribes' (*L2* 510–11). That spring, Lawrence read E.B. Tylor's two-volume *Primitive Culture* (1871) (see *L2* 593). As the editors of the Cambridge edition of *Women in Love* note, Philip Heseltine owned a number of Yoruba or Ere Ibeji figures (*WL* 538 n.74:10).

24 Cecil Gray verifies that Heseltine displayed 'African fetishes' in his Chelsea studio-attic (Gray 1934, 144). Lawrence's friend the painter Mark Gertler had 'also acquired an African carving by 1915', the Benin head which appears in many of his still lifes (*WL* 538 n.74:10). Maurice Beebe speculates that a passage describing African figurines in Gilbert Cannan's novel *Mendel*, the artist-protagonist of which is modelled on Gertler, 'may explain the appearance of a similar scene in *Women in Love*' (Beebe 304). Cournos, who had discussed Gertler in an essay on English painting and sculpture published in the little magazine *Seven Arts* in 1917, probably read and possibly reviewed Cannan's novel (see Cournos 1917b). An anonymous review printed in *Seven Arts* earlier in 1917 finds that *Mendel* 'conveys a very dim, cold, and almost abstract sense of the English society which Mendel is supposed to throw into relief' (Anonymous 252).

25 Ottoline Morrell was Epstein's early patron; she commissioned statuary from him for Garsington Manor (see Gilboa 119). *Female Figure in Flenite* was purchased by the Tate Gallery (now Tate Britain) in 1972.

26 If the African statue in *Babel* is a steal from Lawrence, Cournos' theft raises issues of a different order than the ethical debate about the repatriation of, for example, the Benin bronzes, from institutions such as the British Museum (see Hicks). The artworks in the Rodd townhouse in *Babel* include Futurist paintings titled *The War in the Air* and *Friedrichsbanhof, Berlin*.

27 For modernism and visual culture, see Beasley (2007). Cournos had contributed to Pound's (1914) anthology *Des Imagistes* but he would not be invited to contribute to Lowell's *Some Imagist Poets* anthologies.

28 See the discussion of 'Bohemia in Babel' in Brooker (2007, 23–6).

29 See Hollenberg 129.

30 Compare the text of H.D.'s letter (see Hollenberg 140).

3

Between the lines: Imagism and the Great War

In his extended flashback to the First World War in *Kangaroo*, Lawrence describes 'a gorgeous commotion in Somers' rooms' in Bloomsbury: 'four poets and three non-poets, all fighting out poetry: a splendid time' – until Richard Lovatt Somers, Lawrence's autobiographical protagonist, comes downstairs to find 'three policemen in the porch' (*K* 249). That Lawrence and Frieda were under surveillance following their expulsion from Cornwall in the autumn of 1917 is verified by Richard Aldington, who records in his autobiography that he had 'discovered a strange man lurking on the stairway' of 44 Mecklenburgh Square when the Lawrences were lodging in H.D.'s rooms there: 'I asked him what he was doing, and he astonished me by saying he was from Scotland Yard and engaged in sleuthing Lawrence' (Aldington 1968, 211).

The three 'non-poets' at the gathering reconstructed in *Kangaroo* were Frieda Lawrence, Dorothy Yorke and Cecil Gray; of the four poets present, three – H.D., Aldington and Lawrence– were members of the Imagist school of poetry. John Cournos, a Mecklenburgh Square resident and, with H.D. and Aldington, a contributor to Ezra Pound's *Des Imagistes: An Anthology* (1914), was away in Russia. Robert Nichols – not an Imagist but a Georgian – may have been the fourth poet at the party: Nichols, who had been invalided home with shell-shock when Philip Heseltine introduced him to Lawrence in 1915, would go on to score 'one of the hits of 1917' with his second volume of war verse, *Ardours and Endurances* (Fussell 321).[1] A halfway house and a house of fiction, 44 Mecklenburgh Square was also, as the vignette in *Kangaroo* attests, an open house for poets of various stripes – veterans, combatants, civilians, Imagists and others. This chapter considers the close imbrication of Imagism with the First World War in the poetry of Lawrence, Aldington and H.D.

Lawrence had first met H.D. and Aldington on 30 July 1914, five days before Britain declared war on Germany: meeting him, according to H.D.'s version in

Bid Me to Live, 'happened actually almost identically with the breaking out of the war' (*BML* 86). The occasion was a dinner party at the Berkeley Hotel in Knightsbridge, hosted by American poet and editor Amy Lowell; 'a captain of poets', Lowell had taken over the Imagist helm from Pound, and she now wanted Lawrence on board (Williams 60).[2] It may be that Lawrence, as Helen Carr suggests, 'regarded imagism as an advertising scheme', but he would contribute nonetheless to the three *Some Imagist Poets* anthologies, sponsored by Lowell, which were published between 1915 and 1917, their annual format modelled on that of Edward Marsh's popular *Georgian Poetry* anthologies, in four of the five volumes of which Lawrence's poetry also appeared (Carr 2009, 689). His dealings with Imagists and Georgians alike perhaps imply Lawrence's fealty to neither faction in the poetry wars of the 1910s. But that he had dealings with both proves the point made in the preface to *Some Imagist Poets* (1915) that although they may have been 'banded together between one set of covers' the post-Poundian Imagists did not constitute a 'clique' or an 'exclusive artistic set' (Lowell 1915, vi, viii). Imagism was now to be a 'coöperative venture' and the anthologies were indeed 'democratic', down to their format and financial model: contributors 'were put in alphabetical order' so as 'to avoid any appearance of precedence', each receiving an equal share of royalties (Lowell 1915, vi).[3] There were fewer contributors to Lowell's anthologies than to Pound's *Des Imagistes*, but in other respects Lowell's Imagism formed a broader church than Pound's prewar Imagist cenacle. Writing to Harriet Monroe, the editor of *Poetry*, the Chicago-based journal which had printed the first Imagist poems and manifestos in 1912 and 1913, Pound told her that 'If I had acceded to A.L.'s proposal to turn "Imagism" into a democratic beer-garden, I should have undone what little good I had managed to do by setting up a critical standard', a judgement seemingly borne out by the slide of the strict precepts of Poundian Imagism into the laxer free verse of 'the new poetry' (Pound 1971, 48).[4] But this chapter charts another narrative of Imagism or 'Amygism' in the war years, in which *avant-guerre* experimentalism, under the pressure of contemporary events, forms a new and hybrid idiom: that of war Imagism.[5]

Lawrence had come hotfoot to Lowell's Imagist soirée from *Georgian Poetry* editor Edward Marsh, who had told him, in his capacity as Private Secretary to the First Lord of the Admiralty, Winston Churchill, that 'we shall be in the war' (Aldington 1968, 128). Lawrence's association with Imagism was therefore coterminous with the war from the outset, and his three uncollected war poems – 'Resurrection', 'Eloi, Eloi, lama sabachthani?' and 'Errinyes' – would all be published on Imagist platforms, in the American and British little magazines

Poetry and *The Egoist* and in Lowell's anthologies; Lawrence, as Pound put it, 'was never an Imagist. He was an Amygist' (Jones 25).⁶ Lawrence's relationship to Imagism thus has a different trajectory from that of H.D. and Aldington: whereas Imagism and the war poem are all but synonymous in Lawrence's career, the cool and impersonal classicism of Aldington's and H.D.'s early Imagism would not withstand the traumatic impact of the war on the Western and home fronts. Notwithstanding their different entry points on Imagism's timeline, however, the convergence of Lawrence, H.D. and Aldington on the eve of the war presages their collective re-inflection of Imagist poetics during the conflict.

Following the suppression of *The Rainbow* in November 1915, Lawrence needed every red cent, but his investment in Imagism, not for profit but as a poetics, seems to have been underwritten by his high valuation of H.D.'s verse. 'Don't you realise that this is poetry?', Lawrence had asked H.D. – according to her recreation of events – when they met 'that day at the top floor of the Berkeley' (*BML* 85).⁷ In *Bid Me to Live*, where she replays their encounter, H.D. tells us that Lawrence 'liked her flower poems' ('Sea Lily', 'Sea Iris' and 'Sea Rose', which H.D. had brought with her for inclusion in the maiden *Some Imagist Poets* anthology), and so he 'called her Persephone', after the flower girl of classical mythology. The corollary, for H.D., is that Lawrence is 'Dis of the under-world, the husband of Persephone', a mythical stand-in for H.D.'s actual and all too human husband, Aldington (*BML* 86). The coalescence of poetry, chthonic myth and war in H.D.'s account of their meeting would characterize her lifelong literary relationship with Lawrence. This chapter takes up that conversation between Lawrence and H.D., struck up on the eve of the war and to which Aldington was a third party, in its reappraisal of these three Imagists in time of war.

'How shall we get out of this Inferno?': Lawrence

'The First World War and its subsequent personal and cultural consequences constituted a kind of death for H.D.', Susan Stanford Friedman has suggested, 'a descent to the underworld from which she had to emerge in a process of spiritual rebirth that was decades in the making' (Friedman 1981, 9). Lawrence and Aldington likewise conceived of the world war and wartime London as an underworld. Writing to Cecil Gray from Hampstead on 17 October 1917, shortly before he moved with Frieda to H.D.'s rooms in Bloomsbury, Lawrence complains that:

London is really very bad: gone mad, in fact. It thinks and breathes and lives air-raids, nothing else. People are not people any more: they are factors, really ghastly, like Lemures, evil spirits of the dead. What shall we do, how shall we get out of this Inferno? 'Pray not to die on the brink of so much horror', to parody myself.

(*L3* 170)

Lawrence is parodying his poem 'Craving for Spring', published in his 1917 volume, *Look! We Have Come Through!*[8] His Persephone poem may have been seeded by H.D.'s flower poems, but in his letter to Gray Lawrence alludes to Aldington's 'Lemures', a poem in which the restless spirits of the Roman dead – the *lemures* invoked in Horace's *Epistles* and in Ovid's *Fasti* – are transhistorical travellers, manifesting both in ancient times in 'Thebes of Egypt' and in the 'Now' of wartime London (*CPRA* 29). 'Lemures' had appeared in April 1915 in the first of the *Some Imagist Poets* anthologies; in December of that year, Lawrence told Bertrand Russell that he had been reading J.G. Frazer's *Totemism and Exogamy*, which includes an account of Madagascan lemur-lore according to which the babacoote (a large lemur) is the embodiment of an ancestor-spirit (see *L2* 470). Lawrence had also read *The Golden Bough*, Frazer's compendium of comparative mythology in which belief in the return of the dead is posited as a universal phenomenon, and he draws on Frazer's comparativist myth-kitty – a primary source-book for the Imagists, and in the postwar period, for T.S. Eliot in *The Waste Land* (1922) – in 'Resurrection', an uncollected war poem first drafted in October 1915 and belatedly printed in *Poetry* in 1917 (see *LP3* ciii–civ).

'Frazer's notion of resurrection symbolism being re-enacted by various myths shaped the mythopoeia of both H.D. and D.H. Lawrence', according to Scott Freer. But Freer also differentiates H.D.'s 'syncretic mythopoeia' from Lawrence's 'genealogical method', which 'recovers pagan antecedents' from 'subsequent Christian deformations' (Freer 13, 108). That distinction, while it is valid for the most part, does not hold in 'Resurrection', in which pagan and Judeo-Christian mythologies are composited into the Frazerian archetype of the wounded god. A letter to Cynthia Asquith, written in November 1915, may be read as a gloss on Lawrence's poem: 'My heart is smashed into a thousand fragments, and I shall never have the energy to collect the bits – like Osiris – or Isis', Lawrence says, and he goes on to declare:

> I want to begin all all [*sic*] again. All these Gethsemane Calvary and Sepulchre stages must be over now: there must be a resurrection – resurrection: a resurrection with sound hands and feet and a whole body and a new soul: above all, a new soul: a resurrection.

(*L2* 454)

Lawrence's letter, which connects the Isis and Osiris myth with his own 'whole body' revision of Christian theology, is written under the same Frazerian rubric as 'Resurrection'. The speaker of Lawrence's poem, quoted here from the version printed in *Poetry*, is a Christ-cum-Persephone figure who, even as 'The dead [of the First World War] are burning in the funeral wind', 'like a strange light breaking from the ground, / [...] venture[s] from the halls of shadowy death - / A frail white gleam of resurrection' (Lawrence 1917, 139). The poem's speaker asserts that

> [...] like a cyclamen, a crocus flower
> In autumn, like to a messenger come back
> From embassy in death, I issue forth.
>
> (Lawrence 1917, 139)

'Resurrection' anticipates the underworld mythos of 'Snake' and of Lawrence's *Last Poems*, but in its imagery – of the leaves of the innumerable dead – the poem also looks back to its precursors: to Shelley's 'Ode to the West Wind' and to Shelley's source in canto III of Dante's *Inferno*, behind which, in turn, are anterior journeys to the underworld in the *Aeneid* and *Iliad*.[9] Where Lawrence writes of 'all the lives / That whirl and sweep like anxious leaves away', in Dante the spirits of the dead fall from the banks of Acheron 'As in autumn the leaves drop off one after the other till the branch sees all its spoils on the ground' (Lawrence 1917, 139). Dante's canto, in which the speaker witnesses 'so long a train of people that I should never have believed death had undone so many' (Dante Alighieri 53, 49), is also adduced as an intertext in the evocation of London as a 'dead city' in *Bid Me to Live* and in *The Waste Land*, where 'A crowd flowed over London Bridge, so many, / I had not thought death had undone so many' (*BML* 65; Eliot 1969, 62).

Lawrence is seldom considered in the same allusive terms as Eliot, yet the intertextuality of 'Resurrection' is pointed up when the poem is read in the context of its publication in *Poetry*. The June 1917 number opens with Pound's 'Three Cantos' or Ur-Cantos, the first of which invokes Robert Browning – and Browning's own transtextual transaction with Shelley – Pound's poem enacting the claim in Browning's *Sordello* that 'poets know the dragnet's trick / Catching the dead' (Browning 1:151).[10] For Pound the poet is a resurrection man whereas the first-person speaker of Lawrence's poem presents himself as the Ishmael-like sole survivor of the catastrophe – 'all the lives lost' – of the Great War. But the speaker of 'Resurrection' is also a 'messenger', an emissary from an underworld peopled not only by the war dead but also by Shelley, Dante and Virgil: the 'dead poets' of the past invoked in Eliot's essay 'Tradition and the

Individual Talent', first published in two parts in *The Egoist* in 1919 (Eliot 2021b, 105). As Richard Badenhausen has argued, modernist poets 'expanded the scope of what it means to collaborate' in that, as Eliot's essay proposes, 'a reciprocity exists between dead writer and practicing artist, a relationship that adjusts past and present texts' (Badenhausen 8).

There are contemporary connectivities, too, between 'Resurrection' and Imagist networks. Lawrence had read John Burnet's *Early Greek Philosophy* in July 1915, and Carr proposes that when he met up again with H.D. and Aldington in the autumn of that year in Hampstead, Lawrence's 'keen interest in the Greeks' may well 'have played a part in their growing friendship', a friendship which, in turn, fostered Lawrence's closer connection, from 1915, to the Imagists (Carr 2009, 793). That October, Lawrence sent 'Resurrection' to Harriet Monroe, hailed by F.S. Flint as *'the Editor who discovered Imagism'*, at *Poetry* magazine, telling her to send the poem back if she didn't like it (Flint 1915, 74; see *L2* 417).[11] In March 1917, when a later variant was accepted by *Poetry*, Lawrence sent Monroe the 1915 'Resurrection' again, giving her permission to 'use which you like' (*L8* 22). Using what she liked from both versions, Monroe printed an unauthorized conflation of the two.

Monroe's composite text opens with a (repunctuated) line from the 1915 'Resurrection': 'Now all the hosts are marching to the grave' (Lawrence 1917, 139). In choosing this over the opening of the later version Lawrence had sent her, 'Now like a crocus in the autumn time', Monroe prioritizes the deadly teleology of war and the march of contemporary history over the seasonal cycle of death and rebirth in nature (*LP3* 1522). Her choice may have been informed by the timing of the poem's appearance in *Poetry* in June 1917, the month in which the first US troops were dispatched to Europe. Monroe's own opinions on the war and on America's entry into the conflict, articulated in what Mark Whalan describes as 'a series of extraordinary editorials' in *Poetry*, also inflect her composite 'Resurrection' (Whalan 48). Her editorial for the January 1917 issue, for example, notes that 'men and nations are just about to begin their militant march'. For so many this would be the 'march to the grave' of Lawrence's poem, but Monroe construes the march of history as positive progress 'toward the common goal' of a post-national global federation which, she believed, the war would bring about: 'Through the war the spirit of man is to be reborn', Monroe opines: 'the costly red fertilizer, so lavishly poured out, is to enrich the soil of the new era' (Monroe 1917a, 195). *Poetry*'s 1917 editorials advance that 'common goal', although Monroe still upholds the principle that her magazine will print 'any expression' of the war 'whatever the poet's point of view may be' (Monroe 1917b, 205). *Poetry*, she affirms, supports the 'stand of the individual against immensities' (Monroe 1918, 322).

In printing Lawrence's 'Resurrection', Monroe duly shields the poet's 'little torch' from the wind of war (Monroe 1918, 322). But she also relegates Lawrence's speaker's 'frail flame of resurrection' to the fourth stanza of her conflated text, giving precedence instead to 'The dead [who] are burning in the funeral wind' (*LP3* 1522; Lawrence 1917, 139). Lawrence's final version of 'Resurrection' has now been restored in the Cambridge Edition of *The Poems*, the editor, Christopher Pollnitz, reconstructing its proper stanza sequence and the expressive form – the looping rhythm, interrupted by Monroe's repunctuation – which is the prosodic echo of the poem's Frazerian allegory of resurrection in the seasonal cycle. In its death-and-rebirth imagery, 'Resurrection' closely comports with the attenuated seasonal poem-cycle which concludes Lawrence's 1917 volume, *Look! We Have Come Through!* Holly A. Laird reads the first poem in *Look*'s seasonal triplet, 'Autumn Rain', as a 'Lawrencean complement' to Shelley's 'Ode to the West Wind', the Shelleyan analogue linking 'Autumn Rain' to 'Resurrection' (Laird 1988, 4). 'Autumn Rain' was probably among the poems Lawrence sent to H.D. for inclusion in *Some Imagist Poets* (1917), but it would be printed instead in *The Egoist* in February of that year during H.D's tenure as assistant editor of the journal (see *L2* 664). Composed in tercets made up of uncharacteristically short lines, the poem gestures to Shelley's use of Dantean terza rima in his 'Ode' and is also the most Imagistic of Lawrence's trio, with its opening stanza, 'The plane leaves / fall black and wet / on the lawn', a working model of the Imagist precept that 'the natural object is always the *adequate* symbol' (*LP1* 221). But if 'Autumn Rain' rephrases Pound's prewar iteration of Imagist poetics (the 'petals on a wet, black bough' of 'In a Station of the Metro' (Pound 1990, 111)), the poem's imagery – of 'the sheaves of dead / men that are slain' – picks up on that of Lawrence's uncollected war poems, which were also printed on Imagist platforms.

Like 'Resurrection', 'Ecce Homo', Lawrence's first war poem, is a product of *Poetry* insofar as it was prompted by the magazine's War Poems Prize Award number of November 1914. Lawrence, who had declined an invitation to submit an entry, received his copy of the special issue on 16 November and 'Ecce Homo' was written, in angry response, on the same day. Assistant editor Alice Corbin Henderson's commentary on 'Poetry and War' in the War Poems number defends the anti-war stance then adopted by the magazine:

> The American feeling about the war is a genuine revolt against war, and we have believed that POETRY might help to serve the cause of peace by encouraging the expression of this spirit of protest.
>
> Just as the neutrality of the United States is in no sense passive, so the spirit of her poets is one of active antagonism to the barbaric survival of war.
>
> (Henderson 83)

Lawrence's active antagonism was both to the war and to the protests against it in *Poetry*. 'Today came the War Number of *Poetry*' he informed Monroe in a letter: 'It put me into such a rage'. Lawrence calls out the 'glib irreverence' in the 'dreadful' face of the war of contributions such as Amy Lowell's prose poem 'The Bombardment', reprinted in *Some Imagist Poets* (1915), in which exploding artillery shells shatter not human bodies but 'bohemian glass' (*L2* 232–3; Lowell 1914, 60). Lawrence took exception, too, to Aldington's 'War Yawp', a Whitmanesque apostrophe to '*America!*' which immediately precedes Henderson's editorial and, like it, defends the 'little citadel' of the arts – and, by implication, the Fortress America of a neutral United States – 'Against all wars of the world' (Aldington 1914a, 81). As a corrective to Lowell's and Aldington's efforts, Lawrence enclosed his own 'war poem' in his letter to Monroe, explaining that he 'had' to write it 'because it breaks my heart, this war' (*L2* 232).

His poem, 'Ecce Homo' – which Lawrence told Monroe he had 'typed', ironically enough, 'on a typewriter Amy Lowell gave me' – follows the war 'home to the heart of the individual fighters' in its anatomy of the death-drive of Western civilization or what Lawrence calls 'the *will* to war' (*L2* 233). The 'disturbed soldier-protagonist' (*LP3* cv) who is the poem's speaker and its psychological case-study says of the enemy he has killed in single combat that:

> ... I knew he wanted it, he wanted it
> Like a fierce magnet he drew my bayonet
> Like a spent shaft it sank to its rest
>
> (*LP3* 1515)

The soldier-speaker's more intimate connection is with 'My enemy, my brother' – with his German *brüder* – than with his band of British brothers in arms. 'Woman' and 'our Mothers', meanwhile, rejoice in 'our destruction' and are figured as 'Harpies, Erynnies' and 'Eumenides' (*LP3* 1516). Sarah Cole points out that 'the war's flamboyant all-male theatrics' may 'trouble the smooth narrative of (hetero)normativity' yet need 'not conform to a structure of gender deviance', and it would be reductive to read into the psychosexual drama of 'Ecce

Homo' Lawrence's preference for sleeping with the German enemy over sleeping with his German wife (Cole 140). Nonetheless, the poem's exploration of what Paul Delany identifies as 'the perverse eroticism of violence' (Delany 29) closely prefigures the 'Gladiatorial' chapter of *Women in Love*, a novel in which, Cole acknowledges, Lawrence's treatment of the Birkin-Crich relationship 'transforms the structures of war intimacy' into 'moments of supreme male homoeroticism' (Cole 234).

'Take care how you regard my war poem – it is good', Lawrence told Monroe in a cautionary postscript to his letter, and while 'Ecce Homo' did not appear in *Poetry*, she would solicit further war poems from Lawrence (*L2* 233). When Aldington invited him to contribute to a special Imagist issue of *The Egoist*, Lawrence revised 'Ecce Homo' and retitled the poem 'Eloi, Eloi, lama sabachthani?': where the original title is a Nietzschean reiteration of the words in the Vulgate with which Pilate presents Jesus to the crowd, 'Behold the man', the new Aramaic title reprises Christ's last words on the cross, 'My God, my God, why hast thou forsaken me?' A passion-poem, 'Eloi, Eloi, lama sabachthani?', is an antidote to the 'glib irreverence' of Amy Lowell's entry for *Poetry*'s War Poems Prize Award. But when Lawrence's poem appeared in the Imagist issue of *The Egoist* in 1915, it was Lowell's turn to object, both to its 'pure, farfetched indecency' and to its length: at three pages, 'Eloi, Eloi, lama sabachthani?' hardly meets the Imagist criterion of compression, even in Lowell's looser interpretation of Imagism's dictums (Damon 307–08). A scandalized Lowell refused to distribute the special issue in the United States and 'Eloi, Eloi, lama sabachthani?' would remain under the radar until 1952 when E.W. Tedlock reprinted it as 'A Forgotten War Poem by D.H. Lawrence'.

A few weeks after the Imagist number of *The Egoist* came out, Cynthia Asquith recorded in her diary that 'Lawrence and Beb [her husband, Herbert Asquith, who had joined up in 1914] had war talk, and he accused Beb of unconscious "blood-lust" […]. He has an *idée fixe* that "destruction" is the end, and not the means to an end, in the minds of soldiers' (Asquith 46). The embodiment of Lawrence's *idée fixe* is the first-person speaker of 'Eloi, Eloi, lama sabachthani?', a soldier who, in his psychopathological blood lust, identifies himself as the 'bridegroom of War, war's paramour':

Like a bride he took my bayonet, wanting it,
Like a virgin the blade of my bayonet, wanting it,
And it sank to rest from me in him,
And I, the lover, am consummate,

> And he is the bride, I have sown him with the seed
> And planted and fertilised him
>
> (*LP3* 1518)

The bayoneted soldier-bride is metaphorically feminized and impregnated whereas actual women are at best camp-followers, scavengers who 'Feed on our wounds like bread, receive our blood / Like glittering seed' (*LP3* 1519). The 'seed', the sacrificial blood of the fighting men that will 'expiate' the 'unknowable crime', is seedcorn-cum-semen, its bloody harvest a 'sheaf of self-gathered wounds'. Artillery shells, the speaker says, are 'Like screaming birds of Fate / Wheeling to lacerate and rip up this my body' (*LP3* 1517–19). These are the Harpy bird-women of 'Ecce Homo', who reappear in 'Eloi, Eloi, lama sabachthani?' in company with the Erinyes, the three female Furies who avenge the crime of matricide in Aeschylus' *Eumenides* and in Euripides' *Orestes* and who will take centre stage in 'Errinyes', the third in Lawrence's triptych of uncollected war poems.

Written in 1915, when Lawrence was living as a near neighbour of H.D. and Aldington in Hampstead, 'Errinyes' was published in *Some Imagist Poets* (1916). Like its early version, 'The Turning Back', 'Errinyes' is composed in tercets, a loose approximation of the terza rima of Dante's *Inferno* to which Lawrence looks back in 'Resurrection'.[12] The three-line form in 'Errinyes', the last in his trio of war poems, reflects Lawrence's 'own inveterate habit of "thinking in threes"' (Black 464) and may also be a reflection, in civilian verse, of the triadic thinking which Fussell ascribes to the trench lyric. There is a relationship in the soldier-poetry of the Great War, Fussell finds, between the 'practical, *ad hoc*, empirical principle of three in military procedure and the magical or mystical threes of myth, epic, drama, ritual, romance, folklore, prophecy, and religion' personified in, for example, the 'three Furies, three Graces, and three Harpies' (Fussell 136–38). It is suggestive, then, that, of the poems by Robert Nichols he read in manuscript, Lawrence praised 'A Triptych', subsequently included in Nichols' *Ardours and Endurances* (see *L2* 446).

'The Turning Back', the first version of 'Errinyes', forms the first part of a 'poem-letter' which Lawrence sent to Cynthia Asquith on 2 November 1915 (*LP3* 1826). The poem, which is a call for peace ('We let the weapons slip from out our hands') and even for unconditional surrender ('The foe can take our goods and homes and land'), ends with the entreaty 'Let us go back, the only way is love' (*LP3* 1525–526). In the letter to Asquith in which the poem is enclosed, Lawrence writes: 'about the "downing tools" [...] I send you the poem, which might help to convince you'. 'I very much want you to tell me what you think, because it is a question for the *women* of the land now to decide': 'I still have some hope of the women: they should *know* that only love matters, now' (*L2* 424–25). What Lady Cynthia thought about 'poor Lawrence's last extraordinary letter' is made plain in her diary entry for 5 November 1915: 'He appears to think that *I* could stop the war, if only I really wanted to', presumably by appealing, on behalf of 'the women', to her father-in-law Herbert Henry Asquith who, as Prime Minister, had taken Britain into the war the year before (Asquith 95). Lawrence's 'hope for the women' and his belief in the pacifying power of their 'love' has dissipated in 'Eloi, Eloi, lama sabachthani?' in which the speaker reverts, now with bitter pathos, to the naïve sentiments of 'The Turning Back': 'I had dreamed of love, oh love, I had dreamed of love' (*LP3* 1518).

'Errinyes', as the new title indicates, ups the mythological ante, as the harmless 'homeless ghosts' of fallen soldiers are transfigured into the malevolent Erinyes: 'Out of blood rise up new ghosts'; 'The more we slay and are slain, the more we raise up new ghosts against us' (*LP3* 1525, 1527). As Pollnitz points out, 'Errinyes' is both a debate with the Asquiths and a dialogue with the soldier-protagonist of 'Eloi, Eloi, lama sabachthani?', 'who proclaims that the Errinyes will only sink "Like blood in the earth again" if he or his enemy sheds the blood of the other' (*LP3* cv). 'Eloi, Eloi, lama sabachthani?' and 'Resurrection', together with their early versions, are psychodramas, monologues spoken in the first-person singular. But 'Errinyes' and 'The Turning Back' deploy the first-person plural, a public mode of address which implies that the war, as it is in Lawrence's 1916 poem-sequence of that title to which I turn in the following chapter, is a matter for 'All of Us':

> […] we are mad with terror, seeing the slain
> Victorious, grey, grisly ghosts in our streets;
> Grey, unappeased ghosts seated in the music-halls

'How shall we now appease whom we have raised up?' Lawrence asks (*LP3* 1527).

'A fiercer hell': Aldington

The same question is asked by Aldington, but from the different perspective of the veteran. His war novel, *Death of a Hero*, shares the mythos of Lawrence's 'Errinyes' and 'Eloi, Eloi, lama sabachthani?' in its warning that 'a million murders egged on, lauded, exulted over, will raise a legion of Eumenides about your ears. The survivors will pay bitterly for it all their lives' (*DH* 245). In 'Eumenides', from Aldington's postwar volume *Exile and Other Poems* (1923), that survivor's guilt is embodied in the Eumenides or Erinyes which 'glide about' the first-person speaker, these chthonic goddesses of vengeance manifesting as 'Fearful memories': 'Men, men and the roar of shells' and 'that horrible night in Hart's Crater' at Loos are among 'the thousand images I see / And struggle with and cannot kill'. 'What is it I agonise for?', Aldington asks. His reply, releasing the repressed anger symptomatic of survivor's syndrome, is that it is not 'The dead' but

> It is myself that is the Eumenides,
> That will not be appeased, about my bed;
> It is the wrong that has been done me
> Which none has atoned for, none repented of,
> Which rises before me, demanding atonement.
>
> Tell me, what answer shall I give my murdered self?
>
> (*CPRA* 153–54).

The narrator of *Death of a Hero* pays tribute to Lawrence's definitive account in 'The Nightmare' chapter of *Kangaroo* – a novel published in the same year as Aldington's nightmare-poem, 'Eumenides' – of the post-traumatic effects of the war on civilians. But Lawrence, who did not experience the fighting at first-hand, had little apprehension of the actuality of the trenches: as Aldington recalls in his biography of Lawrence, 'when I sent him word that I was returning to the Front he received the news with serene equanimity' (Aldington 1950b, 202). Lawrence even told Cecil Gray in a letter that he believed Aldington was 'glad to go' back, given that 'It is harder to bear the pressure of the vacuum over here than the stress of conjestion [*sic*] over there' (*L3* 233). A gauge of the experiential distance between 'here' and 'over there' is the different sonics of the shells that are 'Droning over' Lawrence's soldier-protagonist in 'Eloi, Eloi, lama sabachthani?' (*LP3* 1517) but which 'roar' in Aldington's 'Eumenides'. Direct experience had been established as a prerequisite for 'war art' during the First World War itself (Hynes 159) and would persist as a primary criterion until recent reframings such as Santanu Das', which show that 'the scope of First World War poetry is far wider than that of the trench lyric' (Das 2013b, 4). But even in an expanded canon a distinction between combatant and civilian war poetries still obtains. In 'Ecce Homo' Lawrence attempts to channel direct experience through his soldier-protagonist when he says 'I ran across to the trenches' and yet his speaker's avowal, 'Let me kill my self, in all honor' (*LP3* 1516), aligns more closely with Lawrence's own theory of war as 'the pure *suicide* of humanity' than with the de facto 'suicide' in battle of the protagonist of *Death of a Hero* or Aldington's furious elegy, in 'Eumenides', for his 'murdered self' (Asquith 89; *DH* 23).

Aldington's career had been launched in the early 1910s by Pound, in his self-assigned role as *Poetry* magazine's 'Foreign Correspondent'. H.D. was the figurehead for Imagism in its prewar phase and in the January 1913 issue of *Poetry* in which her 'Three Poems' – 'Hermes of the Ways', 'Priapus' and 'Epigram' – appeared, she is synonymous with it: Monroe's editorial 'Notes' introduce '"H.D., *Imagiste*"' as 'an American lady resident abroad, whose identity is unknown to the author' (Monroe 1913, 135).[13] Aldington was the 'original Imagist', however (Gates 4): the youngest pupil to be enrolled in Pound's new School of Images, he was not yet of age when his 'Three Poems' – 'Choricos', 'To a Greek Marble' and 'Au Vieux Jardin' – came out in *Poetry* in November 1912. His subsequent disavowal of Pound and the 'verse revolutionaries' – 'I claim no share whatever in the so-called "revolution of 1912"' – is characteristic of Aldington's later and deliberately Lawrentian self-fashioning as a 'servant of the life impulse' who is unaffiliated with the 'cliques of Paris and London' (*CPRA* 13; Aldington 1935, 19, 33). Aldington's vitalist tonic for the 'hyperaesthesia' of high modernism, of which '[t]he music of atonality, the painting and sculpture of super-realism, the literature of the stream of consciousness, the aestheticism of concrete and cocktails' are symptoms, is advertised in the title of his autobiography: *Life for Life's Sake* (Aldington 1935, 33).

Whether or not he played a walk-on part in the verse revolution of 1912, Aldington was the most active of the post-Poundian Imagists in promoting the new poetry on avant-garde platforms from the mid-1910s through to his editorship of the swansong *Imagist Anthology 1930*. Aldington had supplied the (unsigned) preface for the first of Lowell's *Some Imagist Poets* anthologies in 1915, the year in which *The Egoist*, of which Aldington was then assistant editor, issued its special Imagist number. Aldington's own volumes of the war years and into the postwar period – *Images: 1910–1915* (1915), *Images Old and New* (1916), *Images* (1919), *Images of War: A Book of Poems* (1919) and *Images of Desire* (1919) – all appeared under Imagism's nominal aegis. There is a paradigm shift nonetheless between *Images* and *Images of War*, a transition which is already underway in the 1915 edition of *Images* in home-front war poems such as 'Lemures' and 'In the Tube'. In the latter, the speaker – a man of fighting age but not yet in khaki – who is stared down by 'A row of hard faces' in the London Underground reads in the passengers' eyes the question, posed again by the narrator of Aldington's war novel, *Death of a Hero*, "'What right have you to live?'" (*CPRA* 49).

The Imagist's right to live was likewise called into question, even by a fellow-traveller such as A.R. Orage, editor of the avant-garde little magazine *The New Age* to which Aldington had himself contributed before the war and which, Anne Fernihough observes, 'had fostered the emergence of the imagists in 1908 and 1909' (Fernihough 2013, 42).[14] Writing in October 1914, Orage expresses 'the hope' that 'the war will put an end to "Imagism" in poetry and all such nonsense'. His wish that 'the Imagists and such-like triflers' will 'perish in the war' would be granted by T.E. Hulme, founder of the first 'School of Images' and art critic for *The New Age*, who was killed in the trenches in 1917 (Hynes 64).[15] Intemperate remarks such as Orage's forecast the hostile climate in which *The Rainbow* was prosecuted in 1915, when the Bow Street Magistrates' Court upheld a reviewer's judgement that Lawrence's novel had 'no right to exist in the wind of war' (Douglas 94). In Aldington's differing opinion, the suppression of *The Rainbow* was 'an infamy', a manifestation of 'war-time hysteria' and the beleaguered Lawrence would thenceforth be exempted from the contempt in which Aldington held other non-combatant literary contemporaries such as Eliot and Pound (Aldington 1950a, 20). Aldington has Pound in his sights in 'In the Tube', a poem that stages a face-off between the civilian poet and public opinion which is also a riposte to Pound's *ur*-Imagist lyric 'In a Station of the Metro':

> The apparition   of these faces   in the crowd :
> Petals   on a wet, black   bough .
>
> (Pound 1913b, 12)

Aldington's gentler parody of Poundian Imagism, 'Penultimate Poetry: Xenophilometropolitana', had appeared in *The Egoist* in January 1914 and concludes with a spoof on 'In a Station of the Metro' which nonetheless conveys the shock of the new poetry:

> The apparition   of these poems   in a crowd:
> White faces   in a black   dead faint.
>
> (Aldington 1914b, 36)

Pound's poem – the envoi to his 'Contemporania' sequence printed in *Poetry* in April 1913 – places chthonic mythology in a contemporary setting in locating the underworld in the Paris Métropolitain. Aldington similarly configures the

London Underground as an underworld, but 'In the Tube' also indicates the speed at which contemporary events have overtaken the 'contemporania' of the *avant-guerre*. As Jane Goldman observes, 'In the Tube' forms a 'grim counter' to Pound's exquisite *hokku*, its 'superfluity of adjectival contempt' (Goldman 134) – the faces in Aldington's crowd are 'hard', 'Immobile', 'plethoric', 'Immobile' (again) and 'brasslike' (*CPRA* 49) – flouting Pound's veto in 'A Few Don'ts by an Imagiste' against the 'superfluous word' or 'adjective' (Pound 1913a, 201). Stared down by his fellow commuters, Aldington's speaker looks up instead at 'A row of advertisements' in the tube train carriage (*CPRA* 49) in what may be another poke in the eye for the Pound who had warned the would-be Imagist to avoid 'the way of the advertising agent' – this notwithstanding the advertising stratagems Pound himself deployed in his savvy marketing of modernism (Pound 1913a, 203).[16]

Pound, with Eliot, bears the brunt of the 'Resentment' which Aldington expresses in a poem of that title which is included in the 'Images of War' subsection of his *Complete Poems*. Titled 'Civilians' in *War and Love*, the poem had appeared as 'People' in the *Some Imagist Poets* anthology of 1916, published in May, a month before Aldington joined up. In its first iteration the poem's civilian speaker denounces other civilians, people who 'hiss your hatred about me', but the meaning of the poem alters with Aldington's own changing circumstances, his initial 'resentment' towards his fellow civilians morphing into the combatant's resentment of the civilian population per se (Aldington 1916, 11).[17]

The war on the home front is Aldington's subject again in *Images* in 'Hampstead Heath (Easter Monday 1915)'. The poem is a verbal counterpart to Mark Gertler's painting *The Merry-Go-Round*, discussed in Chapter One: both are set at the funfair held on the Heath in early April 1915. In Gertler's painting, clouds mass like missile tracks above the carousel: in Aldington's poem, the night sky is 'Pierced through / By a swift searchlight, a long white dagger', a deadly portent of the Zeppelin raids on London which would commence that May. In the poem and in the picture, fairground attractions which should offer a temporary respite from the war merely replicate its horrors. The riders in military uniform turn Gertler's merry-go-round into a mechanized fighting machine, while 'The black murmuring crowd' in Aldington's poem, oblivious to the Damoclean 'dagger' above its head, 'flows' between 'the banks of noisy booths'. These booths are carnival shooting galleries, pleasure-ground proxies for the killing fields of Flanders: April 1915 would prove one of the cruellest months of the war, with some 69,000 allied troops lost in the Second Battle of Ypres. In the meantime, on this 'Khaki Bank Holiday', the stream of punters 'flows on' between the banks of booths like a river: like Lethe, perhaps, the mythological river of forgetfulness, if, as it seems, Easter Sunday's promise of resurrection has already been forgotten, or like Acheron, the infernal River of Hades (*CPRA* 50).[18]

Aldington's home front Imagism culminates in 'Captive' (1917), 'Sunsets' (1916) and 'The Faun Captive' (1919), a triptych which charts the poet's change in status from civilian to soldier. All three poems postdate *Images* and *Images Old and New* but are grouped together at the end of the 'Images' section of Aldington's *Collected Poems* (1929) and his *Complete Poems* (1948) as a segue to the 'Images of War' sequence which follows.[19] 'Sunsets', in which 'the wind / Blowing over London from Flanders / Has a bitter taste', augurs Aldington's imminent transfer from the home front to the front line (*CPRA* 68). The sunset, Fussell notes, had been 'a staple of pre-war Georgian poetry and of the literature of the Celtic "Twilight"' as a signifier of the sublime, and would swiftly be redeployed to 'ironic effect' in First World War verse (Fussell 59–60) – and in fiction, in the 'bloody smear of red sunset' in Aldington's *Death of a Hero* (*DH* 269). Aldington's poem's variation on the sunset trench lyric is a disenchanted reply to his own prewar verse, which, as his friend the Irish poet and critic Thomas MacGreevy astutely observes, is shadowed by the literature of 'the so-called "Celtic" twilight' evoked in W.B. Yeats' *The Wind Among the Reeds* (1899) (MacGreevy 15, 10). 'Choricos', the first of Aldington's 'Three Poems' printed in *Poetry* in 1912, is a choral paean to 'Death' – 'youth's glamorous vision of death', as Harriet Monroe puts it – figured as a 'healing wind' which carries 'us' into the chthonic shades: a myth indeed, and one blown away, in the closing lines of 'Sunsets', by the 'bitter' wind of war (*CPRA* 22; Monroe 1929, 42).

The opening lines of Aldington's poem also allude to and overwrite the first lines of T.S. Eliot's 'The Love Song of J. Alfred Prufrock', which had appeared in *Poetry* in 1915, in the June issue which also carried an obituary for Rupert Brooke (a soldier-poet who had emanated 'a sunset glow', in the words of Wilfred Gibson's elegy 'The Going', which would be printed in *Poetry* in August 1915) (Gibson 239).[20] Eliot's opening simile, in which 'the evening is spread out against the sky / Like a patient etherised upon a table', itself defamiliarizes conventional sky-at-night imagery (Eliot 1969, 13), but in Aldington's savage redaction of Eliot's lines – 'The white body of the evening / Is torn into scarlet, / Slashed and gouged and seared' – the evening sky signifies the war's violation of the human 'body' (the bodies which are 'torn, gouged' in *Death of a Hero* (321)) and of the integrity of the modernist lyric (*CPRA* 68). Aldington's poem thereby preempts Wallace Stevens' point, made in the course of the Second World War, that war confronts us with 'events' that are 'beyond our power to tranquillize them in the mind' but which 'engage us in what is direct and immediate and real' (Stevens 656). 'Sunsets' also anticipates the open antagonism towards Eliot in the postwar period which would culminate in Aldington's satirical biofiction of Eliot as the beatified Father Jeremy Cibber in *Stepping Heavenward: A Record* (1931). Eliot had taken over the editorship of *The Egoist* in 1917; when *Prufrock and Other Observations* was issued by the Egoist Press in June of that year, Aldington was in officer training camp.

As McGreevy observes 'men who had been in the war', such as Aldington and MacGreevy himself, had been forced to 'hand over the literary laurels of their generation' to those like Eliot, Joyce and Lawrence who 'had not seen the great tragedy anything like as closely as they themselves had' (MacGreevy 38). Writing to Clement Shorter, editor of *The Sphere*, in 1919, Aldington asked him 'I wonder if you realize what a gulf there is in my generation between the men who fought and those who didn't?' (Zilboorg 2013, 168 n.3). In the same year, in the 'Epilogue' to *Images of War*, Aldington again articulates a 'combat gnosticism' when he speaks in the collective voice of the men who fought to those who didn't, like the Eliot who had taken the epigraph for 'Prufrock' from Dante's *Inferno*.[21] 'We are of those that Dante saw', Aldington's chorus of veterans insists:

> [...] we have passed athwart a fiercer hell,
> Through gloomier, more desperate circles
> Than ever Dante dreamed.
>
> (*CPRA* 122)

Eliot would represent the war dead by way of Dante in *The Waste Land*, in the vision of 'crowds of people, walking round in a ring' in 'The Burial of the Dead'. This first part of Eliot's poem also stages a more intimate encounter between the speaker and a demobbed veteran, one who, like the speaker of Aldington's postwar poem 'The Return', bears with him 'a flavour of the grave' (Aldington 1926, 104): 'There I saw one I knew, and stopped him crying: "Stetson! / You who were with me in the ships at Mylae!"' (Eliot 1969, 62).[22] In superimposing the First Punic War upon the Great War in these lines Eliot is drawing the 'parallel between contemporaneity and antiquity' which, in his essay on '*Ulysses*, Order, and Myth' (1923), he identifies with modernism's 'mythical method', a method also practiced, in the 1910s, by the Imagists (Eliot 2021b, 478). Take, for example, Aldington's poem from *Images*, 'Interlude', in which a tin whistle player 'piping by the Red Lion' pub in London summons up for the speaker a vision of dancing girls from Attica (*CPRA* 50); in the same way, in an aural fold of time into Elizabethan London, Eliot's speaker in *The Waste Land* can 'hear / Beside a public bar in Lower Thames Street, / The pleasant whining of a mandoline' (Eliot 1969, 69, 63). The speaker of Aldington's 'Interlude' pays the piper and in the final line of the poem gives the beggar his due, acknowledging him as '"*Mon semblable, mon frère*"' – words, borrowed from Baudelaire, which are reiterated in the last line of 'The Burial of the Dead' (*CPRA* 50). *The Waste Land* has been described as a 'hall of mirrors' and it may be that Eliot's citation of Baudelaire is a reflection of Aldington's citation. If it is striking that two English-language and Francophile poets should assimilate the identical phrase from *Les Fleurs du Mal*, it is more striking still that in Eliot's poem Baudelaire's words conclude a passage in which the first-person speaker greets a returned soldier (Levinson 247).[23]

Aldington and Eliot did meet after the war, not on London Bridge but when Aldington acted as managing editor of Eliot's literary review *The Criterion*, a post from which he resigned in November 1923 following a spat with Eliot on the topic of Joyce and modernism's mythical method.[24] In 1925, in a letter to poet-critic and *Criterion* contributor Herbert Read, Aldington would tell him that 'I am rebelling against a poetry which I think too self-conscious, too intellectual, too elliptic and alembique': signing off, Aldington declares that he himself will now write 'on opposition lines' (Gates 122). Arguably Aldington had been writing on 'opposition lines' since 1916, insofar as his joining-up poems seemingly share what Samuel Hynes identifies as 'the wartime inclination to regard pre-war Modernism as an historical mistake that had been terminated by the war' (Hynes 103). That the war might indeed, as Orage had hoped, put an end to Imagism is Aldington's subject in 'Captive'. The speaker, a self-pitying substitute for the Aldington who had stoically 'stripped for the medical examination' (Aldington 1968, 163) when he signed up for the army, is forcibly divested of the Hellenistic trimmings and trappings of his prewar Imagism:

> They have torn the gold tettinx
> From my hair;
> And wrenched the bronze sandals
> From my ankles.

The speaker, who is issued with army khaki instead, complains that 'The Muses have forgotten me' (*CPRA* 68).

The dilemma of the Imagist at war is the subject of 'Proem', the prologue to *Images of War*. 'Out of this turmoil and passion, / This implacable contest',

Aldington says, 'I would gather something of repose / Some intuition of the inalterable gods'. But try as he might to work the old Imagist magic, the poet confesses that

> Each day I grow more restless,
> See the austere shape elude me,
> Gaze impotently upon a thousand miseries
> And still am dumb.
>
> (*CPRA* 73)

Hellenic 'repose' is unattainable amid the 'turmoil' of the battlefield and yet the human face of the war stymies speech. 'Proem' invokes classical precedents in proems to war verse from Homer to Lucan but the 'parallel between contemporaneity and antiquity' won't hold; instead the crisis of expression which is Aldington's subject is signalled in the semantic prolapse, in 'Proem', of the poem into the pro(se) (p)oem. For stretches of his two-and-a-half years' war service, prose poetry would be the only medium other than translation or *faux* translation in which Aldington would or could write, the two modes meeting in his privately printed little book of prose poetry, *The Love of Myrrhine and Konallis*, discussed in the following chapter. The prose poem had long been a bona fide mode of Imagism – see Allen Upward's and John Cournos' contributions to Pound's *Des Imagistes* – and after the war Aldington himself would vigorously defend the form against Eliot and other detractors, but in the prologue to *Images of War* prose poetry is deemed a prosaic and even a profane substitute for 'the holy wisdom of poets' (*CPRA* 68). 'For me silence; or if speech, then some humble poem in prose' as Aldington would put it later in 'Discouragement', a 1918 prose poem located at 'Officers' Camp, Fressin'. He is 'too impotent', Aldington confesses, 'to dare' either 'the cool / rhythm of prose' or 'the sharp / edges of poetry' (Aldington 2002, 143).

'Richard was managing to do a little writing between guns', nonetheless, H.D. reassured Amy Lowell in a March 1917 letter, and many of the poems, in prose and in verse, which Aldington jotted down in the 'small pocket-book' he later gifted to Lowell are self-reflexive meditations on the conundrum of the Imagist at arms (Zilboorg 2003, 24). In 'Insouciance', for example, the soldier-poet-speaker, who is 'in the dreary trenches', 'make[s] for myself little poems / Delicate as a flock of doves'. These trench-*hokku* 'fly away like white-winged doves' but are ineffectual as missals of peace; they are the origami-like tokens, rather, of what the title of the preceding poem in *Images of War* terms 'A Moment's Interlude' in the fighting. Making his 'little poems' in the momentary lull, Aldington lends a soldierly pragmatics to the Imagist criterion of compression (*CPRA* 80). Other poems in *Images of War* interpret another Imagist dictum – 'Direct treatment of the "thing"' – from a combatant's point of view (Flint 1913, 199). 'The effect of the war on Aldington', according to MacGreevy, was to bring his 'work closer to an objective reality'. That reality effect is manifested in a poetics of 'absolutely direct statement devoid of every kind of poetic trimming' (MacGreevy 32, 24). 'A Village', for example, displays a stricter adherence to Imagist codes than that achieved in much of Aldington's prewar verse:

> [...] when you've pondered
> Hour upon chilly hour in those damned trenches
> You get at the significance of things,
> Get to know, clearer than before,
> What a tree means, what a pool,
> Or a black wet field in sunlight.
>
> (*CPRA* 90)

The nod in 'a black wet field' to Pound's 'Petals on a wet, black bough' is friendly enough but in 'A Village' Aldington applies the Imagist rule that 'the natural object is always the *adequate* symbol' to ends that are more Lawrentian than Poundian (Pound 1913a, 201). 'How good love of earth is' Aldington's soldier-speaker says, as he finds 'life again, rich life' in 'homely things', even in the unpropitious environment of the trenches (*CPRA* 90–1).

'Trench Idyll', by contrast, is battlefield anti-pastoral, the poem's tautological title encapsulating the 'binary vision' characteristic of canonical First World War literature (Fussell 98). Written for the most part in direct speech 'Trench Idyll' manipulates to grimly ironic effect that polarity between civilian and soldierly experience which, in 'Proem', had struck the poet 'dumb'. The poem's speaker tells us that he 'sat together in the trench' with his commanding officer as the two men talked – as Winterbourne talks with Evans, in Aldington's *Death of a Hero* – 'Of how pleasant London was, / Its women, restaurants, night clubs, theatres' before their conversation turns to the theatre of war closer to hand: to the 'men / Who'd hung for six months on the wire / Just over there' (*CPRA* 88). Paul Nash's woodcut for 'Trench Idyll' in Cyril Beaumont's limited first edition of *Images of War* – a remarkable collaboration between verbal and visual war art – shows three bodies looped in barbed wire entanglements. Nash, who had fought on the Ypres Salient prior to his commission as a war artist, is drawing here on the first-hand witness which also informs his ink-and-watercolour *Wire* (1918). On his return from the Passchendaele Front Nash had 'set down his anguished reactions in image after image', telling his wife in a letter home that 'I have seen the most frightful nightmare of a country more conceived by Dante or Poe than nature, unspeakable' (Cork 198).

'We are of those that Dante saw': in the 'Epilogue' to *Images of War* Aldington, like the better-known soldier poets – and war artists – who were his contemporaries, holds the line between those who fought in the war and those who didn't (*CPRA* 122). Yet in redeploying Imagism as a war idiom, Aldington also crosses the line which still divides the camps and canons of modernist and First World War poetries. In consequence, and more than a century after the Armistice, *Images of War* is stranded in a definitional no man's land, Aldington's reputation as a Great War writer resting more securely on the 'cool / rhythm of prose' in *Death of a Hero* than on 'the sharp / edges of poetry' in *Images of War* (Aldington 2002, 143).

'Hell must open' H.D

In May 1918, Aldington, caught in a binary between love and desire, had written to H.D. to tell her that 'The truth is: I love you & I desire – *l'autre*' (Zilboorg 2003, 49). H.D. would record Aldington's words four decades later in *Bid Me to Live*, where she also comments on the poems he would publish as *War and Love* in 1919.[25] We are told that 'Julia', the H.D. figure in the novel, 'knew about the poetry, a love-and-war sequence, because Rafe [Aldington] had left copies of the last lot with her; "Read them", he had said, "they're written for Bella [Dorothy "Arabella" Yorke]"' (*BML* 57). On reading Aldington's 'hyacinth-myrrh' 'Love' poems, as she calls them (*BML* 57), H.D. found a cloying cliché of her own 'flower-text', embedded in pastiche Elizabethan love lyrics and embodied in Bella – in the 'poppied kisses' of 'An Interlude', the 'crushed flower' of 'Her Mouth', the 'breast-flower peering from our bed' in 'Daybreak' and 'her flower-like body' in 'Sleep' (Aldington 1919b, 5, 78, 86, 87, 89).[26] Incarnating H.D.'s flower-texts in Bella's body parts – her word made Bella's flesh – Aldington adds textual insult to sexual injury: 'as the poets have always known', Jerome McGann points out, the 'sexual event' is 'a model of the textual condition' (McGann 1991, 3).

Commenting on H.D.'s 'flower-pieces' in *Tendencies in Modern American Poetry* Amy Lowell observes that '"H.D." is peculiarly a poet of flowers, and in the very manner in which she uses her flowers, we have hints of that changed technique', the technique of the Imagist experiment of the 1910s for which 'H.D.' was the abbreviated signifier (Lowell et al. 1917, 270). H.D. had drawn on 'the time-honoured language of flowers as tropes for femininity' in her first volume, *Sea Garden* (1916), but she also tropes on the gendered flower trope: as Miranda Hickman suggests, her sea rose, sea lily and sea violet, while they may be 'frail', have 'the ability to weather adversity'. 'We imagine her strange blooms as individuals, likely women', Hickman says, 'scarred and deepened by experience, managing to survive in inhospitable circumstances' (Hickman 193). H.D. would reprise *Sea Garden*'s flower lexicon in her response poems to Aldington's affair, before Bella, with Florence ('Flo') Fallas. Aldington had joined up with his writer friend Carl Fallas, Flo's husband, in 1916, and in July H.D. found lodgings close to their training camp in the village of Corfe Castle in Dorset. She drafted 'Amaranth', 'Eros' and 'Envy' there, a triptych which in its structure and subject matter replicates the love triangle between H.D., Flo and Aldington – the 'we three' of 'Amaranth' – while 'Envy', the envoi to her 'Dorset Trio', also anticipates Aldington's imminent transfer to the front (*CPHD* 311).

'The hurt I have suffered has freed my song', H.D. confessed to John Cournos in a September 1916 letter and in the 'Amaranth' poems she was then composing the epigrammatic objectivity of early Poundian protocols gives way to open and more expressive forms (Hollenberg 135). Louis L. Martz 'suspects that this tendency toward greater openness was encouraged by her friendship with D.H. Lawrence', and indeed the two poets were exchanging manuscripts in this period, commenting in their correspondence on one another's works-in-progress (*CPHD* xix). H.D., however, recoiled when she read the manuscript of Lawrence's marriage-cycle, *Look! We Have Come Through!*, telling him that the poems 'won't do at all; they are not *eternal*, not sublimated'. If, as she judged, there was 'too much body and emotions' in his poems, then Lawrence, tit for tat, would warn H.D. that her 'languid lily of virtue nods perilously near the pit' (*L3* 102; *BML* 47).[27] The imagery of Lawrence's letter to H.D. is adumbrated in his 'Craving for Spring', the poem with which *Look! We Have Come Through!* concludes.[28] A plea for release from 'the winter of the world' at war, 'Craving for Spring' is a Persephone poem, but its first-person speaker repudiates H.D.'s 'lily of virtue', calling on 'life' to 'thaw' the 'cool portentousness' of the 'flowers of the penumbra'. It 'gives me pleasure to destroy the chill Lent lilies', Lawrence's speaker declares: 'Enough of the virgins and lilies' (*LP1* 223–5; *L2* 424).

The caveat in Lawrence's letter to H.D. about the proximity of the lily to the pit implies a causal connection between her abjuration of sex following the stillbirth of their baby daughter in 1915 and Aldington's carnal sins. This is the scenario sketched out in 'Amaranth', the first poem in H.D.'s 1916 Dorset Trio, where the first-person speaker identifies with the *amaranthus caudatus* (or

'Love-Lies-Bleeding') which, like the lily, is a symbol of purity and in classical floriography of eternity and of the underworld (the 'pit'). Like the asphodel, another of H.D.'s chthonic flowers, the amaranthus grows in the Elysian Fields, the domain of the virtuous dead, while in Aesop's fable, as in tamer neoclassical receptions of pagan flower lore, the duller amaranth outlasts the bloom of its gaudier rivals.[29] In her own troubling and self-sacrificial twist on the flower fable, H.D.'s speaker praises 'the love of my lover for his mistress', letting her lover 'take beauty / as his right', even if the mistress (in a biographical reading the 'Florence' whose name has its etymological root in *florens*, or 'flowering') has '*a lesser beauty / and a lesser grace*' than that of the speaker (*CPHD* 313–15). It was not Flo's beauty that concerned H.D. but rather her 'commonness' which, H.D. feared, might taint Aldington's poetry (Guest 78). 'I had thought myself frail', H.D.'s speaker says in 'Eros', but like the 'frail' sea violet in *Sea Garden*, she weathers adversity nonetheless: as another *Sea Garden* poem insists 'beauty, / beauty without strength, / chokes out life' (*CPHD* 318, 20).

'Everybody was so damned outspoken': so Julia, in *Bid Me to Live*, complains of Rafe's love-and-war sequence (*BML* 57). Rafe tells Julia to read the poems he has written for Bella, but H.D. herself had suppressed the poems she had drafted the year before in response to Aldington's affair with Flo Fallas: 'Amaranth', 'Eros' and 'Envy' 'were bound as a trio and were among the unpublished manuscripts she left at her death' (Pearson 587).[30] There was 'too much body and emotions' or 'body and limbs' in the originals – 'My mouth is wet with your life', 'have I not cried in agony of love, / birth, hate, / in pride crushed?' – and so H.D. pulled the poems to pieces, finding in the Sapphic fragment both a formal correlative and a lesbian mask for the disintegration of the Aldington marriage (*CPHD* 313, 316, 320). 'Eros' concludes with the statement that 'to sing love, / love must first shatter us', and like their speaker, who is 'shattered, cut apart, / and slashed open', 'Amaranth', 'Eros' and 'Envy' would be 'shattered, cut apart', their shards re-presented in H.D.'s postwar volume *Heliodora* (1924) as 'Fragment Forty-one (… *thou flittest to Andromeda*. – Sappho)', 'Fragment Forty (*Love … bitter-sweet*. – Sappho)' and 'Fragment Sixty-eight (… *even in the house of Hades*. – Sappho)' (*CPHD* 319, 311). Poems that in their initial iteration were too 'outspoken' are now spoken through the mask of Sappho.

'Eurydice', too, is spoken through a Greek mask and yet it is the most outspoken of the poems H.D. composed at Corfe Castle in 1916. The poem takes up the Orpheus-and-Eurydice leitmotif from 'Amaranth' and 'Eros' – 'Turn, for I love you yet, / though you are not worthy my love'; 'Where is he taking us / now that he has turned back?' – but if it is a pendant to the 'Amaranth' sequence

'Eurydice' is also a radical rescripting of the myth to which 'Amaranth', 'Eros' and 'Envy', in their ethic of female self-sacrifice, more closely conform (*CPHD* 314–15). Refusing the passive, non-speaking role of 'lost' girl or *raptus virginis* to which Eurydice is relegated in the classical canon, H.D.'s speaker insists instead in the furious finale to her monologue that

> hell must break before I am lost;
>
> before I am lost,
> hell must open like a red rose
> for the dead to pass.
>
> (*CPHD* 55)

The 'Amaranth' sequence stayed *sub rosa* but 'Eurydice' would come out, in *Some Imagist Poets* in April 1917 and in *The Egoist* that May, the poem's transmission into print ratifying the turn its speaker takes from abjection to anger and creative agency.

Interpretation of 'Eurydice' as 'a manifesto for a feminist poetics' is, by definition, premised on the poem's appearance on public platforms and yet Helen Sword's point, that 'Eurydice' is a manifesto-poem in 'appropriating hell – the negative space of literary marginality into which the female poet has been driven – as a source of power', confines H.D. instead to that private space defined by Virginia Woolf as the ground zero for women's writerly autonomy (Sword 413–14). If women are to write, that is, they must have an underworld, a (basement) 'room' of their own. But for H.D. as for her modernist contemporaries the underworld is an echo-chamber, resonant with the voices of the dead poets of the past, of ancient and early modern precursors from Homer and Virgil to Dante and Milton. H.D.'s is a sound-reflecting poem, Eurydice's retort to Orpheus that 'my hell is no worse than yours' – 'I have the flowers of myself, /And my thoughts, no god / can take that' (*CPHD* 54–5) – echoing the inversion of values in Satan's statement, in *Paradise Lost*, that 'The mind is its own place, and in itself / Can make a heaven of hell' (Milton 76). And H.D. makes a heaven of hell again when, in the closing lines of her poem, she expropriates the unfolding rose, Beatrice's flower and the culminating symbol of heaven in Dante's *Paradiso* (and, for Freud, a female sex symbol), for her vision of the opening of hell.[31] According to Alicia Ostriker, in 'Eurydice' H.D. 'angrily attack[s]' not only Orpheus 'but the venerable literary tradition of the egocentric male as hero, lover, poet' and yet H.D.'s speaker calls out Orpheus by calling on the mythopoetic tradition which Orpheus, the *ur*-poet, exemplifies (Ostriker 50). Her poem presents a feminist variant of 'colonial mimicry': 'mimicry', Homi

Bhabha argues, 'is always produced at the site of interdiction'; it is a 'forked tongue' discourse, 'uttered between the lines and as such both against the rules and within them' (Bhabha 89, 85). '[F]emale mimicry', as Rita Felski suggests, may not be 'a sign of women's entrapment in a male world' but may constitute instead 'a sly unravelling of male authority' (Felski 75). In its reversal of the gaze of Orpheus, 'Eurydice' is a feminist exercise in revisionist mythography but H.D.'s poem is also a (re)writing, not in its margins, but of and within the male-authored tradition itself.

H.D. herself was hardly a marginal presence in the modernist print culture of the 1910s. Coeditor with Aldington of Lowell's Imagist anthologies, H.D. was also, again with Aldington, assistant editor of *The Egoist*, a role she would perform solo following his enlistment in 1916 through the printing of the May 1917 issue in which 'Eurydice' appears. As Cynthia Pondrom notes 'H.D.'s editorial position with the journal places her among the significant editors of the day' (Pondrom 38). Her editorial remit also informs H.D.'s contribution, *qua* poet, to the Imagist venture. In placing 'Eurydice' in *The Egoist* and in the 1917 Imagist anthology, H.D. exercises the double authority of editor and of author, its reversal of the male gaze rendered all the more potent in her poem's face-off in the public forum of print with Aldington, her Orpheus-poet-husband. 'Literary works do not know themselves, and cannot *be* known, apart from their specific material modes of existence/resistance', McGann insists (McGann 1991, 11). In the material mode of *Some Imagist Poets* (1917) 'Eurydice' exists and resists in relation and as a reply to Aldington's 'Images'. H.D. had first read 'Images' at Corfe Castle in 1916, not in manuscript like the love poems Aldington would later write for Bella, but in the pages of the August issue of *Poetry Review of America*.[32] On reading Aldington's poem there (and his 'Inarticulate Grief', which is also reprinted in the 1917 Imagist anthology), H.D. wrote to Cournos to tell him that she now realized that 'what you and I thought was perhaps a mild and distracting flirtation [with Flo Fallas] was apparently very intense passion' (Hollenberg 132–33). The day before, H.D. had informed Cournos in another letter that she had begun 'writing a long, very long poem, or rather series of poems' which had left her 'torn and tired' (Hollenberg 132): the 'Amaranth' sequence, on the theme of wifely self-sacrifice, which also informs H.D.'s correspondence with Cournos in this period.[33] In 'Eurydice', by contrast, written after she had read Aldington's poems for Flo Fallas, H.D. spurns what Sword defines as 'woman's traditional Eurydicean role as long-suffering wife' and instead goes head to head, poem to poem, with her Orpheus-husband, besting him in the poetic contest (Sword 409). A sequence of short-form stanzas or variations on the speaker's adulterous 'desires' for his 'beloved', Aldington's 'Images', as its title suggests, looks back in formal terms to his first volume, *Images (1910-1915)* (*CPRA* 38). In 'Eurydice', however, H.D. tests the possible limits of her marriage and of the Imagist lyric alike. Turning on Orpheus Eurydice tells him that 'I have more fervour / than you': even 'against the blackness', she insists, 'I have more light' (*CPHD* 54).[34]

'Eurydice' is reprinted in the May 1917 issue of *The Egoist* in which Aldington's poem 'Daughter of Zeus' also appears. Dedicated to 'J.C.' (John Cournos), 'Daughter of Zeus' would subsequently be included in *Images of War*, where in the Beaumont edition it is printed without the epigraph from Marinetti, '*Tuerons la lune*', of *The Egoist* version (*CPRA* 86).[35] The poem's opening lines, 'No! / We will not slay the moon. / For she is the fairest of the daughters of Zeus' (*CPRA* 86), refute Marinetti's proclamation in 'Let's Murder the Moonlight' (1909) that men's 'nerves demand war and despise women' (Poggi 186). Opposing what Wyndham Lewis would call Marinetti's 'play-boy operations upon the art-front in the preliminary sham-war' with the reality of the 1914–18 conflict (Lewis 46), Aldington makes common cause instead with his poem's dedicatee, Cournos, whose article on 'The Death of Futurism', a critique of Marinetti's 'masculomaniac' movement, had been published in *The Egoist*'s January 1917 number. Noting in his piece 'how closely war is allied with sex' Cournos finds that 'the Futuristic juxtaposition of the glorification of war and "contempt for women" is no accident' (Cournos 1917a, 6-7). 'Daughter of Zeus' reverses that Futurist equation in its glorification or sublimation of woman as goddess in time of war. Zeus' moon-daughter gazes down on the 'dead men' on the battlefield and 'Yet for us', the poem concludes, 'she is still a frail lily / Floating upon a calm pool – / Still a tall lady comforting our human despair' (*CPRA* 86). These last lines of the poem, Gates suggests, 'bring to mind both Imagism and *haiku*' (Gates 60), 'calm' and palliative prewar poetic modes – epitomized in F.S. Flint's untitled paean to the moon 'and the glow her passing / sheds on men' in the 1914 anthology *Des Imagistes* – now embodied, in Aldington's trench lyric, in Artemis, goddess both of the moon and of the hunt (Pound 1914b, 31). Artemis is also the goddess of chastity and in this aspect and in her figuration as 'a frail lily' and 'a tall lady' (*CPRA* 86) she is, quite evidently, H.D.'s avatar (Lawrence's lily of virtue, H.D. was sized up by Cournos as being 'a little too tall' (Cournos 1935, 269)).

If she is to comfort men this daughter of Zeus first needs their protection and so 'We will not slay the moon', Aldington avers, speaking in the second-person plural on behalf of Cournos, too, as an ally against Marinetti's rhetorical warmongering and as Aldington's and H.D.'s close mutual friend. 'Please look after H.D. in my absence', Aldington had asked Cournos in a letter of December 1916, the month he was transferred to the front (Risk 13). In October, H.D. had written to Cournos to say that 'You and he [Aldington] are guardian lovers to me. Protect me' (Hollenberg 140).[36] Her letter reveals the 'romantic thralldom' which Rachel Blau DuPlessis has identified in H.D.'s relationships with her male 'Initiators', Aldington and Cournos among them, a thralldom which is palpable in her 'Two Poems', 'The God' (I–IV) and 'Adonis', published in the January 1917 issue of *The Egoist* which also carries Cournos' article on 'The Death of Futurism'.[37] As Diana Collecott notes, however, in the subsection of H.D.'s *Collected Poems* (1925) titled 'The God', the 'Two Poems' initiate a '*series*' which 'progresses' from 'poems that address [male] divinities' to disenchanted women's monologues (Collecott 1999, 144–45). That same serial narrative shapes H.D.'s contribution to the 1917 *Some Imagist Poets* anthology, in which she is represented, in order, by 'The God', 'Adonis', 'Pygmalion' and 'Eurydice'. All four were also published as standalone poems in *The Egoist* between January and May 1917, and in 'Eurydice', positioned there vis-à-vis with Aldington's 'Daughter of Zeus', the paternal protection his poem promises is construed as reckless endangerment and abandonment: 'So you have swept me back, / I who could have walked with the live souls / above the earth' (*CPHD* 51).

'Eurydice' transcends its subtext in the troubled Aldington marriage, Sword insists, albeit that the poem 'can be read on the most obvious biographical level as H.D's personal cry of rage and despair against an unfaithful husband, also a poet' (Sword 414). But if it is the most obvious level on which the poem may be read, the biographical also forms the base layer of H.D.'s palimpsestic writing practice; in 'Eurydice', Susan Stanford Friedman points out, as in 'many of H.D.'s subsequent poems, Greek times, places and names serve as palimpsestic analogues to the modern world and the people in her circle' (Friedman 1990a, 66). H.D.'s account of the composition of 'Eurydice' in *Bid Me to Live* reveals the intricate interlacing of her interpersonal and intertextual relationships with the people in her circle, including Aldington as husband and as poet, and Lawrence. 'Rafe', the Aldington figure in the novel, asks 'Julia' (H.D.) about 'This thing you wrote for Rico [Lawrence]?', to which Julia replies that she has 'sent it in a letter' to Rico. She shows Rafe the 'discarded pages' of a draft of the 'thing' instead – an early version of 'Eurydice', composed as a prose poem (Aldington's own medium in his privately printed *Reverie: A Little Book of Poems for H.D.* (1917)). Reading the draft, Rafe critiques the 'Victorian' inversion in Eurydice's parting words, 'Go, Orpheus, look not back'. Julia's response is that it is 'only the preliminary scribbling': 'I saved that only for the other-side of the page, the paper', she explains (*BML* 28–30). The wartime paper shortage was real enough, but Julia is using the other side of the page, the blank reverse, as a blind for the reverse myth told in 'Eurydice', a poem which, in its final iteration, is marked by the inversion not of syntax but of gendered power relations.

H.D. may at first have sequestered 'Eurydice' from Aldington, as she had the 'Amaranth' poems, but she would utter her personal cry in the public face of modernism nevertheless: she would publish 'Eurydice' and be damned, without Aldington's say-so and with Lawrence's – mixed – blessing.[38] In *Bid Me to Live*, 'Rico' is the secret sharer of the text, apparently an Orpheus-and-Eurydice diptych, which Julia has sent him in her letter. In his reply – in a letter tentatively dated 23 March 1917 in *The Letters of D.H. Lawrence*, the text of which is taken from *Bid Me to Live* – Lawrence responds to H.D.'s poem:

> Your frozen altars mean something, but I don't like the second half of the Orpheus sequence as well as the first. Stick to the woman speaking. How can you know what Orpheus feels? It's your part to be woman, the woman vibration. Eurydice should be enough. You can't deal with both.
>
> (*L8* 23)[39]

Lawrence's double standard is exposed in *Bid Me to Live* when Julia asks: 'if he [Rico] could enter, so diabolically, into the feelings of women, why should not she enter into the feelings of men?' For Julia, the '*gloire*' – a loan word from Lawrence and from Virginia Woolf, which, in H.D.'s idiolect, connotes aesthetic vision – is 'both' (*BML* 36, 107). The creative mind is androgynous for H.D., as it is for Woolf (and as Anaïs Nin claimed it was for Lawrence too) and 'Eurydice' is a speaking model of how to be 'both' (Nin 49). H.D. would take Lawrence's advice and 'Stick to the woman speaking' in her poem and yet the woman who speaks is well versed in the Orphic tradition of Virgil, Dante and Milton – and of Lawrence, if we hear the 'inverted echo' of Lawrence's 'Resurrection' in 'Eurydice' (Kinkead-Weekes 418). A version of Lawrence's Orphic poem was turned down by the editorial committee for the 1917 *Some Imagist Poets* anthology in which 'Eurydice' was first printed, so as editor, as well as in her persona as Eurydice, H.D. effectively silences Lawrence, omitting his poem from the anthology but including her own 'Eurydice', a poem Lawrence had influenced but which also rounds on him.[40]

In the October 1916 letter in which she nominates Aldington and Cournos as her 'guardian lovers' H.D. had also called on them to 'Protect me' from 'another', who is unnamed but understood to be Lawrence: 'You, no doubt, know of whom I write as a cruel-fire!', H.D. tells Cournos, who would later reproduce her letter in *Miranda Masters*: 'There is a power in this person to kill me. I mean literally', H.D. insists; she is locked in a deadly yin-and-yang with the person in question who 'sees in me its *exact* compliment [*sic*]' (Hollenberg 140). Cecil Gray would indeed accuse Lawrence, if not of killing then of keeping his 'women' in thrall by 'allowing himself to become the object of a kind of esoteric female cult, an Adonis, Atthis, Dionysos religion of which he was the central figure, a Jesus Christ to a regiment of Mary Magdalenes' (Gray 1985, 133). Replying to Gray in a letter written in H.D.'s rooms at 44 Mecklenburgh Square on 7 November 1917, Lawrence refutes his allegation:

> Jesus himself was frightened of the knowledge which subsisted between the Magdalen and him, a knowledge deeper than the knowledge of Christianity and 'good', deeper than love, anyhow … It seems to me there is a whole world of knowledge to forsake, a new, deeper, lower one to *entamer* … And my 'women', Esther Andrews, Hilda Aldington etc, represent, in an impure and unproud, subservient, cringing, bad fashion, I admit – but represent none the less the threshold of a new world, or underworld, of knowledge and being.
>
> (*L3* 180)

Gray, an inveterate womanizer, who, in his autobiography, asserts the 'natural' superiority of 'the male', emerges from this spat as the unlikely forerunner of second-wave feminists such as Simone de Beauvoir, who says of Lawrence's 'woman' that 'worshipping man in a mystical cult, she loses and finds herself in his glory' (de Beauvoir 629).[41] A woman-is-to-nature-as-man-is-to-culture equation, according to which 'woman', as the feminine unconscious, must remain under the earth to nurture the ascendant male principle, does underpin the quite literal subordination of woman in Lawrence's postwar version of the Orpheus and Eurydice myth in 'Medlars and Sorb-Apples', first published in the *New Republic* in 1921 and included in his 1923 volume, *Birds, Beasts and Flowers*. If Lawrence shares the mask of Orpheus with Aldington in H.D.'s 'Eurydice', then in 'Medlars and Sorb-Apples', Lawrence is the singular Orpheus whose backward glance consigns Eurydice to the earthy 'underworld', which, as per his letter to Gray, is woman's proper place:

> So, in the strange retorts of medlars and sorb-apples
> The distilled essence of hell.
> The exquisite odour of leave-taking.
>   *Jamque vale!*
> Orpheus, and the winding, leaf-clogged, silent lanes of hell.
>
> (*LP1* 236)

Lawrence's Orphic poem looks back to H.D.'s 'Eurydice', restoring the gender status quo which her poem had reversed and proving Sword's point that 'As Orpheus, Lawrence would gladly follow his Eurydices down to their Underworld; he refused, however, to value too highly their contribution to his quest or to grant them, worse yet, reciprocal access to his own upper world of male privilege' (Sword 413).[42]

Orpheus' and Eurydice's 'unfusing into twain' in 'Medlars and Sorb-Apples' marks the parting of the ways between Lawrence and H.D., Pollnitz suggests (Pollnitz 127).[43] The friendship between the two poets which had developed during and in response to the First World War had ended, like the war itself and as a home front casualty of it, in 1918, when, to Lawrence's disapproval, H.D. left London and her broken marriage to live with Gray in Cornwall, conceiving his (unacknowledged) child there. As I show in my coda to this book, however, textual reciprocities – and tensions – between H.D. and Lawrence would survive their biographical rift, complicated gendered readings of the work of both. H.D. found in Lawrence's heterodox interpretation of Imagists dos and don'ts and in his harping on the 'woman vibration' provocations for the formal and the feminist turn in her poetics dramatized in 'Eurydice'. In return, as Aldington says, 'anyone can see from his *Collected Poems*' that 'even Lawrence was for a time influenced by H.D.' (Aldington 1968, 127). Her flower and fruit poems offered Lawrence an object lesson in how to construct an underworld mythopoesis out of acts of close botanical attention – 'Pomegranate', the Persephone poem with which *Birds, Beasts and Flowers* opens, is an example, and even 'Medlars and Sorb-Apples' finds provender for its 'Delicious rottenness' in the 'fallen' autumn fruits of H.D.'s 'Orchard' (*LPI* 235; *CPHD* 29). And in 'Bavarian Gentians' from *The Last Poems Notebook* the dying Lawrence 'guide[s]' himself 'with the blue, forked torch of a flower' 'down the way Persephone goes' into 'the halls of Dis' (*LP1* 611).

Like H.D. in 'Eurydice' Lawrence had insisted in his 1917 letter to Gray that 'The old world must burst, the underworld must be open' (*L3* 180). Lawrence valued H.D. not only or merely as one of his kept 'underworld' 'women' – the Eurydice to his Orpheus or the Persephone to his Dis – but as 'one of the poetesses whose poetry' Lawrence, like his autobiographical protagonist in *Kangaroo*, 'feared and wondered over' (*K* 248). In the war years H.D., Lawrence and Aldington were fighting out poetry, on the gender line, on the home front and on the front line.

Notes

1. For Lawrence and Nichols in 1917, see *L8* 23. Vivien Whelpton has suggested that the fourth poet at the party may have been F.S. Flint (email to the author, 15 September 2022).
2. The 30 July dinner took place a fortnight after another dinner party, also hosted by Lowell, at the Dieudonne Restaurant in Ryder Street, to celebrate the publication of Pound's 1914 anthology *Des Imagistes*.
3. On the 'democracy' of the Imagist anthologies, see Lowell (2008, 254).
4. What Monroe termed 'the new poetry' would become synonymous with free verse per se, although the intention of the anthology *The New Poetry* (1917), edited by Monroe and Alice Corbin Henderson, had been 'to oppose and correct Amy Lowell's *Some Imagist Poets*' (Williams 188).
5. Pound coined the unsavoury term 'Amygist'. See Espey 25.
6. For Imagism as a transatlantic network, see Fernihough (2013, 41).
7. Lawrence's high estimation of H.D.'s Imagism is confirmed in his letters. See *L2* 203 and *L3* 61.
8. In the manuscript version the poem's penultimate line reads 'Ah, do not let me die on the brink of so much hope!' (*L3* 170 n.20).
9. For recensions of the leaves trope, see Bloom 125–43.
10. Pound's poem is an early version of what would become canto II in *A Draft of XVI Cantos* and subsequent editions of his epic.
11. The version Lawrence sent Monroe in 1915 is printed as 'Resurrection [2]' in *LP3*.
12. 'Errinyes' as it appears in Lowell's Imagist anthology is arranged in sestets, which is likely a 'typist or compositor's error' (*LP3* 1827).
13. In a letter of 24 October 1913, H.D. asked Monroe 'to cut "the affectation of 'Imagiste'" from her signature when her poems were printed in *Poetry* for February 1914' (Williams 41 n.18).
14. For a discussion of Orage and the *New Age*, see Ardis and Jackson.
15. Ezra Pound coined the term 'School of Images' in his Prefatory Note to 'The Complete Poetical Works of T.E. Hulme' (1912) (Pound 1990, 266). Orage had attended Hulme's Tuesday evening gatherings at Frith Street and Hulme himself would continue to contribute to *The New Age* from the front in his 'War Notes' column, signed 'North Staff', in which he called out those literary men of the Bloomsbury group who refused to enlist.
16. On Imagism and advertising, see Materer.
17. For 'People' and its variants, see Gates 143.
18. 'Khaki Bank Holiday' is the title of a Topical Budget newsreel of the Hampstead Heath funfair held during the August 1915 bank holiday; see Shail 181.

19 'Captive', its companion-poem 'The Faun Captive' and 'Sunsets' are the 'one or two newer poems' which conclude the 1919 Egoist Press edition of *Images*. Richard Aldington, 'Note', in *Images* (Aldington 1919a, n. pag.). 'Captive' is included in *Some Imagist Poets* (1917).
20 For the dating of 'Prufrock', see Eliot (2015, 363).
21 For 'combat gnosticism', see J. Campbell.
22 Aldington's 'The Return' is located and dated '*London*, 1919'.
23 Pound acknowledges Aldington's war experience at Hill 70 in canto XVI which also elegizes sculptor Henri Gaudier-Brzeska and Imagist T.E. Hulme (Pound 1964, 75).
24 In '*Ulysses*, Order and Myth' Eliot counters the 'criticism which Mr. Aldington directed upon *Ulysses* several years ago'. Eliot is referring to 'The Influence of Mr. James Joyce', Aldington's 1921 *English Review* essay which had 'treated Mr. Joyce as a prophet of chaos'. Aldington had invited Eliot to answer his essay from an opposite point of view and Joyce himself urged Eliot to respond to Aldington's criticism 'that *Ulysses* represented chaos chaotically' (Read 190). Eliot would criticize the critic – without naming Aldington – in his 'Lettre d'Angleterre', published in May 1922 in *La Nouvelle Revue Française*, and he would take up the argument with Aldington explicitly in his defence of Joyce's mythical method in '*Ulysses*, Order, and Myth' (Eliot 2021b, 478–80).
25 Aldington's intention had been to publish *Images of War* and *Images of Desire* as a single volume. Brought out as discrete books instead in England in 1919, the two sequences would be brought together in the same year in an American edition, *War and Love*. In his Foreword, Aldington explains that the volume is a far cry from the 'subtleties' of *Images*, its two parts exploring the 'conflict' between 'the delight of the flesh' in the sexual act and that 'agony of the flesh which is known only to infantrymen of the line'. *War and Love* is dedicated to F.S. Flint, who, as a fellow-Imagist and veteran, 'will be most likely to understand' that this is 'a book by a common soldier for common soldiers' which 'expresses the soldier's mood': a 'disregard of rules for conduct, a yearning of the flesh, a wild grasping at life' (Aldington 1919b, 5–6). Accordingly the 'life'-affirming 'Love' sequence of *War and Love* takes its epigraph not from Dante's *Inferno* but from his *Vita Nuova* and yet, although the poems' love object is his mistress, Dorothy Yorke, it is H.D. whom Aldington addresses as 'my Beatrice' in a June 1918 letter, written during his second tour of duty, in which he says that 'those who love each other best hurt each other most' (Zilboorg 2003, 52).
26 I borrow the term 'flower-text' from von Glinski (32).
27 H.D. would nonetheless accept Lawrence's 'New Heaven and Earth' from *Look! We Have Come Through!* for *Some Imagist Poets* (1917). First printed there as 'Terra Nuova', the poem was Lawrence's sole contribution to that year's anthology.
28 Pollnitz speculates that 'Craving for Spring' was probably written in February 1917 and so may not have been included in the version of *Look! We Have Come Through!* which Lawrence sent to H.D. that month (see *LP2* 975).

29 For the symbolic language of the amaranth, see Seaton 50. 'The Rose and the Amaranth' is numbered 369 in Perry's Index of Aesop's *Fables*.
30 The first, posthumous, publication of 'Amaranth', 'Eros' and 'Envy' was in 1969 in an H.D. special issue of *Contemporary Literature*.
31 For the symbolic rose, see Seward 7.
32 See Norris (2015b, 104). Aldington had sent the uncensored original of 'Images' to Flint, 'the patient keeper of my confessions!' in a letter in May 1916. The (untitled) original is printed in Gates 178–79. See Whelpton (2013, 122).
33 In her 5 September 1916 letter H.D. asks Cournos 'would it be a good and wise sacrifice, to try to get her [Flo] to come here, to have her live, as she suggested, with me?' (Hollenberg 34).
34 An earlier sequence also titled 'Images' had appeared in Aldington's *Images (1910–1915)*.
35 The epigraph is retained in *War and Love* and is restored in Aldington's *Complete Poems* where the dedication is dropped instead.
36 'Don't brood too much over R. and don't surround him with too much tenderness', Flint had advised H.D. in a September 1916 letter (Hollenberg 135).
37 See DuPlessis (1979).
38 See Morrisson's study of *The Public Face of Modernism*. According to his biographer Aldington certainly did not see the 'Amaranth' poems 'at the time of their composition' (Whelpton 2013, 136).
39 The editors of volume VIII of his *Letters* note that Lawrence 'was in correspondence with Hilda Aldington about the anthology, *Some Imagist Poets* (Boston and New York, 1917), to which both had contributed' and in which 'Eurydice' – one half, it seems, of the original manuscript – appeared. The editors suggest that these comments may come from the same letter, the text again taken from *Bid Me to Live*, in which Lawrence advises H.D. to 'Kick over your tiresome house of life, our languid lily of virtue nods perilously near the pit … love-adept, you are a living spirit in a living spirit city' (*L8* 23–4).
40 The rejected version of Lawrence's poem is printed as 'Resurrection' [3] in *LP3*. Lowell explains of the *modus operandi* of the Imagist anthologies that 'any poem could be excluded by one veto' (Lowell 1917, 254).
41 Gray's view was that 'In marriage there can be no equality; one or the other must dominate, and nature has agreed that it should be the male' (Gray 1985, 61).
42 Eurydice's words, '*Jamque vale!*' (and now farewell) are those spoken by Virgil's Eurydice in book IV of the *Georgics* and by the ghost of Aeneas' dead wife, Creusa, in book II of the *Aeneid*, in which Aeneas recalls the sack of Troy.
43 'Medlars and Sorb-Apples', like other 'Fruits' poems in *Birds, Beasts and Flowers*, may also have been prompted by Lawrence's brief affair, in Tuscany in 1920, with Rosalind Baynes.

4

Translation, global modernism and the Great War

In October 1915, an advance notice for the Poets' Translation Series (PTS) appeared in *The Egoist*. The little magazine, then under Richard Aldington's editorship, had brought out its special number on Imagism in May and the Imagist agenda, of renovating poetic diction and reinterpreting the classics in a modernist idiom, is carried over into the PTS. The aim of the Imagists who were the series' editors, Aldington and H.D., was to promote 'unhackneyed poetry' which is 'proof of the amazing vitality of the Hellenic tradition' (Aldington 1915, 163).

The first pamphlet issued by the PTS was Aldington's translation of Anyte of Tegea, the poet commemorated by Antipater of Sidon as the 'woman-Homer' (Aldington 1930, n. pag). Sappho's poems and fragments followed in Edward Storer's version and the third number, H.D.'s *Choruses from Iphigeneia in Aulis*, came out in 1916. From the outset, women's voices, solo and in chorus, are the leading voices in a series which challenges the chauvinistic co-option of the classics to the war effort. 'How would 1917 London have acclaimed such anti-war propaganda'? H.D. wonders in her unpublished 'Notes on Euripides' (H.D. 2003, 277). Her own translation of the choruses from Euripides' *Iphigeneia*, published the year before, turns the heroic 'Troy on the Western Front' trope into an alternative 'anti-war' analogy between the Trojan War and the Great War focalized and vocalized through the suffering and sacrifice of women (Vandiver 2010, 232).

D.H. Lawrence's 'little book' of verse translations, 'All of Us', was written during the war, but the poems were published only in bits in his lifetime (*L3* 233). Lawrence was not a contributor to the PTS and his translations are not from the Greek but are adapted from German transcriptions of the Arabic songs of the Egyptian fellaheen, labourers on excavations carried out on behalf of the Berlin Museum in the Upper Nile region in 1900. When he revised these folk songs in 1916 as 'All of Us', Lawrence repurposed the sequence as 'war *literature*' for 'the people' (*L3* 51). But if there are significant differences, there are also striking affinities between Lawrence's translations and those issued by the PTS. In these unaligned yet allied projects, an Imagist poetics is transferred into a war idiom in verse very often spoken by women: prompted perhaps by H.D.'s translation of Euripides, Lawrence planned another 'little book' of poems, a sequel of sorts to 'All of Us' to be called 'Chorus of Women'.

This chapter tracks 'the triple path-ways' of translation – to borrow a phrase from H.D.'s adaptation of Anyte in 'Hermes of the Ways' – taken by H.D. herself, by Aldington and by Lawrence in the war years and the postwar decade (*CPHD* 37). In the first part of the chapter, I draw on the scholarship of Caroline Zilboorg, Elizabeth Vandiver and Eileen Gregory to consider Aldington and H.D. as partners in the 'joint venture' of the PTS before tracing, between the lines of their own translations, quasi-translations and adaptations the parting of the ways between the two poets. The second part of the chapter uses translation theory to map the intersection between translation and the global Great War in Lawrence's 'All of Us'.

'It all began with the Greek fragments': H.D. and Aldington

From the outset H.D.'s and Aldington's partnership as poets was premised on translation.[1] Aldington's 1912 poem 'To Atthis' is an early product of their collaborative working practice: subtitled '(*After the Manuscript of Sappho now in Berlin*)' its base text is a 'new' Sapphic fragment which had appeared, in J.M. Edmonds' 'restoration', in the *Classical Review* in 1909 (Edmonds 99).[2] Aldington was 19 years old in 1912, too young to be issued with a reader's card for the British Library, and so H.D., who was six years his senior, accessed and transcribed Edmonds' text there on his behalf. Ezra Pound submitted 'To Atthis' for publication in *Poetry* magazine but the editor, Harriet Monroe, rejected it on the advice of Paul Shorey, Professor of Greek Language and Literature at the University of Chicago, that Aldington's translation was inaccurate.[3] Monroe and Shorey missed the point of Aldington's supposed 'mistranslation', but Ezra Pound, who defended 'To Atthis' as 'quite beautiful scholarship or no scholarship', anthologized the poem in *Des Imagistes* in 1914 and would publish his own version of the fragment as 'O Atthis' in 1916.[4] Edmonds' opinion was that in 'these torn pieces of papyrus or vellum there is something to be supplied, before, even as fragments, they can be in any way complete' and indeed half the words in his 'conjectural restoration', as Pound called it, are supplied by Edmonds himself (Edmonds 99). Pound, by contrast, valued the Sapphic fragment *qua* fragment, finding in the pieces of Oxyrhynchus papyri published by the Egyptian Exploration Society and in the vellum scraps of the Berlin Manuscript an ancient prototype for a modernist poetics of rupture and concision.[5] Pound's 'O Atthis', at seven lines, is pithier than Aldington's eighteen-line 'To Atthis', albeit that the ellipses with which Aldington's version peter out gesture to the incompleteness of the Sapphic original.

Aldington and H.D. would break with Pound and his Imagist school in 1914, but the PTS would take up Pound's agon with Shorey and his scholarly ilk. The editorial objective of the series was to reclaim, via new 'translations of Greek and Latin poetry and prose', a literature that 'has too long been the property of pedagogues, philologists, and professors'; the 'wrangling of grammarians', the editors opined, has obscured the 'human quality' of the classics (Aldington 1915, 163). In her unpublished essay 'The Wise Sappho', H.D. salutes the archaeologists who are 'searching to find a precious inch of palimpsest among the funereal glories of the sand-strewn Pharaohs' (H.D. 1982, 69) and in her 'Notes on Euripides' she concedes that 'we need scholars to decipher and interpret the Greek': but we also need poets, H.D. insists, 'to see *through* the words, the word being but the outline' (H.D. 2003, 278). Her distinction between poets and professors is endorsed by T.S. Eliot, in whose judgement H.D.'s choruses are 'much nearer' to the Greek than the translations of Professor Gilbert Murray (Eliot 2021b, 198).[6]

Euripides, Gregory points out, 'is the central figure within H.D.'s Hellenism', although her 'female literary precursor' Sappho has been foregrounded in feminist approaches to H.D.'s reception of the classics (Gregory 5–6, 105). Unlike Aldington and Pound, however, H.D. 'never dared to quote openly from the new finds'; her engagement with Sappho, if not with the new finds, would come after the war, in indirect response to the end of her marriage to Aldington (Goldschmidt 53). H.D.'s early verse draws on the *Greek Anthology*, a collection of epigrams first assembled by Meleager of Gadara in 60 BCE and subsequently expanded in multiple recensions. The *Anthology* 'inaugurated literary modernism', according to Gideon Nisbet, who identifies J.W. Mackail's 'stripped-down' version of 1906, *Select Epigrams from the Greek Anthology*, as a 'touchstone' for the Imagist experiment with epigrammatic brevity in the *avant-guerre* (Nisbet vii, xxiv–xxv). From 1914, however, the epigrams, many of which are epitaphic or funerary, would be deployed to different ends, the *Anthology* now serving as a manual for war memorializing and as a handy source of war-mongering slogans.

H.D.'s 'Hermes of the Ways' was published in *Poetry* in 1913 as the first of 'Three Poems' introduced as 'Verses, Translations, and Reflections from "The Anthology"'. When Pound read the poem in the tearoom of the British Museum, he appended the *per pro* signature 'H.D., *"Imagiste"*' to the draft, and that is how 'Epigram', the third of her 'Three Poems' in *Poetry*, is signed. This origin story of Imagism is one of several competing narratives; in another account Imagism came about in a Kensington bun shop. That H.D.'s emergence as a poet is located in the classical translation and adaptation is a matter of record, however, as the tagline to her 'Three Poems' in *Poetry* proves; 'It's straight talk, straight as the Greek!', Pound insisted when he recommended the poems to Harriet Monroe (Pound 1971, 11).[7] 'Hermes of the Ways' was written in 1912, three years before Aldington published his translation of the same Anyte epigram under the same title. If she acted as his occasional amanuensis or scribe Aldington's translations also drew on H.D.'s creative practice, the two 'Hermes' versions indicating that 'the process of translation – into Aldington's poetic modern English version and into H.D.'s new poem – was a joint process of more complex interrelation than has yet been examined' (Zilboorg 1991, 94).

'Hermes of the Ways' is reprinted in H.D.'s first volume, *Sea Garden*, a gathering of her early verse and her flower poems which nods to Meleager's arrangement of his *Greek Anthology* as a 'garland of poetic flowers' (Aldington 1930, 13).[8] Aldington would translate *The Poems of Meleager of Gadara* for the second postwar set of the PTS, but for her PTS pamphlet, published, like *Sea Garden*, in 1916, H.D. takes her source text from the genre of Greek tragedy. Euripides, H.D. observes, 'lived through almost a modern great-war period' (H.D. 2003, 277), and she found 'a mirror' in the chorus of women in his *Iphigeneia in Aulis*, Gregory says – a speaking mirror – 'for the visceral and bewildering experience of war' (Gregory 25). The women of Chalcis lament that 'nothing will ever be the same', but as with the Trojan War, so with the First World War, H.D.'s translation implies (*CPHD* 76).

The subject of *Iphigeneia in Aulis* – a woman sacrificed in the manly pursuit of war – struck both a public and a personal chord for H.D. in 1916, the year Aldington joined the army and embarked on an affair with Flo Fallas.[9] Euripides' Iphigeneia consents 'to do sacrifice', to be put to death to appease the goddess Artemis who has becalmed the Greek fleet at Aulis, preventing it sailing to Troy. Iphigeneia's role is reprised in less drastic fashion by the first-person speaker of H.D.'s 1916 poem 'Amaranth', discussed in the previous chapter, who attests that she will 'sacrifice' herself for 'my lover, Atthis'. The Euripidean topos of female sacrifice is refracted through Sappho's fragment forty-one (in H.T. Wharton's numbering) in H.D.'s poem, where Atthis, the unfaithful lover, is the avatar of the unfaithful Aldington, who had been Sappho's translator in 'To Atthis' and is now a soldier.[10] If he is to make the ultimate sacrifice on the battlefield – and since 'Those who are about to die fear only chastity', as Aldington claims in his poem 'Thanatos' – then H.D.'s first-person speaker deems it her duty to 'do sacrifice' by acknowledging 'the love of my lover for his mistress' (*CPHD* 83, 310–13; Aldington 1926, 59).[11]

H.D. chose not to publish 'Amaranth' or its companion poems, 'Eros' and 'Envy', but she would rework the 1916 Dorset Trio in her postwar volume *Heliodora* (1924) across four 'Fragment' poems: 'Fragment Thirty-six' (*'I know not what to do: / my mind is divided. – Sappho'*), 'Fragment Forty' (*'Love … bitter-sweet. – Sappho'*), 'Fragment Forty-one' (*'… thou flittest to Andromeda. – Sappho'*) and 'Fragment sixty-eight' (*'… even in the house of Hades. – Sappho'*). The headings for *Heliodora*'s 'Fragment' poems are taken from Wharton's prose translations; H.D.'s 'self-sanction against translating Sappho' means that she avoids 'a direct textual encounter, insisting rather on literary mediation' (Gregory 148, 151).[12] Mediated through Wharton, the headings are cue-lines for the poems which follow; 'after Sappho' on the page, the poems are H.D.'s remediations, under Sappho's aegis, of her own wartime verse.[13] The 'Fragment' poems are not translations and nor are they 'restorations' of lost lyric originals; indeed, the heading for 'Fragment Forty-one' reproduces only the second of the two surviving lines from Sappho *'… thou flittest to Andromeda'*. The line left out – given by Wharton as *'But to thee, Atthis, the thought of me is hateful'* (98) and by Storer in his PTS pamphlet *Poems & Fragments of Sappho*, as 'So you hate me now, Atthis […]' (Aldington and Storer 16) – is translated by H.D. herself in 'The Wise Sappho' as 'Ah, Atthis, you hate even to think of me' (H.D. 1982, 65).[14] Atthis had been named in 'Amaranth' – 'my lover, Atthis' – but in 'Fragment Forty-one' his name is redacted from the heading and from the main body of the poem (*CPHD* 311). As Jason Harding and John Nash point out, however, modernist 'non-translation' very often 'involves a re-translation back into subjective experience' (Harding and Nash 17) and Atthis remains an unspoken presence in the 'Fragment' poems in which H.D. mediates her relationship with Aldington – their early collaboration as poet-translators and his subsequent infidelities – through the medium of their shared 'Sapphic intertextuality' (Gregory 148). In a letter to H.D. from behind the front line in 1918, Aldington had asked her to 'pardon your old lover all his faults and all his pettiness and remember only that part of him that you used to love – Atthis!' (Zilboorg 2003, 57).

Women poets have spoken of lesbian love through Sappho's mask, but like her own bisexual identity, H.D.'s reception of Sappho is open to interpretation.[15] As Sarah Parker notes, her critics 'disagree on whether H.D. uses the homoerotic Sappho "mask" to disguise biographical content regarding her husband, Richard Aldington, or whether "the revisions made before publication masked [...] the lesbian content"' of her translations. But this is a false binary, according to Parker, who points out that the early drafts of 'Amaranth' 'switch the pronoun of the poem's addressee from male to female and back again' in a gender-fluid grammar which allows H.D. 'to avoid being tied down to one kind of definition or sexological category' (Parker 29).[16] In 1918, after the break-up of her marriage to Aldington and the end of her affair with Cecil Gray, H.D. formed a relationship with Bryher (Winifred Ellerman). A correspondingly queer trajectory has been traced in H.D.'s postwar poetry in which *Heliodora* is read, most recently in Susan McCabe's joint biography, as the 'love story' of 'We Two': of H.D. and Bryher (McCabe 3). That love story is told in the *Heliodora* poem titled 'We Two', H.D.'s paean to the 'shelter' she had found in her relationship with Bryher, but 'Fragment Forty-one' may more plausibly be read as the story of 'you two' (Aldington and Flo Fallas) and of 'we three' (the love triangle formed between Aldington, Flo and H.D.) (*CPHD* 181–82). The 'Sappho fragments', McCabe says, 'punctuate *Heliodora* as voice-over of H.D.'s drama with Bryher' (McCabe 125) but these 'Fragment' poems speak instead, in H.D.'s and Aldington's common language of classical reception and translation, to the wartime drama of a marriage in shatters.

The first of H.D.'s 'Fragment' verses appear in *Hymen* (1921). Dedicated to Bryher and to H.D.'s daughter, Perdita, the volume has been read as an 'anti-epithalamium' (McCabe 120). But like the *Heliodora* fragments the single Sappho fragment poem in *Hymen*, 'Fragment 113 "*Neither honey nor bee for me.*" – Sappho', speaks to 'old desire' and 'old pain' (*CPHD* 131) – to H.D.'s sexual and textual intimacy with the Aldington who, in the 'Images' sequence published in *Some Imagist Poets* (1917), had figured himself translating the same Sapphic fragment:

Here alone I scribble and re-scribble
The words of a long-dead Greek poet:
'*Love, thou art terrible,*
Ah, Love, thou art bitter-sweet!'

(*CPRA* 63)

The 'sun's fire', H.D. writes in her adaptation of 'Fragment 113', 'gathers such heat and power, / that shadow-print is light, / cast through the petals / of the yellow iris flower' (*CPHD* 131). In the same way the 'shadow-print' of earlier writing – Sappho's fragment, Wharton's translation of Sappho, Aldington's translation and retranslation of the fragment and 'Eros', the second poem in H.D.'s Dorset Trio – is legible through the lines of her poem.[17] 'The palimpsestic layering of personalities inherent in any reading of Sappho sets the stage for the rhetorical encoding of H.D. and Aldington's own relationship', Erika Rohrbach argues, and 'Fragment 113' proves her further point, that H.D. 'turned this palimpsestic reading relationship into a writing style' (Rohrbach 194, 184). As Rohrbach rightly concludes 'if we are to interpret H.D.'s fragment poems by her life, we should read with the Aldington rift and not the Bryher refuge in mind' (Rohrbach 189).

'It all began with the Greek fragments', H.D. recalls (H.D. 1979, 41). In the title poem of *Heliodora* she looks back to her first attempt, in collaboration and competition with Aldington, to translate epigrams from the *Greek Anthology*: 'He and I sought together, / over the spattered table, / rhymes and flowers' (*CPHD* 151).[18] His phrases, H.D.'s speaker remarks in an aside, were 'not as good as mine' but in another parenthesis she credits him with coming up with the compound words – '(He wrote myrrh-curled, / I think, the first)' – that have become synonymous with H.D.'s own verse (*CPHD* 151, 154). The poems of *Sea Garden* are located in liminal and littoral spaces, on the 'wor(l)d-edge' where 'sea-grass tangles with shore-grass' (*CPHD* 26, 39), but these characteristic compounds also conjoin H.D.'s lexis with Aldington's:

He said:
'I will make her a wreath;'
he said:
'I will write it thus:

I will bring you the lily that laughs,
I will twine
with soft narcissus, the myrtle,
sweet crocus, white violet,
the purple hyacinth, and last,
the rose, loved-of-love,
that these may drip on your hair
the less soft flowers,
may mingle sweet with the sweet
of Heliodora's locks,
myrrh-curled.'

(*CPHD* 153)[19]

The prewar scene of translation to which 'Heliodora' returns indicates that Aldington's *Meleager of Gadara*, issued by the PTS in 1920, had its origins before the war in a joint venture with H.D. Compare the verse version of Meleager's 'The Garland' written by the 'he' in 'Heliodora' with Aldington's prose translation:

> I will bind the white violet and the gentle narcissus with myrtles, laughing lilies and the soft crocus; and I will bind with them the dark-blue hyacinth and the amorous rose so that the garland about the temples of myrrh-tressed Heliodora may strew flowers on her bright loose hair.
>
> (Aldington 1930, 19)

The love poems to Heliodora in Meleager's *Greek Anthology* constitute 'a kind of autobiography', Zilboorg suggests, or a 'A Love Story in Bits and Pieces', as Regina Höschele puts it, a story H.D. adopts and adapts in *Heliodora* in the title and 'Fragment' poems and in 'Nossis', in which H.D. gives her own version of Meleager's 'Garland' (Zilboorg 1991, 84).[20] His 'wreath', Meleager says in 'Nossis', is 'wrought' of '*memories with names of poets*', '*red-lilies for Anyte, / for Sappho, roses*' and, for Nossis, '*the myrrh-iris*' (*CPHD* 156–57). The prominence of women poets in Meleager's *Anthology* was 'vitally important to H.D.', Rachel Blau DuPlessis explains, in demonstrating that 'Greek women lyricists were "in some subtle way co-workers with men"' (DuPlessis 1986, 22).[21] *Heliodora*, like the *Greek Anthology*, celebrates Anyte, Sappho and Nossis; voicing their 'woman-tongued' poetics in a modernist idiom, H.D. also affirms that women, in modernity as in antiquity, are co-workers with men (Nisbet 100).

Aldington, whose career as a translator began with the Greek fragments, would go on to produce standard translations of de Bergerac, Laclos, Voltaire, Remy de Gourmont, Theophrastus and Boccaccio. The PTS suspended its operations when he entered the army: Aldington's *Greek Songs in the Manner of Anacreon*, issued in the second set of the PTS in 1919, is 'entirely a "war work"' but since 'A small and imperfect dictionary was the only one light enough to carry on active service' translation proper proved impractical (Aldington 1930, 57).[22] Aldington would fall back instead on forms of *imitatio* and *faux* translation: stationed in France, he also drew on the French tradition of the prose poem, the medium deployed in *The Love of Myrrhine and Konallis* for his imitations of Greek lyrics of lesbian love. Privately printed in 1917 in a run of forty copies and reissued in an expanded trade edition in 1926, *The Love of Myrrhine and Konallis* is subtitled, in its first version, 'A Cycle of Prose Poems after the Greek Manner'. It is a work, not of translation but of ersatz Sapphistry in which Myrrhine, an H.D-like hetaira, and Konallis, a goat-girl, celebrate their same-sex desire.[23] The eroticism of the sequence – the voyeurism of the male gaze on girl-on-girl action – is pointed up in Frank Mechau's Aubrey Beardsley-inspired designs for the (yellow) book jacket and end sheets of the 1926 edition. The illustrated version of *The Love of Myrrhine and Konallis* invites comparison with French poet Pierre Louÿs' *The Songs of Bilitis* (1894), a pseudotranslation of ancient lesbian love lyrics printed with sexually explicit art deco illustrations in a privately circulated English edition in 1926. 'Perhaps they are a perversion', Aldington admitted of his imaginary women in a 1917 letter in which he defends himself with the troubling explanation that 'from shadows they became so real to me that human beings seemed very shadows by comparison' (quoted in Gates 47–8). The sexual politics of the *Myrrhine and Konallis* poems *are* complicated, however, by the speculation that they were 'written in part by H.D.', in which case, Zilboorg points out, the cycle suggests a possible 'collaboration much less common and more complex than the joint translations on which we can be more certain both Aldington and H.D. worked' (Zilboorg 1990, 28–9).[24] For all its cod classicism and, perhaps, 'perversion', May Sinclair would praise *The Love of Myrrhine and Konallis* as 'a sequence of the most exquisite love poems in the language' (Sinclair 403).

Like *The Love of Myrrhine and Konallis*, Aldington's *Reverie: A Little Book of Poems for H.D.* was privately printed by the Clerk's Press in Cleveland, Ohio, in 1917.[25] In a letter to the Reverend Charles C. Bubb – the improbable printer of this little book and of the risqué *Myrrhine and Konallis* – Aldington described *Reverie* as 'representing the best of my trench work' (quoted in Gates 47). The title poem locates him behind the lines: 'Not far away as I now write / The guns are beating madly upon the still air' (*CPRA* 101). *Reverie*'s 'Sorcery of Words' is reprinted in the 1926 edition of *Myrrhine and Konallis* as one of 'Nineteen Prose Poems' appended to the original sequence but together with his translations, improper and proper, the majority of his prose poems are excluded from Aldington's *Collected* and *Complete Poems*.[26] 'Sorcery of Words' is not itself a translation but a prose poem prompted by 'words, remembered from some aesthetic essay'. Those words, '"The poetry of winter"', are remembered from Walter Pater's essay on Renaissance poet and translator Joachim du Bellay who, in response to the higher status of prose in the French literary tradition, had defended poetry as 'rhyme in prose' (Aldington 1926, 72; du Bellay 15).[27] After du Bellay, as Aldington would point out in 1921 in his 'A Note on Poetry in Prose', the *'poème en prose'* – unrhymed prose poetry – would be recognized by French critics as 'a distinct literary *genre*'. English critics, likewise, Aldington insists, 'must seek our poetry among the prose poets' (Aldington 1921, 16, 19). Aldington's PTS translations are in prose and his defence of the prose poem in English is informed by the French example. In 'Sorcery of Words', however, poetry and poetry in prose are not, as he would later insist, 'interdependent'; rather, the medium of Aldington's prose poem is its message, that the poem in prose is prosaic, a poor substitute for pure poetry (Aldington 1921, 17). At 'Base Camp Calais', where 'Sorcery of Words' is located, those remembered words, 'the poetry of winter', return as an 'ironic / phrase', an 'echo' of the prewar past. For Pater, du Bellay, although 'coming to us through three centuries[…] seems of yesterday', but Pater's own words are now no more than a 'whisper' which comes 'faintly' to the listener 'across the clamour of the age' (Aldington 1926, 73; Pater 113).

The provenance of 'Sorcery of Words' in Aldington's 'Little Book of Poems for H.D.' suggests that the silent listener, the 'You' to whom his prose poem is addressed, is H.D. herself. She is 'clean and warm / with the delicate leisure of a flower-scented / library', whereas the speaker, a soldier at base camp, is 'hungry, sore, unshaven, / dirty' (Aldington 1926, 72–3). The partnership between H.D. and Aldington before the war – when her 'leisure' time was spent working, on his behalf, in a library – is recast, in 1917, as a polarity between civilian complacency and soldierly suffering.[28] Paul Fussell has identified 'irony emerging from anomalous contrasts' as a dominant mode of Great War literature (Fussell 204), and there is an 'ironic persistance [sic]' of irony itself in Aldington's prose poem ('irony', 'ironic', 'ironic / phrase', 'ironically') (Aldington 1926, 72–3). The 'echo' of that 'ironic / phrase "the poetry of winter"' is, to borrow Fussell's phrase, a 'travesty echo' from the world before the world war (Fussell 38).

Aldington's situation in 'Sorcery of Words' is reversed in his postwar prose poem 'In the Library', where, 'now that it is over', the poet-speaker finds himself in the reading room rather than in an army camp. 'What is it / I am reading? Greek? What does / Greek matter?', the speaker asks, as his thoughts force him out of the library and back to the front line: 'I am out again on the muddy / trench-boards' (Aldington 1926, 106). In 'At the British Museum', written before Aldington's war service, the first-person speaker says 'I turn the page and read' and as he does so is transported out of 'the great dome' of the reading room to Dante's Italy, to 'the cleft battlements of Can Grande's castle' (*CPRA* 45).[29] By contrast, 'Sorcery of Words', belying its title, invokes not a 'bewitchment' by literary language but the 'disenchantment' which, Andrew Frayn argues, 'comes to represent First World War experience' (Frayn 2014, 6). But if Pater's phrase about du Bellay, 'the poetry of winter', is ironic, du Bellay himself, a Hellenist and translator of the classics whose original poetry celebrates the everyday 'homeliness' of his native France, may have given Aldington, who honed his French in the trenches, a steer for his own war verse.[30] In his *Images of War* poem 'A Village', I suggest in Chapter

Three, the soldier-poet discovers the beauty of 'homely things'; like the du Bellay who, in Pater's words, created a 'new Italy in France', Aldington declares that the 'drab' French village in which his regiment is billeted is as 'lovely in our eyes / As the prince city of Tuscany' (Pater 113, 40; *CPRA* 90).[31]

Aldington would return to 'Sorcery of Words' in 1930 in *Roads to Glory*, a collection of Great War short stories which, in its formal experimentation with a prose version of Imagism, may be compared to Ernest Hemingway's *in our time* (1924). 'Sorcery of Words' is spliced into the concluding story, 'Farewell to Memories', as a meditation in time of war prompted by a letter the soldier-protagonist has received 'from a woman' who writes of 'how beautiful the first snowdrops looked in the library' and of 'the loveliness of winter twilight over the quiet meadows' (Aldington 1934, 263). In a similar scenario in Aldington's war novel, *Death of a Hero*, the protagonist, George, is in the trenches when he receives a letter from his wife, Elizabeth, telling him that 'She had just been to Hampton Court to look at the flowers' (*DH* 317). Alice Kelly notes in her discussion of First World War correspondence that letters 'attempted to bridge the distance between soldiers and civilians' but in 'Farewell to Memories' and *Death of a Hero*, letters are signifiers instead of the gulf of incomprehension between civilians and soldiers (Kelly 2017, 84).

Aldington often included poems in the letters he sent to H.D. from the front line. 'The Faun Captive', for example, was enclosed in a July 1918 letter signed off with the poets' pet names for one other: 'The Faun sends kisses to his dear Dryad' (Zilboorg 2003, 86).[32] Faun and Dryad, Aldington and H.D. are parodied as a latter-day Pericles and Aspasia in John Cournos' *roman à clef*, *Miranda Masters*. Cournos, who was himself a prose poet, would have been aware of Aldington's praise for Walter Savage Landor's *Pericles and Aspasia* (1836) as 'poetry in prose of unforgettable loveliness' (Aldington 1921, 22).[33] Landor's volume, made up of imaginary letters between Athenian statesman Pericles and Aspasia, the hetaira who was his consort, and between Aspasia and her female friend, Cleone, is a forerunner of Aldington's 'Letters to Unknown Women'.[34] These 'Letters', a series of prose pieces published in *The Dial* between March 1918 and May 1919, are a highfalutin form of fan mail, sent across the centuries to Sappho, Helen, Heliodora and other 'Unknown' women of antiquity. These are dead letters to recipients who lie 'in the cold fields of Persephone' but they are also reflections on the modern reception of the women to whom they are addressed (Aldington 1918b, 598). In his letter to Sappho, for example, Aldington tells her that despite her 'fame as the greatest woman-poet in the world' she remains an 'enigma', her legend 'overlaid by so many men': 'you have been drowned for the sake of a man's love in the Aegean and buried in an Aeolic grave by your girl lovers'. 'Legend upon legend has grown up, H.D. likewise attests in 'The Wise Sappho', 'adding curious documents to each precious fragment' (H.D. 1982, 68). Aldington's 'Letter' adds another curious document to the palimpsest; addressing the Sappho 'who mourned when Atthis left you for Andromeda', Aldington may be remembering his own 'To Atthis' when he tells Sappho that:

> All that we have of you are a few tattered, almost unreadable papyri and such fragments as were quoted by grammarians and critics still extant. But the fate that destroyed your work created your reputation. We are thrilled by those fragments as by no other poetry in the world.
>
> (Aldington 1918c, 430–81)

In his 'Letter' to Helen of Troy, Aldington disparages the moderns as 'a diseased generation' who live 'vicariously, through arts and literature' (Aldington 1918a, 525). His own 'Letters', indeed, engage in 'the same kind of life projection through classical writers that H.D. would accomplish with Sappho' (Rohrbach 185).

Aldington reminds Heliodora in his 'Letter' to her that she 'loved flowers' and was 'beloved by Meleager'. There is an irony, however, in his assurance that 'while Meleager is remembered, Heliodora will not be forgotten' in that it is the *Heliodora* poet, H.D. who is remembered while Meleager's translator, Aldington, is, if not forgotten, then more often remembered as H.D.'s faithless first husband than as her partner in translation (Aldington 1918b, 598). Passages in Aldington's 'Letter' to Heliodora anticipate his *Meleager of Gadara*, the last of the postwar PTS pamphlets and the belated outcome of the collaboration with H.D., begun before the war, which is the subject of her 'Heliodora'. As Zilboorg says of Aldington's *Meleager of Gadara* 'Meleager's life, encoded in his verse, in translation simultaneously encodes Aldington's own experiences': 'not only his love for H.D. but their shared aesthetics' (Zilboorg 1991, 84).

'A tiny book of poems of the present day': Lawrence

Early drafts of the verse translations he would revise in 1916 as 'All of Us' are transcribed in love letters Lawrence sent to his then fiancée, Louie Burrows, in 1910. Unpublished in its entirety in Lawrence's lifetime, 'All of Us' has recently been recuperated in the Cambridge Edition of *The Poems*; in the first volume the sequence is spliced between *Rhyming Poems* and *Unrhyming Poems*, unsettling the binary arrangement established by Lawrence himself in his 1928 *Collected Poems*. The significance – structural, aesthetic, historical – accorded to 'All of Us' in *The Poems* is comparable to that of *Drum-Taps*, the Civil War volume interpellated into the 1867 edition of Walt Whitman's *Leaves of Grass* and is justified by the editor, Christopher Pollnitz, on the grounds that given Lawrence's repeated and vain attempts from 1916 until 1919 to find a publisher for 'All of Us' its inclusion meets the criterion of authorial intent.[35] But Pollnitz's editorial intervention is also motivated by the aesthetic judgement that 'In the very distinctive style of verse it represents, "All of Us" is a valuable addition to the Lawrence canon' (*LP2* 700). 'All of Us', I want to suggest, is no less valuable an addition to the canons and counter-canons of First World War verse and to the poetics of global modernism.

Variants of 'All of Us' have been in circulation since 1919, when *Poetry* magazine printed versions of twelve of the poems as 'War Films' in its After-the-War number. 'War Films' is a selection, made by Harriet Monroe and her cohort of editors, from 'Bits', which is Lawrence's effort to reassemble the poems he had put together in the lost 'All of Us' typescript of 1916. 'Bits' is reproduced in its incomplete entirety in the 1964 *Complete Poems of D.H. Lawrence* and so it is curious that even in its attenuated form the sequence has been met with what Pollnitz describes as 'a critical silence that has been almost total' (*LP2* 700).[36] The exception that proves (and may also explain) the rule is Pollnitz's own 2001 article, coauthored with David Cram, 'D.H. Lawrence as Verse Translator', which clarifies the murky transmission history of what would become 'All of Us', a history that, it turns out, Lawrence himself helped to obscure. The germ of the sequence is found in English translations of German transliterations of Egyptian fellaheen folk songs that Lawrence sent in lieu of love poems to Louie Burrows in 1910. In his correspondence Lawrence attributes the German redactions of the Arabic originals to his German-born uncle, Fritz Krenkow, a part-time Orientalist (see *L1* 230).[37] In fact, as Pollnitz and Cram discovered, the fellaheen songs were translated into German not by Krenkow but by Heinrich Schäfer, an Egyptologist who transcribed the labourers' songs he heard in the course of excavations carried out on behalf of the Berlin Museum at Saqqāra, in the Upper Nile region, in 1900–01. Schäfer's collection of these fellaheen songs, *Die Lieder Eines Ägyptischen Bauern* (*Songs of an Egyptian Peasant*), was published in 1904, with Frances Hart Breasted's English edition appearing in the same year.[38] It may be that the death of Lawrence's mother, which took place just three days after he sent Louie the first of his verse translations, explains his desire to keep it in the family by accrediting the translations to his German uncle; that Lawrence should have suppressed the German connection altogether in his later, First World War, adaptations of the Egyptian songs is easier to understand.

Whatever his motives, in effacing Schäfer from the record Lawrence increases the slippage between source and target text that obtains in any act of translation – and which in the case of 'All of Us' is aggravated by the fact that Lawrence's renditions of the fellaheen songs are translations of translations, English versions of German versions of Arabic originals. Mediated through two European languages the songs of the fellaheen are also transposed, by Lawrence as by Schäfer before him, from an oral into a lexical medium and from the culture of the Orient to that of the Occident.[39] When Lawrence returned to the songs in 1916 they would be adapted yet again and still more radically transfigured; in 'All of Us', the voice of the Egyptian fellaheen is transmitted not as surrogate love poetry but in the voices of men and women in time of war. The proximity of love and death in the fellaheen songs which had reflected Lawrence's personal circumstances when he first translated them in 1910 is now recoded to speak to the collective as well as individual experience of loss brought about by the war. Poems that had been the product of a private correspondence become the property of 'all of us' and what had begun, in one sense of the term at least, as 'pure translation' – Louie Burrows found the eroticism of the songs 'shocking' – gives way in Lawrence's later versionings to oblique or free translation (*L1* 204, 210).

How should we parse 'the politics of translation' in 'All of Us'?[40] On one hand, Lawrence's initial expropriation of the fellaheen songs is a prime instance of Orientalism as defined by Edward Said in which the Orient, or Near Orient in the case of Egypt, offers 'a sort of surrogate or even underground self' for the European who dabbles in its culture (Said 3). To translate the fellaheen songs may not be to talk like an Egyptian but the Eastern promise of the lyrics Lawrence translated for Louie as proxies for the love poetry he could not then write is closely imbricated with their erotic charge. Read in this way, Lawrence's 1910 remediations of the songs belong in a longstanding tradition in which the Orient 'offended sexual propriety' and 'exuded dangerous sex' (Said 167). On the other hand, the very different uses to which Lawrence subsequently put the fellaheen songs may be counted as what Said deems 'exceptions, or if not exceptions then interesting complications, to [the] unequal partnership between East and West'; to the uneven power relationship which affects cultural, no less than political, interactions between Europe and its Middle Eastern Other (Said 153).

In the judgement of translation studies scholar Lawrence Venuti, 'Translating is always ideological because it releases a domestic remainder, an inscription of values, beliefs, and representations linked to historical moments in the receiving situation' (Venuti 2013, 28). Because 'the translator involves the source text in an asymmetrical act of communication' translation inevitably encodes those asymmetries of power identified by Said. Yet translation may also be utopian, Venuti suggests. Invoking Ernst Bloch's utopian theory of culture, according to which cultural forms release a 'surplus' that is supererogatory to their use value, Venuti proposes that 'the domestic remainder inscribed in the foreign text during the translation process' may be construed as a 'utopian surplus' (Venuti 2013, 28). Venuti's 'surplus' or 'remainder' comports with Walter Benjamin's understanding of translation as 'a supplement to the language in which it expresses itself'. In 'The Task of the Translator' Benjamin proposes that:

> Just as the manifestations of life are intimately connected with the phenomenon of life without being of importance to it, a translation issues from the original – not so much from its life as from its afterlife [...]. The life of the originals attains in [translations] to its ever-renewed latest and most abundant flowering.
>
> (Benjamin 79, 72)

The organic metaphor deployed in Benjamin's definition of translation as 'flowering' is applied by Lawrence to art per se in *Study of Thomas Hardy*:

> What then of this excess that accompanies reproduction? The excess is the thing itself at its maximum of being. If it had stopped short of this excess, it would not have been at all. If this excess were missing, darkness would cover the face of the earth. In this excess, the plant is transfigured into flower, it achieves at last itself. The aim, the culmination of all is the red of the poppy.
>
> (*STH* 11–12)

In her gloss of this passage Anne Fernihough explains that Lawrence is 'explicitly opposing art to the network of exchange: art is the "excess" or "waste" symbolized in the poppy's extravagant flowering, that which cannot be recuperated, but falls outside the sway of exchange-value' (Fernihough 1993, 30). The songs of the fellaheen are more troubling manifestations of 'excess' or 'utopian surplus' in that the art of the workers on the Saqqāra excavation is at once supernumerary to and a by-product of their physical toil; the songs are cultural surplus in an Orientalist economy driven by unskilled manual labour (Schäfer tells his reader that 'When the boys sang at the work of excavating, as they were usually inclined to do, they kept strict time, accenting the beats, which, just as in ancient times, were, besides, often marked by clapping the hands and stamping the feet' (xi–ii)). The fellaheen work songs nonetheless exemplify what Hannah Arendt defines as 'human "power", whose strength is not exhausted when it has produced the means of its own subsistence and survival but is capable of producing a "surplus", that is, more than is necessary for its own reproduction' (Arendt 88). In Arendt's analysis 'The force of life is fertility. The living organism is not exhausted when it has provided for its own reproduction and its "surplus" lies in its potential multiplication'. The 'specifically human mode of the life force [...] is as capable of creating a "surplus" as nature itself' (Arendt 108) – as Lawrence likewise suggests in the analogy in *Study of Thomas Hardy* between the 'excess' that is the artwork and 'the red of the poppy' (*STH* 11–12).

Study of Thomas Hardy was begun in September 1914, the month after the outbreak of the First World War and before the poppy became the symbol of the conflict into which many colonized people, including the fellaheen, would be drawn.[41] Some 32,000 fellaheen were (often forcibly) recruited into the Egyptian Labour Corps, divisions of which served in Salonika and Mesopotamia, and on the Western Front. Lawrence's 1916 retranslations of the Egyptian songs into topical anti-war poems therefore speak to the contemporaneous experience of the fellaheen as well as to that of the colonizing culture. In the context of the 1914–18, *Weltkrieg* the 'domestic remainder' identified by Venuti as a property of the translated text is also and inevitably a foreign remainder; as Pollnitz notes, 'All of Us' not only 'represents Lawrence's response to the First World War in surprising forms' but also 'shows that he had previously unrecognised knowledge of its far-flung campaigns' (*LP1* xxxiv). 'War Films', the title of the selection printed in *Poetry*, captures the poems' quasi-cinematic pan of the war's locations from the home front in London ('Zeppelin Nights'), to army training camps in Wiltshire ('Drill on Salisbury Plain in Summer Time'), to Flanders ('Near the Mark'), to the Dardanelles ('Antiphony') and to the East African front ('The Well of Kilossa').

In his revisionist history *The World's War: Forgotten Soldiers of Empire* David Olusoga notes that 'The unglamorous history of labour and of labour migration is an essential, if often unwritten, aspect of the First World War'. To procure labourers, 'those powers that could drew on the resources of their empires' (Olusoga 32). The 'All of Us' poem 'Foreign Sunset', with its descriptive subtitle '*Coloured labourers behind the fighting-line complain that they are done up*', gives voice to that silenced history, deploying the trench verse sunset trope to very different ends (*LP1* 148). A composite translation of Schäfer's Lieder nos. 34 and 36, 'Foreign Sunset' superimposes upon the fellaheen workers at the Saqqāra excavations coloured labourers behind the front line, who may themselves be fellaheen conscripted into the Egyptian Labour Corps or members of the British West India or French North African regiments, all of whom performed behind-the-line duties such as digging and reinforcing trenches and securing supply chains (a West Indian soldier is featured in the foreground of Wyndham

Lewis' 1918 painting, *A Canadian Gun Pit*).[42] Linguistic superimposition infers solidarity between the experience of the coloured labourers and that of another subaltern group: the colliers of Lawrence's own Nottingham mining country. Embedded in the poem's opening line, 'Oh master, let it be loose-all, it is enough' (*LP1* 148), is a dialect term from the East Midlands collieries, 'loose-all' meaning the end of a working shift. Mining was a reserved occupation during the war, so like the coloured labourers the coal-blackened miners were also working behind the line, if in domestic coalfields rather than in foreign fields.[43]

Grafting a white working-class idiom onto the tongue of coloured labourers, the poem courts the charge of ethnocentrism levelled at translations that replace or domesticate source language idioms with target-language equivalents. Equivalence is a contested concept for translation studies theorists and for critics of modernist primitivism like Marianna Torgovnick, who insists that homologies between 'primitive' peoples (like the fellaheen) and subaltern groups in the domestic culture (like miners and the working class) are inevitably false since 'systems of us/them thinking [...] structure all discourse about the civilized and the primitive'. That binary only collapses when the 'us' itself is shown to be 'fragmented along lines of gender, national origin, class, political sympathies, race' (Torgovnick 4).[44] The vernacular speech act in 'Foreign Sunset' not only articulates the way in which transnational surplus 'exceeds the ideologies of the dominant class' (Venuti 2013, 28) but also posits a wider, far from ethnocentric, equivalence between workers in a war which was 'the first in which peoples and nations from across the globe fought and laboured alongside one another, rarely in equality other than equality of suffering' (Olusoga 15).

Vernacular language as Matthew Hart defines it is a 'carrier of culture that links voice to labor and a whole way of life' (Hart 6). In 'Foreign Sunset' the vernacular is an intercultural carrier and as such bears closer comparison with the discourse Hart calls 'synthetic vernacular' than with Rudyard Kipling's Cockney khaki or Lawrence's own dialect ballads. A dialect of modernism deployed by, amongst others, J.M. Synge and Hugh MacDiarmid, synthetic vernacular 'signals a poet's attempt to sublate the tension between local languages' and what Said describes as the '"new inclusiveness" [...] marking modernism's late imperial engagement with the non-Occidental world' (Hart 9). The colour line and class lines are clearly drawn in 'Foreign Sunset' but if these lines fracture Torgovnick's 'civilized' consensus they also converge in the service of Said's new inclusiveness. The three-way comparison in Lawrence's translation between the coloured labourers, English miners and the fellaheen connotes a capacious understanding of 'us', set against the 'them' not of the native Other but of a military-industrial complex that subjugates white and coloured labour and colonial subjects alike.

The collusion of industry and empire is exposed again in 'All of Us' in 'Drill on Salisbury Plain in Summer Time', where wartime conscription is equated with the 'forced labour' (*corvée*) of the fellaheen and in 'Munitions Factory', a proletarian protest poem located at the war machine's hub (Schäfer 28).[45] The opening salvo of 'Munitions Factory' is a disenchanted repurposing of the first line of Schäfer's 'Lied. No. 29', from the 'At Work on the Excavations' section of his *Songs*, 'For Allah's sake, let us eat dinner, ye, who stand behind us!' (Schäfer 32):

> For God's sake, let us stop, Oh you who stand behind us,
>   Let us eat the last meal!
> Would you have us go on till we drop, Oh you who stand
>   behind us?
>
>   (*LP1* 147)

The not so casual blasphemy that differentiates the complaints of the English factory workers from those of the Arabs at work on the excavations anticipates Lawrence's assertion, in *Kangaroo*, that 'machine warfare is a blasphemy against life itself' (*K* 221). The spiritual drought brought on by the war is registered again in 'All of Us' in the bitter irony of prayer-poems such as 'Benediction' and 'Supplication' and in 'The Well of Kilossa', Lawrence's version of Schäfer's 'The Well Zemzem [*sic*]'. In Lawrence's translation, the holy water of the Zamzam well at Masjid al-Haram, taken by pilgrims making the hajj to Mecca, reverts to water as a basic necessity of life; the poem's subtitle is '(*A thirsty soldier in East Africa praises the well at which he drank*)' (*LP1* 140).[46] But if Lawrence's transposition of the Zamzam well to the godforsaken terrain of the East Africa Campaign secularizes or desacralizes the Islamic original the fellaheen songs themselves often combine the spiritual with the sexual, the sacred with the profane: in his annotation to 'The Well Zemzem', for instance, Schäfer tells us that well also 'means a girl' (Schäfer 12). In other translations psychological likeness transcends religious difference: the all-too-human lapse of piety in 'Allah's house', which is the subject of Schäfer's 'Inattentive Devotions' (Schäfer 22), is transposed in Lawrence's translation, 'Straying Thoughts', to the 'cathedral church' of St. Paul's, both poems' speakers violating W.H. Auden's dictum, that 'To pray is to pay attention' (*LP1* 141; Auden 694). The speakers of 'Munitions Factory' and Schäfer's work song represent very different constituencies but identify a common oppressor nonetheless in the 'you who stand[s] behind us', an overseer figure in whom the twin imperatives of industrialism and imperialism are embodied. The 'us', meanwhile, comprised of English factory hands and the Egyptian labourers, constitutes one of the 'communities fostered by translating' identified by Venuti (2013, 28). Transplanting the Egyptian songs into the wartime environment of 'All of Us', Lawrence carries out what Benjamin identifies as the key task of the translator: to preserve the 'vital connection' between the source text and its 'afterlife' in the target text (Benjamin 72).[47]

Connectivities between source and target cultures make 'All of Us' a complex instance of what postcolonial theorists of translation term 'overwriting', where the 'suppressed identity' of the colony is 'overwritten by the colonizer' (Munday 125, 131). Fernihough's point that the 'anti-imperialism implicit in Lawrence's critique of "white consciousness" is central to his aesthetics' indicates that overwriting works to dissident ends in Lawrence: 'All of Us' is a palimpsestic kind of overwriting, a writing over earlier writing the vestiges of which remain legible (Fernihough 1993, 13). Jahan Ramazani discusses modernist poems that incompletely assimilate the '"alien" cultural materials' on which they draw and thus 'reflect in their diction, syntax and sound the pressure of other languages' (Ramazani 2012, 296, 302). In 'All of Us' that pressure produces the effect that Venuti calls 'foreignisation', which in English-language translations, operates as 'a form of resistance against ethnocentrism and racism' (Venuti 1995, 20). In 'Fragile Jewels', for instance, the foreign cadences of Schäfer's 'Lied no. 14' survive the song's translocation from an Egyptian leave-taking to its equivalent in wartime England:

> Oh brother, put me in your pouch
> As you would a fresh, sweet locust-pod.
> For I am frail as a flask of glass,
> As a fine grey egg, or a slender rod.
>
> (*LP1* 141)

Schooled in Frazer and Frobenius, Lawrence was prone to syncretize 'primitive' peoples such as Celts, Etruscans and Native Americans. 'All of Us' is different, its substitutions and surrogations between subaltern and subnational population groups revealing global connectivities rather than effacing ethnic and experiential differences. Take 'Gipsy', for example, a poem that Lawrence translated from Schäfer and subsequently readapted, but which is omitted from the 'All of Us' typescript.[48] The 1910 translation is spoken in the local vernacular of an East Midlands labourer – 'Shalt see me come home with steaming hair, / Shalt know then the worth of that money there' (*L1* 196) – who is reincarnated as the 'Gipsy' we encounter in *New Poems* in 1918.[49] In its final *New Poems* version, the translation completes what Torgovnick would call its 'set of substitutions' between categories of the 'primitive' by looping back, by way of the etymological association between 'gipsy' and 'Egyptian', to the culture of the source text (Torgovnick 159). 'Star Sentinel (*A young woman muses on her betrothed, who is in Mesopotamia*)' and the 1919 'Bits' poem 'Mother's Son in Salonika' likewise effect a return to the original song's Middle Eastern provenance.[50] If 'All of Us' domesticates the foreign, it also foreignizes the domestic, interanimating English and Egyptian experience and expression.[51]

Olusoga holds the 'literary war' – in particular the canon of First World War poetry – responsible for erasing the 'multinational, multi-ethnic, multi-racial dimension' of the conflict (Olusoga 39). Lawrence, who refused to join up to that literary war, conceived of 'All of Us' as an alternative 'kind of cosmopolitan folk poetry' (*LP2* 698) in much the same way that Schäfer presented his 'Lieder' as 'songs really sung by the people' (Schäfer ix–x). 'Give it the people as the "war *literature*" they are looking for', Lawrence advised his agent, J.B. Pinker: 'they will find themselves in it' (*L3* 51, Lawrence's emphasis). Lawrence shared Ezra Pound's objections to 'war *literature*' of the kind featured in *Poetry* magazine's War Poems Prize Award number, discussed in Chapter Three, which had appeared somewhat prematurely in November 1914, only three months after the commencement of hostilities. If the *Poetry* special issue was in poor taste (it appeared during the First Battle of Ypres) so were the publications advertised in its back pages; *The Masses*, with its 'War on War' slogan, promised the reader 'Shrapnel Cartoons' and 'Rifle-fire stories by our staff of Literary Sharpshooters'.[52] As a non-combatant who was deemed unfit for active service, Lawrence would subsequently be excluded from what would form the canon of First World War verse, which privileged soldier-poetry over its civilian counterpart.[53] Canonical war poetry, for instance that of Wilfred Owen and Siegfried Sassoon, was valorized for its first-hand witness, a criterion that remains firmly in place in Paul Fussell's influential 1975 study, *The Great War and Modern Memory*. Fussell, himself a veteran of the Second World War, critiques the poet and artist David Jones, a survivor of the First World War, for refracting war through myth in his *In Parenthesis* (1937). Civilian poetry, meanwhile – such as Pound's *Cathay* (1915) and *Homage to Sextus Propertius* (1919) – is wholly excluded from Fussell's remit. *Cathay* and the *Homage*, moreover, are like 'All of Us' translations and as a mode of mediation, translation, like Jones' mythical method, violates the principle of immediacy observed even in the most dissident of canonical soldier-poems.

Pound scholarship has received *Cathay* as First World War verse since the publication of Hugh Kenner's *The Pound Era* in 1971, whereas Lawrence's war poems have been sidelined and deemed unquantifiable. For example, in a recent essay reframing the field to accommodate the writing of non-combatants Santanu Das, who makes only passing reference to Lawrence due to 'pressure of space', judges that his 'war' verse 'is unlike anything else in First World War poetry' (Das 2013b, 22). Yet as a 'tiny book of poems of the present day' (*L3* 51) 'All of Us' bears comparison with *Cathay*, published in its first edition with 'heavy tan wrappers' in a material allusion, perhaps, 'to the military apparel of World War I' (Pound 2011, 292). In *Cathay*, as Christine Froula notes, 'Pound attuned the Chinese poems' modalities of loss – leave-takings, homesickness, exile, loneliness, lament, desolation – to *Cathay*'s wartime moment. [...] vivid, singular, expressive, yet impersonal and choral, *Cathay*'s plaints resounded in London's wartime vortex' (Froula 212) – and 'in the trenches', where Pound's friend, the sculptor Henri Gaudier-Breszka, 'immediately identified his situation with that of the Bowmen of Shu' (Moody 271). Through comparable processes of translation and translocation, 'All of Us' exposes the global and multiethnic dimensions of the First World War that the 'literary war' served to obscure.

If the longstanding exclusion of texts like Lawrence's and Pound's from dominant definitions of war poetry has been premised, at least in part, on the fact that they *are* translations – since the surplus generated by translation is itself surplus to the sparer and starker requirements of war poetry – then *as* translations 'All of Us', like Pound's wartime work, meets Steven Yao's definition of the period of modernism as 'an age of translations' (Yao 5). As Rebecca Beasley insists, 'Central to any account of global modernity and its modernisms are analyses of the flow of cultural material across the globe – which is to say, analyses of translation' (Beasley 2012, 552). For Pollnitz and Cram, however, the modernism of 'All of Us' modifies its achievement and even explains Lawrence's 'prevarications' about his sources:

> Revising the Fellaheen songs during the rise of modernism, Lawrence might have had a premonition that the global literary protocol he was helping construct would be sufficiently powerful to absorb and reconfigure all that was local, folkloric and ingenuous. [...] While Lawrence's use of his folk source was more secretive than the thefts and borrowings of other modernists, his evasiveness might be attributable to his disquiet about the direction modernist practice was taking him, away from the Romantic myth of the poet as the sole source of sincerity and vision, and away from the poet as the champion of folk spontaneity and directness.
>
> (Cram and Pollnitz 149)

Lawrence found in folk song, both fellaheen and German, a mode of resistance to the deadly technologies of industry and the war and yet 'All of Us' is also a working model of the way in which the folk tradition evolves in response to modernity. The Egypt transmitted in the fellaheen songs is far from the Pharaonic, premodern Egypt evoked in *Women in Love* and *The Ladybird*. Indeed, the subsistence lifestyle of the fellaheen was in direct competition with the dynastic Egypt that Orientalists sought to conserve; the nitrogenous earth taken by peasant farmers from ancient sites to fertilize their fields contained fragments of the papyri sought by archaeologists, Schäfer among them.[54] It is in taking liberties with the originals that Lawrence remains faithful to the spirit of the fellaheen songs which, reconfigured and translocated as they are, remain collective and topical expressions of lived experience in which 'the people themselves speak' (Schäfer vii). Concerns of the kind expressed by Pollnitz and Cram should also be set against Ramazani's warning that 'Criticism that reduces high modernist and later cross-regional "appropriations" to orientalist theft or primitivist exoticism may risk circumscribing instead of opening up possibilities for global and transnational analysis' (Ramazani 2009, 11). The distinction between a globalizing aesthetic and the local and folkloric – if not that between light-fingered modernists and sincere Romantics – has been queried in recent studies of global modernism which 'recast modernism's internationalism on a transcontinental landscape of multiply located agencies' (Friedman 2015, 6). Despite 'geopolitical discrepancies', Ramazani suggests, poets nonetheless 'fashion a locally responsive poetics, paradoxically, by virtue of a bypass through the global' (Ramazani 2009, 10).

Translation – itself a bypass through the global – was crucial to the development of modernism and of Great War modernism. 'All of Us', like *Cathay*, also proves Yao's point that in the modernist era translation served as a vehicle for exploring the relationship between poetry and gender (Yao 5). *Cathay* juxtaposes the plaints of the River-Merchant's wife and the courtesan of 'The Jewel Stairs' Grievance' with those of the Bowmen of Shu while the majority of the speakers and personae in 'All of Us' are women. 'The Grey Nurse' is Lawrence's adaptation of Schäfer's 'Lied no. 7', 'The Prophet in the Rose-Garden'. This, one of the loveliest of the fellaheen songs, is derived from medieval Persian poet Sa'di's *Gulistān*:

> The grey nurse entered a rose-garden
> And the roses' shadows sheltered her.

> Her apron was brown with blood. She prayed;
> And roses listened to her prayer.
>
> (*LP1* 142)

Since *Gulistān* means rose garden it may be that the nurse in Lawrence's translation finds a temporary sanctuary from war in poetry itself, the roses, like 'the red of the poppy', representing the utopian surplus of the artwork. But Lawrence's translation also displays the dystopian residue of the war; the nurse's apron, brown with dried blood, is the stained wartime substitute for the Prophet's gold-embroidered prayer shawl of the original.

'The Grey Nurse' is the first part of a diptych completed by 'The Saint (*Litany of grey nurses*)'. The latter is Lawrence's version of 'To the Saint at Tanta' which follows 'The Prophet in the Rose-Garden' in Schäfer. In Lawrence's poem the Sufi saint – Es-Seyyid Ahmed el-Badawi, an intercessor between mankind and the Prophet – is gendered as the 'Sister' petitioned by the nurses, who are the descendants of those Sisters of Mercy who went with the original grey-uniformed nurse, Florence Nightingale, to the Crimean War:

> Sister, Oh holy sister,
> Thou door into Heaven, Sister!
> Thou of the tall, bright Tomb!
> Thou splendid door to the Angels!
> Thou silver portal to the Presence!
>
> (*LP1* 143)

In counterpoint to the nurses' litany a solo voice addresses the 'beloved' who – if he is the same soldier we have heard praying on the battlefield in 'Supplication', the poem immediately preceding the nurse verses in 'All of Us' – may already have been killed in action: 'If here I am left in life, beloved, I'll come / And kindle my lamp at the innermost flame, beloved, of thy tomb' (*LP1* 143). The tomb of the Tanta saint is reimagined here as a war grave.

Contrary to the received view that Lawrence did his 'real poetic work during the First World War' in *Look! We Have Come Through!* (1917), in which the Great War is displaced onto the battle of the sexes, 'All of Us' gives voice to the wartime experience of men and more often of women, whether nurses who staffed field hospitals behind the lines or the women who worked and waited on the home front (Palmer and Minogue 230). Of these, the widowed and unmarried – those 'left in life', as the speaker in 'The Saint' puts it – are 'surplus women', so called after the 1921 Census revealed the more than two million population gap between the genders in the postwar period.⁵⁵ The women of 'All of Us', the surplus product of the war who also embody the cultural surplus generated in the process of translation, populate the domestic and the foreign remainder of the text and connect 'All of Us' to the wider matrix of Lawrence's poetic war work. There is a crossover, for example, in the 'All of Us' poem 'Star Sentinel' of the sexualized bayonet imagery of Lawrence's war poem 'Eloi, Eloi, lama sabachthani?', discussed in the previous chapter. 'Star Sentinel' is spoken, its subtitle tells us, by '*A young woman [who] muses on her betrothed, who is in Mesopotamia*' and who asks 'Do I see your bayonet twinkle with answering love?' (*LP1* 139). The sword-phallus, a weapon of war in 'Eloi, Eloi, lama sabachthani?', is reimagined as the instrument of love in 'All of Us', a collection in which Lawrence's 'hope of the women' in wartime is articulated in the voices of women themselves (*L2* 425).

Lawrence may have pitched his translations of the fellaheen songs as 'tours de force' which 'might have a real popular success', but his private prediction that the establishment would find his 'doubtful little pills' hard to swallow would be borne out when Cyril Beaumont, who was the publisher of the first edition of Aldington's *Images of War*, rejected 'All of Us' and subsequently mislaid the typescript (*L3* 51, 234). Beaumont brought out Lawrence's *Bay* instead, a volume which moves 'from the old pre-war days, and from the old country pre-war sleep, gradually into war' (*L8* 29). In 1918, when he had completed *Bay*, which would appear belatedly in 1920, Lawrence planned to make 'other little books of poems' 'à propos of the war', the classical model for which was Euripides' *Trōades* or *The Trojan Women*, the story of four women of Troy – Hecuba, Cassandra, Andromache, Helen – who lament over the body of Hector in the final book of the *Iliad* (*L3* 238, 233). Pollnitz explains that the new sequence, which Lawrence thought of calling 'Chorus of Women' or 'Choir of Women', was to be 'made up of monologues or portraits of women who, as in *The Trojan Women*, had been devastated by war' (*LP2* 710). Lawrence's title indicates that his work-in-progress would have woven these monologues or word portraits into a contemporary equivalent of Euripides' chorus of Trojan women, preempting – like H.D.'s *Choruses from Iphigeneia in Aulis* – W.B. Yeats' preference for the vitality of the 'tragic chorus' over the 'passive suffering' of First World War soldier poetry (Yeats 199). 'Chorus of Women' also anticipates the rich modern reception of *The Trojan Women* in the twentieth-century theatre of war and anti-colonial resistance, albeit that this little book would, like 'All of Us', be a casualty of the conflict that incited it.⁵⁶ Now reassembled out of its 'Bits', 'All of Us' – the surplus product of the war machine and of the translation process – deserves new attention as we rethink the relationship between 'war *literature*' and global modernism.

Notes

1. For modernist translation and collaboration, see Davison. On the collaboration between S.S. Koteliansky and Lawrence as translators, see Hyde.
2. The fragment adapted by Aldington in 'To Atthis' is fragment 96 in the Loeb numbering (see D. Campbell 120–21).
3. On Monroe and Storey, see Williams' history of the first decade of *Poetry* (Williams 253). Pound himself would fall foul of another Chicago Professor of Classics, William Gardener Hale, who attacked Pound's mistranslations in the sections of his 'Homage to Sextus Propertius' which were printed in *Poetry* in 1919.
4. Ezra Pound's remarks are made in a letter to Harriet Monroe of November 1912 (Kenner 55). Aldington's 'To Atthis' was first printed in 1913 in *The New Freewoman*, the forerunner to *The Egoist*, and is reprinted in Pound's 1914 anthology, *Des Imagistes*. Pound's 'O Atthis' appears as 'Ἰμέρρω' in his 1916 volume *Lustra*, which also includes 'Papyrus', his poem based on a (vellum) scrap first published in the Berlin Manuscript in 1902.
5. Aldington's 'To Atthis' 'took Pound to Greek' (Kenner 55). Pound's 'Papyrus' is a version of the Gongula fragment printed in the issue of the *Classical Review* following that in which the Atthis fragments appear.
6. Eliot wrote two further pieces on H.D.'s choruses: 'Classics in English' (1916) and an unpublished review, in French, of her *Choruses from Iphigeneia in Aulis* (1916). See Eliot (2021a, 493–96, 497–503).
7. See Aldington's different account in his autobiography (Aldington 1968, 122). For rival accounts of the formation of Imagism, see Carr (2009, 1).
8. As Nisbet notes, '*anthologia* literally means flower-gathering' (xii).
9. See the chapter titled 'The Sacrifice of Iphigeneia' in Robinson's biography of H.D. In Robinson's overdetermined reading of H.D.'s adaptation of Euripides 'The situation is that Paris (Richard Aldington) has taken Helen from her first husband, Menelaus (Ezra Pound). […] Consequently the Greeks (including Lawrence personified as Achilles) are going to war to reclaim Helen (H.D., the poet) from Paris' (Robinson 101). H.D.'s translation, Robinson contends, shows her 'realization that Ezra Pound had "sacrificed" her for the spirit of poetry' (Robinson 104).
10. H.T. Wharton's 'Fragment Forty-One' is fragment 131 in the Loeb Classical Library numbering.
11. See Vandiver's discussion of the 'Varieties of Sacrificial Experience' in First World War poetry (Vandiver 2010, 196–201).
12. Gregory cites the assertion of the poet and translator Hipparchia, in H.D.'s *Palimpsest*, that it 'was desecration to translate' Sappho (H.D. 1968, 72).
13. See Selby Wynn Schwartz's novel *After Sappho*, in which Sappho is muse to women from Sarah Bernhardt to Virginia Woolf. Curiously, H.D. is not among these women.

14 Storer's translation was first printed in a standalone PTS pamphlet in 1915.
15 Victorian poets Katherine Harris Bradley and Edith Emma Cooper, the aunt and niece who published together under the pseudonym 'Michael Field', were co-'translators' of Sappho. See Prins.
16 Atthis in Sappho's poetry is a woman; Attis, a male fertility god, is identified with Adonis, the mortal lover of Persephone, who is a figure for Aldington in H.D.'s mythopoesis. In her 1991 article on the PTS, Zilboorg comments on 'the extensive attention recently given by feminist scholars to H.D.'s interest in Sappho, scholars who have generally minimized or misinterpreted or ignored Aldington's interest in Sappho and influence on H.D.' (Zilboorg 1991, 95 n.27).
17 Wharton's fragment 113 is fragment 130 in the Loeb Classical Library numbering.
18 Angela K. Smith notes that in 'Heliodora' H.D. and Aldington 'are configured as nameless, competitive but still collaborating poets' (A.K. Smith 15).
19 On compound words in Aldington and H.D., see Zilboorg (1991, 76). Holly A. Laird detects H.D.'s influence on the 'hyphenated word combinations' in Lawrence's 1923 volume, *Birds, Beasts and Flowers* (Laird 2020, 216).
20 See Höschele, 'Meleager and Heliodora: A Love Story in Bits and Pieces?'
21 DuPlessis is quoting from H.D.'s unpublished essay 'Notes on Ancient Lyric Poets'.
22 On Aldington and translation at the front, see Vandiver (2019, 15).
23 The H.D. figure in Cournos' *Miranda Masters* is described as 'a hetaira, a companion to poets' (Cournos 1926, 176).
24 The possible coauthorship to which Zilboorg refers is mooted by Dale Davis in 'The Matter of Myrrhine for Louis'.
25 A precedent and perhaps a blueprint for *Reverie*, Aldington's 'Little Book of Poems for H.D.', is her former fiancé Ezra Pound's handbound manuscript, 'Hilda's Book' (1905–7).
26 Aldington observed a strict separation between his original and his translated poetry whereas H.D. who, as Steven Yao says, regarded translation as 'constitutive' of her poetics includes her translations in her 1925 *Collected Poems* (Yao 85). 'Sorcery of Words' is included in Cyril Beaumont's first limited edition of *Images of War* (1919) but is omitted from the expanded George Allen and Unwin edition (1919) and from the Four Seas Company US edition (1921). On Aldington's exclusion of translations from his *Complete Poems* see Gates 139.
27 See Pater 113. In the second sonnet of *The Regrets*, du Bellay says that what he writes should be 'prose in rhyme or rhyme in prose' (du Bellay 12).
28 Compare Siegfried Sassoon's 'Repression of War Experience', a poem addressed to the civilian 'you' who is 'summering safe at home' (Sassoon 2022, 28–9).
29 Cangrande della Scala (1291–1329), the Veronese nobleman who appears in Boccaccio's *Decameron*, was Dante's patron and builder of the castle at Soave. Amy Lowell borrowed the title of her prose poem 'Can Grande's Castle' and that of the 1918 volume in which it appears from Aldington, taking lines from his 'At

the British Museum' as the epigraph to her book of '"polyphonic prose"' pieces which, she explains, 'owe their existence to the war', although 'They are scarcely war poems, in the strict sense of the word' (Lowell 1918, n. pag.).

30 In a 1918 letter to H.D., Aldington told her 'I am learning to write all over again'. His 'method', he explained, was to 'write on a sheet of paper a line of French prose upon which I "meditate" until out of the confusion of my senses & thoughts & emotions something definite frames itself' (Zilboorg 2003, 62).

31 Aldington, who credits Pater's essay with the recovery of du Bellay, 'this once forgotten French poet', notes that du Bellay's 'Jeux Rustiques' are written 'in imitation' of Italian poets Andrea Navagero and Marc-Antonio Flaminio who themselves 'wrote epigrams in imitation of those in the Greek anthology' (Aldington 1924, 33, 34).

32 In his previous letter Aldington had thanked H.D. for 'doing the typing of my "proses"', so she had acted as his amanuensis once again (Zilboorg 2003, 82). Zilboorg suggests that these 'proses' are probably 'Prayers and Fantasies I-VIII', a prose-poem sequence published in *Poetry* in November 1918.

33 Havelock Ellis, the 'Philosopher of Love' and a friend of H.D., edited a 1903 edition of *Pericles and Aspasia* (see Peterson 174–75). Aldington also praised Landor's *Hellenics* (1846), a collection of epigrams, idylls and dramatic passages. Landor is a forerunner of the Imagists in that his 'laconisms', as Aldington observes, 'are an attempt to achieve Greek brevity' (Aldington 1924, 145).

34 May Sinclair noted of his 'sources and affinities' that 'Richard Aldington owes and immense debt to Walter Savage Landor. There is no other writer of "prose poetry" with whom he can be more fitly compared' (Gates 6).

35 Lawrence's arrangement of his *Collected Poems* is preserved, with the addenda of *Pansies, Nettles, More Pansies, Last Poems* and *Uncollected Poems*, in Vivian de Sola Pinto and Warren Roberts' 1964 *Complete Poems*. Whitman's *Drum-Taps* was republished as a standalone volume by Chatto & Windus in 1915 'with an introduction reprinted from the *Times Literary Supplement* (1 April 1915) connecting the work with the current war'. That connection would be played out in the literary war, too, with poets Ivor Gurney and Isaac Rosenberg and the American nurse-poet Mary Borden turning to Whitman as 'a counter-example' to the sacrificial idealism embodied by Rupert Brooke (Palmer and Minogue 234–35). The guiding aim of *The Cambridge Edition of the Works of D.H. Lawrence* is 'to provide texts which are as close as can now be determined to those [Lawrence] would have wished to see printed' (*LP1* xi).

36 'All of Us' is mentioned only in passing in the two major studies of Lawrence's poetry (Laird, Gilbert) and in the standard work on Lawrence and translation (Hyde). The new Cambridge Edition of *The Poems* has prompted new work on 'All of Us' (see McLoughlin).

37 Fritz Johann Krenkow (1872–1953) was married to Lawrence's aunt Ada. Krenkow, a businessman in the East Midlands hosiery trade, would be appointed to a

professorship at the Aligarh Muslim University in India in 1929–30, subsequently taking up a post at the University of Bonn in 1931–5.

38 Lawrence's reference to 'the book' in a letter to Louie Burrows must mean Schäfer's book, indicating that Schäfer's *Die Lieder Eines Ägyptischen Bauern* is the German source of Lawrence's translations of the Arabic songs (*L1* 205).

39 The fellaheen songs were written down to the dictation of the excavation's watchman, Mahmûd Mohammed el-'Itr, and then 'rewritten at his dictation, so that all these printed texts give his pronunciation'. Mahmûd insisted 'that none of the songs was composed by himself' (Schäfer viii).

40 See Spivak, 'The Politics of Translation'.

41 Fussell remarks that two years before the war the focus of Georgian poetry 'was appearing to narrow down to the red flowers, especially roses and poppies, whose blood-colors would become an indispensable part of the symbolism of the war' (Fussell 243–44). Fussell's example of the full-blown flower symbolism of the war years is the opening stanza of Lawrence's poem 'Bombardment' from his 1920 volume, *Bay*: 'The Town has opened to the sun. / Like a flat red lily with a million petals / She unfolds, she comes undone' (*LP1* 125).

42 See Cork 209. The Egyptian Labour Corps (ELC) was founded in 1915 'to fill the crucial manpower for logistics and supply of the fighting men in all the fronts of the Great War'. By 1917, some 23,000 members of the ELC, most of whom were recruited from Upper Egypt, had been sent to the Western Front; others were dispatched to Gallipoli, Salonika and Suez. Coercive recruitment fostered anti-British sentiment and contributed to the 1919 uprising for Egyptian independence from British rule (Rogan 14–15).

43 Miners were also deployed to dig tunnels under No Man's Land. See Wood.

44 In his discussion of 'Translation and the Trials of the Foreign' Antoine Berman argues that 'to play with "equivalence" is to attack the discourse of the foreign work' (Berman 287).

45 *Corvée* or forced labour was abolished in 1889. In a 1915 letter to Cynthia Asquith, Lawrence recalls that in July 1914, after a walking tour in Westmorland, 'we came down to Barrow in Furness, and saw that war was declared […] Messrs. Vickers Maxim call in their workmen – and the great notices on Vickers' gateways' (*L2* 268). Vickers was an armaments manufacturer, principally of machine guns.

46 Kilossa is in Tanzania, then German East Africa, a region that in the 1910s was ravaged by drought and famine as well as by war. Kilossa was taken by the British in August 1916.

47 McLoughlin astutely notes that in 'Finding continuities between those exploited and oppressed by the first global armed conflict and the quotidian sorrows and sufferings of a colonized people, Lawrence constructs a supra-nationalism grounded in labour' (McLoughlin 61).

48 The association of the 'gipsy' with Egyptian ethnicity is implied again in Lawrence's 1923 novella *The Ladybird*. On Lawrence, gipsies and Egyptians, see Ruderman 124–48.
49 See de Sola Pinto and Roberts' edition of Lawrence's *Complete Poems* (974).
50 Both the 'All of Us' poem 'Star Sentinel' (1916) and the 'Bits' poem 'Mother's Son in Salonika' are revised versions of a lost *ur*-poem, Lawrence's original translation of Schäfer's 'Lied no. 68'.
51 Jed Esty places Lawrence in the English tradition of autoethnography, which in its nineteenth-century practice 'often featured a mutual allegorization between the "folk" at home (rural peasants or urban working class) and the "folk" abroad (tribal, primitive, or colonized working class)'. By the 1930s 'autoethnographic writing tended not so much to trade between these two "others" of metropolitan intellectuals as to *replace* the primitivist with the domesticated version of the folk' (Esty 239). Lawrence, who was dead in 1930 and who was no metropolitan intellectual, can hardly be held responsible for the trade-off Esty describes.
52 See *Poetry* 5.2 (1914), n. pag.
53 See Kendall's discussion of 'Civilian War Poetry'. In a composite review of 'Other Poets of the War' in *Poetry*'s After-the-War number, Harriet Monroe discriminates between 'the work of soldiers' and 'war verse written by outsiders' (Monroe 1919, 223). Both kinds of war poem are represented in the issue in which Lawrence's 'War Films' follows Richard Aldington's 'In France: 1916–1918'. Aldington uses a cinematic metaphor in *Death of a Hero*: in the 'hallucinated memories' of the soldier-protagonist, 'images and episodes met and collided like superimposed films' (*DH* 297).
54 The tussle over papyri between Oxford University Egyptologists Grenfell and Hunt and local fellaheen in 1896 is dramatized in Tony Harrison's 1988 play *The Trackers of Oxyrhynchus*; on Schäfer's turn-of-the-century search for papyri, see Verner 159. Lawrence dedicated 'All of Us' to Cynthia Asquith, the model for Daphne Apsley in *The Ladybird*. The daughter-in-law of Herbert Asquith, Prime Minister from 1908 to 1916, Cynthia, who undertook war work with the wounded, may be a model for 'The Daughter of the Great Man' in the 'All of Us' poem of that title: 'The daughter of the great man rolls her khaki wool, / And in her hands the sparkling needles fly' (*LP1* 145). In *The Ladybird*, Daphne sews shirts of 'fine white flannel', embroidered with the crest of his 'family insect', for Count Johann Dionys Psanek, the prisoner of war who is 'like an Egyptian king-god in the statues' (Lawrence 1992, 175, 217, 212).
55 On 'surplus women', see Nicholson 23. The postwar 'man shortage' is the subject of Aldington's 1931 novel *The Colonel's Daughter* (Aldington 1986, 42).

56 Staged in 415 BCE, at the height of the Peloponnesian War, *The Trojan Women* is a barely coded commentary on the atrocities – tantamount to genocide – committed in Athens' brutal subjugation of the island of Mêlos. Euripides' play would be staged every year between the two world wars and adapted to contemporary contexts in the postwar period. *Les Troyennes* (1965), Jean-Paul Sartre's last play, was prompted by Jacqueline Moatti's literal translation, staged during the Algerian War, of the classical original; Sartre's freer adaptation is a dissident commentary on other colonial wars in French Indochina and Vietnam (see Goff 801).

Coda

Squaring the circle

Like 'The Man Who Died', in his posthumously published novella of that title, D.H. Lawrence has come back. Blacklisted by Kate Millett in 1970 for the 'murderous' sexual politics of stories such as 'The Woman Who Rode Away', Lawrence has ridden out second-wave feminism to reemerge, unexpectedly enough in 2020s cancel culture, as the cover boy in a cluster of recent books written by women (Millett 292).[1] The jacket of Lara Feigel's *Look! We Have Come Through! Living with Lawrence* (2022) on which he is figured, in David Mann's design, in Warhol-esque multicoloured multiples serves as a visual signifier of Lawrence's recent repeat appearances as a literary icon. Feigel's *Look!* book, Frances Wilson's *Burning Man: The Ascent of D.H. Lawrence* (2021), Rachel Cusk's *Second Place* (2021), Alison MacLeod's *Tenderness* (2021) and Alison Moore's *Missing* (2018) and *The Retreat* (2021): these remarkable works of creative criticism, biography, fiction and biofiction are all – either directly or, in Moore's case and Cusk's, more obliquely – about Lawrence. Tapping the vein of life-writing opened by Lawrence in the years of the Great War all these works also dither generic distinctions. In this coda, I want to compare receptions of Lawrence in twenty-first-century women's writing with Lawrence's long afterlife in H.D.'s fiction and poetry.

Lara Feigel's 'bibliomemoir', described in its blurb as 'interweaving literary criticism, biography and memoir' in its 'exhumation of an author', is written in the form of a journal of the plague year of 2020 in which Lawrence – who came through his own lived experience of lockdown during the First World War – is a COVID buddy who shares her support bubble (Feigel n. pag.). Although she admires Millett, Feigel tells us that she also 'admired Lawrence's writing of women': his 'repetitions and circlings were the rhythms of female thought' (Feigel 3). Reading Lawrence, Feigel experienced 'the moment of conversion that so many readers – among them so many women – have had', not least Doris Lessing: 'What do we care about his pronouncements on the sex war?', Lessing demanded to know. Feigel's answer is that now, half a century after Millett's *Sexual Politics* knocked Lawrence off the pedestal F.R. Leavis had put him on in the mid-twentieth century, we 'are freed … to read him on our own terms' (Feigel 3, 8, 10).

Our terms, however – or the terms of Feigel's bibliomemoir, in which her reading of Lawrence is intimately informed by her own lived experience – are also Lawrence's terms, since he was 'someone who lived his life though his fiction and his fiction through his life – with the art shaping the life at least as much as the life shaped the art' (Feigel 76). 'I am unable to distinguish between Lawrence's art and Lawrence's life'. Frances Wilson admits in *Burning Man*, her partial biography beginning in 1915, the year in which, with the suppression of *The Rainbow*, Lawrence began his descent into the inferno of the First World War. Wilson describes her book as a work of 'non-fiction which is also a work of imagination' and, inverting the roles of literary biographer and her subject, the centrepiece of her work of imagination is an extended discussion of Lawrence's own and only exercise in biographical writing, his *Memoir of Maurice Magnus*, published in 1924 (Wilson 2021a, 3).

Rachel Cusk's *Second Place* is a work of imagination which 'owes a debt' to Mabel Dodge Luhan's 1933 memoir of Lawrence, both books reframing Lawrence's lethal portrait of Luhan as the woman who rode away (Cusk 2021, n. pag.). Lawrence had travelled to Luhan's little arts colony in Taos, New Mexico, in 1922, to collaborate with her on 'an American novel': 'he wanted to write it around me', Luhan explains in *Lorenzo in Taos*, 'my life' (Luhan 59). The project stalled, but as Luhan's biographer suggests, 'Mabel's quest for spiritual and emotional redemption became the central theme' of Lawrence's American stories such as 'The Woman Who Rode Away', in which Luhan's attraction to the Native American culture of New Mexico is imagined as a fatal attraction (Rudnick 199). The 'L' figure in Cusk's novel is a painter, not a writer – a common enough transposition in author-fictions and in fictional representations of Lawrence – but Cusk's pen portrait amounts to much more than another Lawrence biofiction. Her novel rescues Luhan from Lawrence's murderous take on her life story and succeeds where Lawrence himself had failed in successfully translating Mabel's 'life' into the medium of the novel. But as a novel that owes a debt to Luhan's memoir, *Second Place* is a Lawrence-like hybrid of fiction and biography which comports with Cusk's Lawrence-like comment that 'For me, writing and living are the same thing' (Cusk 2014a).

Alison MacLeod's *Tenderness* is 'a "dialogue" across time' with *Lady Chatterley's Lover*. Taking her title from Lawrence's working title for his book MacLeod takes the story beyond the timeframe of the original to the new life led by Lady Chatterley and her lover in the New World. In another transatlantic move MacLeod weaves another narrative thread into her story in which Jackie Kennedy – a 'Lady' in waiting, who will become First Lady in 1961 – attends the 1959 court case in which Grove Press successfully contested the decision of the Postmaster General of New York to suppress a trade edition of *Lady Chatterley's Lover*. MacLeod's novel is 'a work of fiction' which also incorporates 'factual' and found materials, both real and fabricated, like letters and legal documents, including lengthy extracts from the transcript of the Chatterley Trial at the Old Bailey in 1960, when Penguin Books won its case against the Crown to publish the first unexpurgated English edition of *Lady Chatterley's Lover* (MacLeod 595).[2]

Alison Moore's novel *The Retreat*, a psychological portrait of a woman who loved islands, is a feminized take on 'The Man Who Loved Islands', Lawrence's fictionalized case study of his sometime friend, the novelist and islomaniac Compton Mackenzie. The protagonist of Moore's *Missing*, meanwhile, is a literary translator who is given the Lawrentian first and last names of 'Jessie' and 'Noon' (after Lawrence's first lover, Jessie Chambers, who is the model for Miriam Leivers in *Sons and Lovers*, and the autobiographical protagonist of Lawrence's unpublished novel *Mr. Noon*). Moore's Jessie Noon, it seems, lives the dream of the woman in Cusk's *Outline* who says that 'I would like to be a D.H. Lawrence character, living in one of his novels' and for whom *Sons and Lovers* is 'the book that has inspired me more than anything else in my life' (Cusk 2014b, 209–10). Moore's Jessie Noon, whose name couples Lawrence's life with his fiction, is an obsessive reader of biographies of Lawrence in which his life story, up to and including the inevitable deathbed scene in which 'Lawrence had to die all over again', is replayed on repeat (Moore 2018, 14).[3]

In the wake of his real-time death in 1930, Lawrence had been brought back to life (only to die all over again) in a clutch of biographies, memoirs and biofictions; genres which, almost a century on, are reanimated and recombine in the new crop of Lawrence-related titles.[4] More broadly, Lawrence's latest ascent is in step with the recent rise of autofiction, the chosen medium for a (post) feminist identity politics in, for example, Sheila Heti's *How Should a Person Be? A Novel from Life*; first published in 2010 and longlisted for the Women's Prize for Fiction in 2013, Heti's book reproduces and transcribes 'real world' emails and conversations.[5]

The synergy between the recent wave of women's autofiction and the new vogue for Lawrence is a seeming conundrum, one that Jessica Ferri seeks to resolve in her double review, printed in the *Los Angeles Times* in 2021, of Wilson's *Burning Man* and Cusk's *Second Place*. Ferri contends that 'today, when "autofiction" is the rage' women writers such as Wilson and Cusk 'turn the toxic male author [Lawrence] into rich material' but her argument falters in the face of what Wilson and Cusk have to say about Lawrence (Ferri). Where Ferri calls Lawrence out for his toxic masculinity, for Cusk, who has said in an interview that 'I would love to have had him as my friend', it is more a case of Lawrence-and-me than of Lawrence#MeToo (Cusk 2014a). For her part, Wilson claims that the hybrid formula of autofiction, far from being a form of *écriture feminine*, was concocted in the first instance by Lawrence himself. In the introductory 'Argument' to her *Burning Man* biography – a paratextual nod to the 'Argument' prefacing Lawrence's *Look! We Have Come Through!*, the 1917 autobiographical poem-cycle from which Feigel's book takes its title – Wilson acknowledges that 'I am unable to distinguish between Lawrence's life and his work'. In consequence, she explains, 'I read his novels, stories, letters, essays, poems and plays as exercises in autofiction, which genre he pioneered to get around the restrictions of genre' – with Lawrence's memoir of Maurice Magnus proving the biographical exception to Wilson's autofictional rule (Wilson 2021a, 3).

In promoting him as a pioneer-practitioner of autofiction, Wilson makes Lawrence newly relevant to twenty-first-century readers who may view in the more forgiving light of selfie aesthetics what a hostile contemporary such as Cecil Gray saw as Lawrence's 'ludicrously Narcissist self-portraits' (Gray 1985, 137). But in representing her burning man as a solitary volcano – prone as Lawrence was to violent eruptions – Wilson may also be rekindling an older myth of 'solitary genius'.[6] The rude health of life-writing today means that the 'death of the author' is old or even fake news, perhaps, but the current cult of writerly personality lends a new timeliness, too, to Jerome McGann's warning that a 'hypnotic fascination with the isolated author has served to foster an overdetermined concept of authorship, but (reciprocally) an underdetermined concept of literary work' (McGann 1983, 122).

My intention is not to put Lawrence *redivivus* back in his box nor is to restore him to his pre-poststructuralist eminence as Author-god. My interest, rather, is in the relationship of life to 'literary work' in Great War modernism. As Martin Amis reminds us, 'writing fiction about real men and women is an extraordinary thing to go and do'. 'D.H.L. started it', according to Amis, who nominates Lawrence as the 'first serious life-writer', remarks made in *Inside Story*, Amis' autobiography that is advertised, in its subtitle, as 'A Novel' (Amis 83). If writing about real people is an extraordinary thing to do, it is all the more extraordinary that Lawrence started to experiment with life-writing in the years of the Great War; in the context of that deadly conflict, life-writing was indeed a 'serious' business, not – despite Lawrence's silly theories of the solar plexus – an exercise in literary navel-gazing. An autobiographical mode, life-writing is social *and* subjective, the story of the self and of the lives of others.

Of his contemporaries, H.D. is the closest precursor of the women who are writing about Lawrence today. Her autobiofictional novel *Bid Me to Live*, published in 1960, exhumes the Lawrence who has been dead for thirty years in a coming to terms with him in which H.D. also confronts, head on, the troubling 'sex fixations' which had made Lawrence her antagonist in the modernist battle between the genders (*BML* 35).[7] H.D. has emerged as the winner of that contest, hands down: since Susan Stanford Friedman asked 'Who Buried H.D.?' in her groundbreaking article of that title in 1975 the rise of H.D.'s reputation has been in inverse ratio to what until very recently has been the slide in Lawrence's standing (see Friedman 1975). When *Bid Me to Live* came out, however, H.D. still took second place to Lawrence: the release of her novel by Grove Press, which had brought out the first unexpurgated edition of *Lady Chatterley's Lover* the year before, was timed to ride the wave of media attention generated by the *Regina vs. Penguin Books* trial in 1960.

Marketed on the strength of H.D.'s one-time friendship with him, *Bid Me to Live* is testament to the remarkable longevity of her intertextual relationship with Lawrence. 'I have carefully avoided coming to terms with Lawrence, the Lawrence of *Women in Love* and *Lady Chatterley*', H.D. acknowledged in the notebooks she kept during her analysis with Freud in 1933 (H.D. 1970, 134). In her belated coming to terms with him in *Bid Me to Live* H.D. interleaves Lawrence's writing – his fiction, his poetry and, most significantly, his letters, the medium in which Lawrence most vividly came back to life for his contemporaries – into her autofictional palimpsest. Writing to Aldington in 1949, when she had completed the manuscript, H.D. told him:

> I am happy about Lawrence, now I finished my *Madrigal*. […] I felt that I did not have to worry any more to 'place' old Lorenzo, having 'placed' him in time and space and eternity, at last, to my own satisfaction.
>
> (Zilboorg 2003, 306)

Bid Me to Live – for which *Madrigal* was H.D.'s preferred title – 'was roughed out, summer 1939': 'I had been writing or trying to write this story since 1921',

H.D. tells us. Her 'War I' novel – 'a novel in historical time' which is also a 'mythical story' – was completed during 'War II' (H.D. 1986, 180).⁸ H.D. returns to War I again in *The Walls Do Not Fall*, the first volume of her War II sequence, *Trilogy*:

> An incident here and there,
> and rails gone (for guns)
> from your (and my) old town square
>
> (*CPHD* 509)

The 'high, heavy railings' of the old square garden have been recycled for the war effort (*AR* 69) and in the same way H.D. presents herself in *Trilogy* as an Isis figure who will 'collect the fragments' and 'melt down', 're-invoke, recreate' the war-torn past in the war-torn present (*CPHD* 547–8). 'That war, this war. They were exactly superimposed upon one another', H.D. explains in *Magic Mirror* (H.D. 2012, 55).

In *Bid Me to Live* H.D. is 'square haunting' again, circling back in time to Mecklenburgh Square in the First World War in a reckoning and rapprochement with Lawrence begun in her interwar writing. In 'The Poet' (1935), for example, H.D. pays what Louis L. Martz calls 'a calm and measured tribute to the memory of D.H. Lawrence.' 'I think of your song', H.D. writes and she remarks that 'it is an odd thing that we meet here': in 'the dead past' and in the rendezvous with the dead that is one poet's elegy for another (*CPHD* xxviii, 462–63). The Poet's 'shrine' is a 'small coptic temple' (*CPHD* 464), a version of the temple of Isis in H.D.'s *Pilate's Wife*, a prose fiction with close intertextual connections to Lawrence's *The Man Who Died* (1931), a novella or Biblical autobiofiction which the American poet-critic Robert Duncan, in *The H.D. Book*, locates on 'the borderline between [Lawrence's] story-telling and his being' (Duncan 73). *Pilate's Wife* was begun in the 1920s, completed in 1934 and, like *The Man Who Died*, published posthumously (in 2000).⁹ In *Tribute to Freud*, H.D. tells us that when her then lover, Stephen Guest, brought her a copy of *The Man Who Died*, he said to her '"Did you know that you are the priestess of Isis in this book?"' H.D.'s initial reaction was

> a slight feeling of annoyance. I had told friends of a book that I wanted to write, actually did write. I called it *Pilate's Wife*. It is the story of the wounded but living Christ, waking up in the rock-tomb. I was certain that my friends had told Lawrence that I was at work on this theme. My first sudden reaction was, 'Now he has taken my story'.
>
> (H.D. 1970, 141–42)

'It was not my story', H.D. acknowledges on reflection: 'There is the old myth or tradition that Christ did not die on the Cross' (H.D. 1970, 142). If H.D. is indeed the original for Lawrence's priestess of Isis in *The Man Who Died*, the Jesus of her story – 'a sort of poet' and an 'Etruscan sun-god' – is modelled on Lawrence, the man who died and who would be serially resurrected in H.D.'s poetry and prose fiction (H.D. 2000, 49, 100).

Following her analysis with Freud, H.D. would overtly fashion herself as an Isis-figure, her mission to gather the limbs of an Osiris who, Helen Sword suggests, she identified with Lawrence:

> In *Tribute to Freud* [H.D.] chronicles how, during and after her 1933–34 psychoanalytic sessions with Sigmund Freud, she came to recognize Lawrence not only as Orpheus to her Eurydice, leader to her follower, but also as Osiris to her Isis: the twin-brother, mirror-image initial sharer who inspires her artistically but whose shattered image she in turn must gather up, reconstruct, re-member.
> (Sword 420)[10]

In H.D.'s words, 'Lawrence came back with *The Man Who Died*. Whether or not he meant me as the priestess of Isis in that book does not alter the fact that his last book reconciled me to him. Isis is incomplete without Osiris' (H.D. 1970, 149–50). H.D.'s vision in *Pilate's Wife* 'is a collaborative one', Joan A. Burke points out, positing 'an ideal of gender harmony, a realigned, sacred partnership through which H.D. speaks to several precursors and contemporaries, D.H. Lawrence among them' (H.D. 2000, xiv).[11]

H.D.'s necrotextual relationship with the dead Lawrence continues in *Trilogy*, her War II poem-sequence. The last volume, *The Flowering of the Rod* (1946), takes up and transfigures the phallic imagery of Exodus 7 on which Lawrence had drawn in his (post) War I novel, *Aaron's Rod*:

> *This is the flowering of the rod,*
> *this is the flowering of the burnt-out wood,*
>
> *where we, Zadkiel, we pause to give*
> *thanks that we rise again from death and live.*
>
> (*CPHD* 574)

Here, Martz observes, 'the rod of Aaron and the cross of Christ are merged' in the mythopoeic syncretism which led H.D., like Lawrence, to 'correlate faith with faith' (*CPHD* xxxiii, 541). H.D. fashions herself in *Trilogy* as 'Our Lady of the Pomegranate', a Madonna-Magdalene-Persephone who will also 'recover the secret of Isis'. The Lady carries with her the 'Book of Life'; not the novel, which Lawrence had described as 'the book of life', but H.D.'s *Trilogy* itself, offered as an act of poetic intercession in time of war (*CPHD* 541, 569; *STH* 195).[12]

'Whatever afterlife he envisaged', Lara Feigel says of Lawrence, 'he has had an afterlife here with us, in the troubled century' after his death (Feigel 228). Feigel herself in *Look! We Have Come Through! Living with D.H. Lawrence* and Frances Wilson in *Burning Man* have taken over H.D.'s self-appointed role as keeper of Lawrence's creative-destructive flame. The resurrection of The Man Who Died in twenty-first-century biography and autobiofiction brings my own book full circle, back to Lawrence, H.D. and Aldington: Great War modernists who in their writing crossed the line between literature and lived experience.

Notes

1 See Frances Wilson's article in *The Telegraph* titled 'D.H. Lawrence predicted cancel culture – and then became its first victim' (2021).
2 In his review of MacLeod's *Tenderness* Sean Matthews points out that 'This is a work of biofiction which has footnotes and further reading' (Matthews 242).
3 See Walker, 'Shelfie: Alison Moore's "Missing"'.
4 Biographies published in the immediate aftermath of Lawrence's death include John Middleton Murry, *Son of Woman: The Story of D.H. Lawrence* (1931); Catherine Carswell, *The Savage Pilgrimage: A Narrative of D.H. Lawrence* (1932); Dorothy Brett, *Lawrence and Brett: A Friendship* (1933); Mabel Dodge Luhan, *Lorenzo in Taos: The Story of D.H. Lawrence in New Mexico* (1933); and Frieda Lawrence, *Not I, But the Wind …* (1935). On Lawrence's 'lives', see Eggert. Lawrence biofictions of the 1930s include Osbert Sitwell, *Miracle on Sinai* (1933); Keith Winter, *Impassioned Pygmies* (1936); and H.G. Wells, *Brynhilde* (1937). For a discussion of these texts, see Jenkins, 'Lawrence in Biofiction'.
5 The award of the 2022 Nobel Prize in Literature to French writer Annie Ernaux attests to the continuing rise in female-authored autofiction. Although she refuses the autofictional label, Ernaux unsettles the boundary between life and art in, for instance, *The Years* (2018), defined by its author as 'impersonal autobiography' (see Baisnée).
6 See Jack Stillinger, *Multiple Authorship and the Myth of Solitary Genius*.
7 For the battle of the genders, see the second volume, *Sexchanges*, of Gilbert and Gubar's *No Man's Land*, 258–323.
8 H.D. wanted to publish *Bid Me to Live* (as *Madrigal*) under the pen name of Delia Alton: 'I sign *Madrigal*, Delia Alton' (H.D. 1986, 190). 'Alton' is a contraction of

Aldington; 'Delia', an epithet for Artemis, may also allude to the 'Delia' in Ezra Pound's 1916 poem 'Impressions of François-Marie Arouet (de Voltaire)'.

9. Lawrence's *The Man Who Died* was published as *The Escaped Cock* in 1929 by Harry and Caresse Crosby's Black Sun Press; the novella was published as *The Man Who Died* in 1931, in Secker's and Knopf's editions. Despite H.D.'s claim that Lawrence had taken the story from her both Lawrence in *The Man Who Died* and H.D. in *Pilate's Wife* draw on George Moore's tale of a Christ who did not die on the Cross in *The Brook Kerith* (1916).

10. See Pound's 'I Gather the Limbs of Osiris', a work about literary history published in *The New Age* in 1911–12 which is proto-Imagist in its attention to the 'Luminous Detail' (Pound 1973, 21).

11. Diana Collecott likewise suggests that 'Lawrence's late story on the resurrection of Christ serves as shorthand for [H.D.'s] own suppression and recall of the dead Lawrence' (Collecott 1999, 92).

12. As Friedman notes H.D. came to see herself as 'a kind of Vestal Virgin, keeping the flame of divinity alive for mankind' (Friedman 1981, 225).

Bibliography

D.H. Lawrence: Works

Lawrence, D.H. (1917), 'Resurrection'. *Poetry* 10.3, 139–41.
Lawrence, D.H. (1981), *Letters of D.H. Lawrence. Vol. 2, June 1913–October 1916*, ed. George J. Zytaruk and James T. Boulton. Cambridge: Cambridge University Press.
Lawrence, D.H. (1985), *Study of Thomas Hardy and Other Essays*, ed. Bruce Steele. Cambridge: Cambridge University Press.
Lawrence, D.H. (1987), *Women in Love*, ed. David Farmer, John Worthen and Lindeth Vasey. Cambridge: Cambridge University Press.
Lawrence, D.H. (1988), *Aaron's Rod*, ed. Mara Kalnins. Cambridge: Cambridge University Press.
Lawrence, D.H. (1989), *The Rainbow*, ed. Mark Kinkead-Weekes. Cambridge: Cambridge University Press.
Lawrence, D.H. (1991), *Complete Poems*, ed. Vivian de Sola Pinto and F. Warren Roberts (1964). Harmondsworth: Penguin.
Lawrence, D.H. (1992), *The Fox, the Captain's Doll, the Ladybird*, ed. Dieter Mehl. Cambridge: Cambridge University Press.
Lawrence, D.H. (1994), *Kangaroo*, ed. Bruce Steele. Cambridge: Cambridge University Press.
Lawrence, D.H. (1995), *The Woman Who Rode Away and Other Stories*, ed. Dieter Mehl and Christa Jansohn. Cambridge: Cambridge University Press.
Lawrence, D.H. (1998), *The First 'Women in Love'*, ed. John Worthen and Lindeth Vasey. Cambridge: Cambridge University Press.
Lawrence, D.H. (2003), *Studies in Classic American Literature*, ed. Ezra Greenspan, Lindeth Vasey and John Worthen. Cambridge: Cambridge University Press.
Lawrence, D.H. (2004), *Late Essays and Articles*, ed. James T. Boulton. Cambridge: Cambridge University Press.
Lawrence, D.H. (2005), *Introductions and Reviews*, ed. N.H. Reeve and John Worthen. Cambridge: Cambridge University Press.
Lawrence, D.H. (2013a), *The Poems. Vol. 1: Poems*, ed. Christopher Pollnitz. Cambridge: Cambridge University Press.
Lawrence, D.H. (2013b), *The Poems. Vol. 2: Notes and Apparatus*, ed. Christopher Pollnitz. Cambridge: Cambridge University Press.
Lawrence, D.H. (2018), *The Poems. Vol. 3: Uncollected Poems and Early Versions*, ed. Christopher Pollnitz. Cambridge: Cambridge University Press.

D.H. Lawrence: Letters

Lawrence, D.H. (1979), *Letters of D.H. Lawrence. Vol. 1: September 1901–May 1913*, ed. James T. Boulton. Cambridge: Cambridge University Press.
Lawrence, D.H. (1981), *Letters of D.H. Lawrence. Vol. 2: June 1913–October 1916*, ed. George J. Zytaruk and James T. Boulton. Cambridge: Cambridge University Press.
Lawrence, D.H. (1984), *Letters of D.H. Lawrence. Vol. 3: October 1916–June 1921*, ed. James T. Boulton and Andrew Robertson. Cambridge: Cambridge University Press.
Lawrence, D.H. (1987), *Letters of D.H. Lawrence. Vol. 4: June 1921–March 1924*, ed. Warren Roberts, James T. Boulton and Elizabeth Mansfield. Cambridge: Cambridge University Press.
Lawrence, D.H. (1989), *Letters of D.H. Lawrence. Vol. 5: March 1924–March 1927*, ed. James T. Boulton and Lindeth Vasey. Cambridge: Cambridge University Press.
Lawrence, D.H. (1991), *Letters of D.H. Lawrence. Vol. 6: March 1927–November 1928*, ed. James T. Boulton and Margaret Boulton, with Gerald M Lacy. Cambridge: Cambridge University Press.
Lawrence, D.H. (2000), *Letters of D.H. Lawrence. Vol. 8: Previously Uncollected Letters and General Index*, ed. James T. Boulton. Cambridge: Cambridge University Press.

H.D.: Works

H.D. (1968), *Palimpsest* (1926). Carbondale and Edwardsville: Southern Illinois University Press.
H.D. (1970), *Tribute to Freud*. Manchester: Carcanet.
H.D. (1979), *End to Torment*. New York: New Directions.
H.D. (1982), '*Notes on Thought and Vision*' *and* '*The Wise Sappho*'. San Francisco: City Lights.
H.D. (1983), *Collected Poems 1912–1944*, ed. Louis L. Martz. New York: New Directions.
H.D. (1986), 'H.D. by Delia Alton'. *Iowa Review* 16.3, 180–221.
H.D. (1992), *Asphodel*, ed. Robert Spoo. Durham: Duke University Press.
H.D. (2000), *Pilate's Wife*, ed. Joan A. Burke. New York: New Directions.
H.D. (2003), 'Notes on Euripides' (extracts), in H.D., *Hippolytus Temporizes & Ion: Adaptations of Two Plays by Euripides*. New York: New Directions, 277–8.
H.D. (2011), *Bid Me to Live*, ed. Caroline Zilboorg (1960). Gainesville: University Press of Florida.
H.D. (2012), *Magic Mirror, Compassionate Friendship, Thorn Thicket: A Tribute to Erich Heydt*. Victoria: ELS Editions.

Richard Aldington: Works

Aldington, Richard (1914a), 'War Yawp'. *Poetry*, 5.2, 78–81.
Aldington, Richard (1914b), 'Penultimate Poetry: Xenophilometropolitana'. *The Egoist* 1.2, 36.
Aldington, Richard (1915), 'The Poets' Translation Series'. *The Egoist* 2.10, 163.
Aldington, Richard (1916), 'People', in *Some Imagist Poets*, ed. Amy Lowell, et al. Boston: Houghton Mifflin, 11.
Aldington, Richard (1918a), 'Letters to Unknown Women'. 'To Helen'. *The Dial*, LXIV (June), 525.
Aldington, Richard (1918b), 'Letters to Unknown Women'. 'To Heliodora'. *The Dial*, LXV (December), 598.
Aldington, Richard (1918c), 'Letters to Unknown Women'. 'To Sappho'. *The Dial*, LXIV (May), 430–1.
Aldington, Richard (1919a), *Images*. London: The Egoist Press.
Aldington, Richard (1919b), *War and Love*. Boston: The Four Seas Press.
Aldington, Richard (1921), 'A Note on Poetry in Prose'. *The Chapbook: A Monthly Miscellany* 22 (April), 16–24.
Aldington, Richard (1924), *Literary Studies and Reviews*. London: George Allen and Unwin.
Aldington, Richard (1926), *The Love of Myrrhine and Konallis and Other Prose Poems*. Chicago: Pascal Covici.
Aldington, Richard, trans. (1930), *Medallions from Anyte of Tegea, Meleager of Gadara, the Anacreontea, Latin Poets of the Renaissance*. London: Chatto and Windus.
Aldington, Richard (1934), *Roads to Glory* (1930). London: Heinemann.
Aldington, Richard (1935), *Artifex: Sketches and Ideas*. London: Heinemann.
Aldington, Richard (1948), *The Complete Poems of Richard Aldington*. London: Allan Wingate.
Aldington, Richard (1949), *Soft Answers*. Harmondsworth: Penguin.
Aldington, Richard (1950a), *D.H. Lawrence: An Appreciation*. Harmondsworth: Penguin.
Aldington, Richard (1950b), *Portrait of a Genius, but ...: The Life of D.H. Lawrence, 1885–1930*. London: Heinemann.
Aldington, Richard (1954), *Pinorman: Personal Recollections of Norman Douglas, Pino Orioli and Charles Prentice*. London: Heinemann.
Aldington, Richard (1968), *Life for Life's Sake: A Book of Reminiscences* (1941). London: Cassell and Company.
Aldington, Richard (1976), Introduction to D.H. Lawrence, *Aaron's Rod* (1950). Harmondsworth: Penguin, 7–10.
Aldington, Richard (1984), *Death of a Hero* (1929). London: Hogarth Press.
Aldington, Richard (1986), *The Colonel's Daughter* (1931). London: Hogarth Press.

Aldington, Richard (2002), *An Imagist at War: The Complete War Poems of Richard Aldington*, ed. Michael Copp. Madison: Fairleigh Dickinson University Press.

Aldington, Richard and Edward Storer, trans. (1919), *The Poems of Anyte of Tegea and Poems & Fragments of Sappho*. The Poets' Translation Series, Second Set No. 2. London: The Egoist Press.

H.D. and Aldington: Letters

Zilboorg, Caroline, ed. (2003), *H.D. and Richard Aldington: Their Lives in Letters, 1918–61*. Manchester: Manchester University Press.

H.D. and John Cournos: Letters

Hollenberg, Donna Krolik (1986), 'Art and Ardor in World War One: Selected Letters from H.D. to John Cournos'. *The Iowa Review* 16, 126–55.

Richard Aldington and John Cournos: Letters

Risk, R.T., ed. (1978), *The Dearest Friend: A Selection from the Letters of Richard Aldington to John Cournos*. Francestown: Typographeum.

John Cournos: Works

Cournos, John (1917a), 'The Death of Futurism'. *The Egoist* 4.1, 6–7.
Cournos, John (1917b), 'New Tendencies in English Painting and Sculpture'. *Seven Arts* 2.6, 762–78.
Cournos, John (1922), *Babel*. New York: Boni and Liveright.
Cournos, John (1926), *Miranda Masters*. New York: Alfred A. Knopf.
Cournos, John (1935), *Autobiography*. New York: G.P. Putnam's Sons.

Secondary works

Albright, Daniel (2000), *Untwisting the Serpent: Modernism in Music, Literature, and Other Arts*. Chicago: University of Chicago Press.

Amis, Martin (2020), *Inside Story*. London: Jonathan Cape.
Anonymous (1917), review of Gilbert Cannan, *Mendel: A Story of Youth*. *Seven Arts* 2.2, 252.
Ardis, Ann L. (2009), 'The *New Age* under A.R. Orage (1907–1922)', in *The Oxford Critical and Cultural History of Modernist Magazines, Vol. 1: Britain and Ireland 1880–1955*, ed. Peter Brooker and Andrew Thacker. Oxford: Oxford University Press, 205–25.
Arendt, Hannah (1958), *The Human Condition*. Chicago: University of Chicago Press.
Arrington, Lauren (2021), *The Poets of Rapallo: How Mussolini's Italy Shaped British, Irish, and U.S. Writers*. Oxford: Oxford University Press.
Asquith, Cynthia (1968), *The Diaries of Lady Cynthia Asquith, 1915–1918*. London: Century Hutchinson.
Auden, W.H. (2015), 'Work, Carnival and Prayer', in *W.H. Auden: Prose. Vol. 6: 1969–1973*, ed. Edward Mendelson. Princeton, NJ: Princeton University Press, 688–703.
Badenhausen, Richard (2004), *T.S. Eliot and the Art of Collaboration*. Cambridge: Cambridge University Press.
Baisnée, Valérie (2018), '"I am She who does not speak about herself": Annie Ernaux's Impersonal Autobiography *The Years*'. *European Journal of Life Writing* VII, 72–89.
Beasley, Rebecca (2007), *Ezra Pound and the Visual Culture of Modernism*. Cambridge: Cambridge University Press.
Beasley, Rebecca (2012), 'Modernism's Translations', in *The Oxford Handbook of Global Modernisms*, ed. Mark Wollaeger and Matt Eatough. Oxford: Oxford University Press, 551–70.
Beauman, Sally (1985), 'Introduction', in Compton Mackenzie, *Vestal Fire*. London: Chatto and Windus, n. pag.
Beebe, Maurice (1968), 'Lawrence as Fictional Character', in *The Spirit of D.H. Lawrence*, ed. Salgado Gamini and G.K. Das. London: Macmillan, 295–310.
Bell, Clive Bell (2015), *Art* (1914). London: Create Space Independent Publishing.
Benjamin, Walter (1973), 'The Task of the Translator', in *Illuminations*, ed. Hannah Arendt, trans. Harry Zohn. London: Fontana, 70–82.
Berman, Antoine (2004), 'Translation and the Trials of the Foreign', in *The Translation Studies Reader*, ed. Lawrence Venuti. London: Routledge, 276–89.
Bhabha, Homi K. (1994), *The Location of Culture*. London: Routledge.
Binckes, Faith (2016), 'Lines of Engagement: *Rhythm*, Reproduction, and the Textual Dialogues of Early Modernism', in *Little Magazines and Modernism: New Approaches*, ed. Suzanne W. Churchill and Adam McKible. London: Routledge, 21–34.
Black, Michael (1992), *D.H. Lawrence: The Early Philosophical Works. A Commentary*. Cambridge: Cambridge University Press.
Bloom, Harold (1975), *A Map of Misreading*. Oxford: Oxford University Press.
Boldrini, Lucia and Julia Novak, ed. (2017), *Experiments in Life-Writing: Intersections of Auto/Biography*. London: Palgrave Macmillan.
Bollus, Christopher (2008), *The Evocative Object World*. London: Routledge.

Booth, Alyson (1996), *Postcards from the Trenches: Negotiating the Space between Modernism and the First World War*. Oxford: Oxford University Press.

Brooker, Peter (2007), *Bohemia in London: The Social Scene of Early Modernism*. London: Palgrave Macmillan.

Brooker, Peter (2009), 'Harmony, Discord, and Difference: *Rhythm* (1911–13), *The Blue Review* (1913), and *The Signature* (1915)', in *The Oxford Critical and Cultural History of Modernist Magazines. Vol. 1: Britain and Ireland 1880–1955*, ed. Peter Brooker and Andrew Thacker. Oxford: Oxford University Press, 314–36.

Brooker, Peter and Andrew Thacker, eds (2009), *The Oxford Critical and Cultural History of Modernist Magazines. Vol. 1: Britain and Ireland 1880–1955*. Oxford: Oxford University Press.

Brown, Catherine and Susan Reid, eds (2020), *The Edinburgh Companion to D.H. Lawrence and the Arts*. Edinburgh: Edinburgh University Press.

Browning, Robert (1981), *The Poems*, 2 vols, ed. John Pettigrew and Thomas J. Collins. Harmondsworth: Penguin.

Bullen, J.B. (2003), 'D.H. Lawrence and Sculpture in *Women in Love*'. *The Burlington Magazine* 145.1209, 841–6.

Burkman, Katherine H. (2016), *The Drama of the Double: Permeable Boundaries (What Is Theatre?)*. London: Palgrave Macmillan.

Campbell, David A., ed. and trans. (1982), *Greek Lyric: Sappho, Alcaeus*. Loeb Classical Library. Cambridge, MA: Harvard University Press.

Campbell, James (1999), 'Combat Gnosticism'. *New Literary History* 30.1, 203–15.

Cannan, Gilbert (1912), 'Observation and Opinions. 1. – Machines'. *Rhythm* 2.7, 110–12.

Cannan, Gilbert (1916), *Mendel: A Story of Youth*. New York: George H. Doran Company.

Cannan, Gilbert (1920), *Windmills: A Book of Fables*. New York: Huebsch.

Carr, Helen (2009), *The Verse Revolutionaries: Ezra Pound, H.D. and the Imagists*. London: Jonathan Cape.

Carrington, Noel, ed. (1965), *Mark Gertler: Selected Letters*. London: Rupert Hart-Davis.

Carswell, Catherine (1981), *The Savage Pilgrimage* (1932). Cambridge: Cambridge University Press.

Christodoulides, Nephie J. and Polina Mackay, eds (2012), *The Cambridge Companion to H.D.* Cambridge: Cambridge University Press.

Churchill, Suzanne W. and Adam McKible, eds (2016), *Little Magazines and Modernism: New Approaches*. London: Routledge.

Cleaves, Rachel Hope (2020), *Unspeakable: A Life beyond Sexual Morality*. Chicago: University of Chicago Press.

Cole, Sarah (2003), *Modernism, Male Friendship, and the First World War*. Cambridge: Cambridge University Press.

Coleman, Philip, Kathryn Milligan and Nathan O'Donnell, eds (2017), *BLAST at 100: A Modernist Magazine Reconsidered*. Leiden: Brill.

Collecott, Diana (1990), 'Images at the Crossroads: H.D.'s "Scrapbook"', in *Signets: Reading H.D.*, ed. Susan Stanford Friedman and Rachel Blau DuPlessis. Madison: University of Wisconsin Press, 155–81.

Collecott, Diana (1999), *H.D. and Sapphic Modernism, 1910–1950*. Cambridge: Cambridge University Press.

Comentale, Edward P. and Andrzej Gasiorek, eds (2006), *T.E. Hulme and the Question of Modernism*. Aldershot: Ashgate.

Cork, Richard (1994), *A Bitter Truth: Avant-Garde Art and the Great War*. New Haven, CT: Yale University Press.

Corneilson, Paul (1998), *The Science and Art of Renaissance Music*. Princeton, NJ: Princeton University Press.

Costin, Jane (2020), 'Sculpture', in *The Edinburgh Companion to D.H. Lawrence and the Arts*, ed. Catherine Brown and Susan Reid. Edinburgh: Edinburgh University Press, 338–53.

Cram, David and Christopher Pollnitz (2001), 'D.H. Lawrence as Verse Translator'. *Cambridge Quarterly* 30.2, 133–50.

Crawford, Fred (1987), 'Misleading Accounts of Aldington and H.D.'. *English Literature in Transition, 1880–1920* 30.1, 49–67.

Cusk, Rachel (2014a), 'Interview with Kate Kellaway'. *The Guardian*, 24 August, online edition.

Cusk, Rachel (2014b), *Outline*. London: Faber and Faber.

Cusk, Rachel (2021), *Second Place*. London: Faber and Faber.

Damon, Samuel Foster (1935), *Amy Lowell: A Chronicle, with Extracts from her Correspondence*. Boston: Houghton Mifflin.

Dante Alighieri (1939), *The Divine Comedy*, trans. John D. Sinclair. New York: Oxford University Press.

Das, Santanu (2011), *Race, Empire and First World War Writing*. Cambridge: Cambridge University Press.

Das, Santanu, ed. (2013a), *The Cambridge Companion to the Poetry of the First World War*, ed. Santanu Das. Cambridge: Cambridge University Press.

Das, Santanu (2013b), 'Reframing First World War Poetry: An Introduction', in *The Cambridge Companion to the Poetry of the First World War*, ed. Santanu Das. Cambridge: Cambridge University Press, 2–34.

Davis, Alex and Lee M. Jenkins, eds (2015), *The Cambridge History of Modernist Poetry*. Cambridge: Cambridge University Press.

Davis, Dale (1986), 'The Matter of Myrrhine for Louis'. *The Iowa Review* 16.3, 165–73.

Davison, Claire (2014), *Translation as Collaboration: Virginia Woolf, Katherine Mansfield and S.S. Koteliansky*. Edinburgh: Edinburgh University Press.

de Beauvoir, Simone (1972), *The Second Sex* (1949), trans. H.M. Parshley. Harmondsworth: Penguin.

Delany, Paul (1979), *D.H. Lawrence's Nightmare: The Writer and His Circle in the Years of the Great War*. Hassocks: Harvester Press.

Dettmar, Kevin J.H. and Stephen Watts, eds (1996), *Marketing Modernisms: Self-Promotion, Canonization, Rereading*. Ann Arbor: University of Michigan Press.

Dillon, Sarah (2007), *The Palimpsest: Literature, Criticism, Theory*. London: Bloomsbury.

Dillon, Sarah (2018), 'Palimpsesting: Reading and Writing Lives in H.D.'s "Murex: War and Postwar London (circa. A.D. 1916-1926)"'. *Critical Survey* 30, 29-39.

Donaldson, George and Mara Kalnins, eds (1999), *D.H. Lawrence in England and Italy*. London: Palgrave Macmillan.

Douglas, James (1970), review of D.H. Lawrence, *The Rainbow*, in *D.H. Lawrence: The Critical Heritage*, ed. R.P. Draper. London: Routledge, 93-5.

Doyle, Charles, ed. (1990), *Richard Aldington: Reappraisals*. English Literary Studies Monograph Series. Victoria: University of Victoria Press.

Draper, R.P., ed. (1970), *D.H. Lawrence: The Critical Heritage*. London: Routledge.

du Bellay, Joachim (2006), *The Regrets, with the Antiquities of Rome, Three Latin Elegies, and the Defense and Enrichment of the French Language*, ed. and trans. Richard Helgerson. Philadelphia: University of Pennsylvania Press.

Duncan, Robert (2011), *The H.D. Book*, ed. Michael Boughn and Victor Coleman. Berkeley: University of California Press.

DuPlessis, Rachel Blau (1979), 'Romantic Thralldom in H.D.'. *Contemporary Literature* 20.2, 178-203.

DuPlessis, Rachel Blau (1986), *H.D.: The Career of That Struggle*. Brighton: Harvester Press.

Durand, Lionel (1960), 'Life in a Hothouse'. *Newsweek* 55.18, 92-3.

Eatough, Matt (2018), 'Philology Contra Modernism: Translating Izibongo in Johannesburg'. *Modernism/Modernity* Print Plus platform 3.3. https://doi.org/10.26597/mod.0067.

Eder, David (1943), *Memoirs of a Modern Pioneer*. London: Victor Gollancz.

Edmonds, J.M. (1909), 'Three Fragments of Sappho'. *Classical Review* 23.4, 99-104.

Eggert, Paul (2001), 'The Biographical Issue: Lives of Lawrence', in *The Cambridge Companion to D.H. Lawrence*, ed. Anne Fernihough. Cambridge: Cambridge University Press, 157-78.

Einhaus, Ann-Marie and Katherine Isobel Baxter, eds (2017), *The Edinburgh Companion to the First World War and the Arts*. Edinburgh: Edinburgh University Press.

Eliot, T.S. (1969), *The Complete Poems and Plays*. London: Faber and Faber.

Eliot, T.S. (2015), *The Poems of T.S. Eliot: The Annotated Text. Vol. 1: Collected and Uncollected Poems*, ed. Christopher Ricks and Jim McCue. London: Faber and Faber.

Eliot, T.S. (2021a), *The Complete Prose of T.S. Eliot. Vol. 1: Apprentice Years, 1905-1918*, ed. Jewel Spears Brooker and Ronal Schuchard. London and Baltimore, MD: Faber and Faber and Johns Hopkins University Press.

Eliot, T.S. (2021b), *The Complete Prose of T.S. Eliot. Vol. 2: The Perfect Critic, 1919-1926*, ed. Anthony Cuda and Ronald Schuchard. London and Baltimore, MD: Faber and Faber and Johns Hopkins University Press.

Ellis, David, ed. (2006), *Women in Love: A Casebook*. Oxford: Oxford University Press.
Epstein, Jacob (1940), *Let There be Sculpture*. London: Joseph. e-book.
Espey, John J. (1955), *Ezra Pound's Mauberley: A Study in Composition*. Berkeley: University of California Press.
Esty, Jed (2004), *A Shrinking Island: Modernism and National Culture in England*. Princeton, NJ: Princeton University Press.
Farr, Diana (1978), *Gilbert Cannan: A Georgian Prodigy*. London: Chatto and Windus.
Feigel, Lara (2022), *Look! We Have Come Through! Living with Lawrence*. London: Bloomsbury.
Felski, Rita (2003), *Literature after Feminism*. Chicago: University of Chicago Press.
Fernihough, Anne (1993), *D.H. Lawrence: Aesthetics and Ideology*. Oxford: Clarendon Press.
Fernihough, Anne, ed. (2001), *The Cambridge Companion to D.H. Lawrence*. Cambridge: Cambridge University Press.
Fernihough, Anne (2013), *Freewomen and Supermen: Edwardian Radicals and Literary Modernism*. Oxford: Oxford University Press.
Ferri, Jessica (2021), 'D.H. Lawrence Hated Women Writers. Now They Get to Speak: On "Burning Man", a D.H. Lawrence Biography, and Rachel Cusk'. *Los Angeles Times*, 17 August, online edition.
Firchow, Peter E. (1980), 'Rico and Julia: The Hilda Doolittle: D.H. Lawrence Affair Reconsidered'. *Journal of Modern Literature* 8.1, 51–76.
Flint, F.S. (1913), 'Imagisme'. *Poetry* 1.8, 198–200.
Flint, F.S. (1915), 'Chicago'. *The Egoist* 5.2, 74–5.
Frayn, Andrew (2014), *Writing Disenchantment: British First World War Prose, 1914–1930*. Manchester: Manchester University Press.
Frayn, Andrew and Fiona Houston (2023), 'The War Books Boom, 1928–1930'. *First World War Studies*. https://doi.org/10.1080/19475020.2022.2129718.
Freer, Scott (2015), *Modernist Mythopoeia: The Twilight of the Gods*. London: Palgrave.
Freud, Sigmund (2003), *Beyond the Pleasure Principle and Other Writings*, trans. John Reddick. Harmondsworth: Penguin.
Friedman, Susan Stanford (1975), 'Who Buried H.D.? A Poet, Her Critics, and Her Place in "The Literary Tradition"'. *College English* 36, 801–14.
Friedman, Susan Stanford (1981), *Psyche Reborn: The Emergence of H.D.* Bloomington: Indiana University Press.
Friedman, Susan Stanford (1990a), *Penelope's Web: Gender, Modernity, H.D.'s Fiction*. New York: Cambridge University Press.
Friedman, Susan Stanford (1990b), 'Return of the Repressed in H.D.'s *Madrigal Cycle*', in *Signets: Reading H.D.*, ed. Susan Stanford Friedman and Rachel Blau DuPlessis. Madison: University of Wisconsin Press, 233–52.
Friedman, Susan Stanford (2015), *Planetary Modernisms: Provocations on Modernity across Time*. New York: Columbia University Press.
Friedman, Susan Stanford and Rachel Blau DuPlessis, ed. (1990), *Signets: Reading H.D.* Madison: University of Wisconsin Press.

Froula, Christine (2013), 'War, Empire and Modernist Poetry, 1914–1922', in *The Cambridge Companion to First World War Poetry*, ed. Santanu Das. Cambridge: Cambridge University Press, 210–26.

Fussell, Paul (2013), *The Great War and Modern Memory* [1975]. Oxford: Oxford University Press.

Gamini, Salgado and G.K. Das, eds (1968), *The Spirit of D.H. Lawrence*. London: Macmillan.

Gasiorek, Andrzej (2017), '"With Expletive of Whirlwind": *BLAST* Then and Now', in *BLAST at 100: A Modernist Magazine Reconsidered*, ed. Philip Coleman, Kathryn Milligan and Nathan O'Donnell. Leiden: Brill, 17–29.

Gates, Norman T. (1974), *The Poetry of Richard Aldington: A Critical Evaluation and an Anthology of Uncollected Poems*. University Park and London: Pennsylvania State University Press.

Genette, Gérard (1997), *Palimpsests: Literature in the Second Degree*, trans. Channa Newman and Claude Doubinsky. Lincoln: University of Nebraska Press.

Gibson, Wilfred (1915), 'The Going'. *Poetry* 6.5, 239.

Gilbert, Sandra (1990), *Acts of Attention: The Poems of D.H. Lawrence*. Carbondale: Southern Illinois University Press.

Gilbert, Sandra M. and Susan Gubar (1989), *No Man's Land: The Place of the Woman Writer in the Twentieth Century. Vol. 2: Sexchanges*. New Haven, CT: Yale University Press.

Gilboa, Raquel (2009), *… And There Was Sculpture: Jacob Epstein's Formative Years, 1880–1930*. London: Paul Holberton Publishing.

Girling, Anna (2020), 'He Could Have Done Anything: The Failed Career of a Poet and Critic'. *Times Literary Supplement*, 20 March, 12–13.

Goff, Barbara (2008), *Euripides: Trojan Women*. Bristol: Bristol Classical Press.

Goldman, Jane (2003) *Modernism, 1910–1945: Image to Apocalypse*. London: Bloomsbury.

Goldschmidt, Nora (2019), '"Orts, Scraps, and Fragments": Translation, Non-Translation, and the Fragments of Ancient Greece', in *Modernism and Non-Translation*, ed. Jason Harding and John Nash. Oxford: Oxford University Press, 49–66.

Goodman, Nelson (1978), *Ways of Worldmaking*. Indianapolis: Hackett.

Gray, Cecil (1934), *Peter Warlock: A Memoir of Philip Heseltine*. London: Jonathan Cape.

Gray, Cecil (1985), *Musical Chairs* (1948). London: Hogarth Press.

Greene, Ellen, ed. (1996), *Re-Reading Sappho: Reception and Transmission*. Berkeley: University of California Press.

Gregory, Eileen (1997), *Classic Lines: H.D. and Hellenism*. Cambridge: Cambridge University Press.

Guest, Barbara (1985), *Herself Defined: The Poet H.D. and Her World*. New York: Harper Collins.

Harding, Jason and John Nash, eds (2019), *Modernism and Non-Translation*. Oxford: Oxford University Press.

Harrison, Andrew (2003), *D.H. Lawrence and Italian Futurism: A Study of Influence*. Amsterdam: Rodopi.

Harrison, Andrew (2018), 'D.H. Lawrence, Rananim and Gilbert Cannan's *Windmills*'. *Review of English Studies* 69.292, 953–66.

Hart, Matthew (2010), *Nations of Nothing but Poetry: Modernism, Transnationalism, and Synthetic Vernacular Writing*. New York: Oxford University Press.

Henderson, Alice Corbin (1914), 'Poetry and War'. *Poetry* 5.2, 82–4.

Hickman, Miranda (2015), 'Early Eliot, H.D., and Pound', in *A History of Modernist Poetry*, ed. Alex Davis and Lee M. Jenkins. Cambridge: Cambridge University Press, 186–203.

Hicks, Dan (2021), *The Brutish Museums: The Benin Bronzes, Colonial Violence and Cultural Restitution*. London: Pluto Press.

Hoberman, Ruth (2012), '"Making Life into Art": The Three-Way Conversation of Gilbert Cannan, Mark Gertler, and D.H. Lawrence', in *Reading Texts, Reading Lives: Essays in the Tradition of Humanistic Cultural Criticism in Honour of Daniel R. Schwarz*, ed. Helen Maxson and Daniel Morris. Newark: University of Delaware Press, 31–49.

Höschele, Regina (2009), 'Meleager and Heliodora: A Love Story in Bits and Pieces?', in *Plotting with Eros: Essays in the Poetics of Love and the Erotics of Reading*, ed. Ingela Nilsson. Copenhagen: Museum Tusculanum Press, 99–134.

Hulme, T.E. (1913), 'Mr Epstein and the Critics'. *The New Age* 14.8, 251–2.

Hussey, Mark (2021), *Clive Bell and the Making of Modernism*. London: Bloomsbury.

Hyde, G.M. (1981), *D.H. Lawrence and the Art of Translation*. Totowa, NJ: Barnes and Noble Books.

Hynes, Samuel (1992), *A War Imagined: The First World War and English Culture*. London: Pimlico.

Jackson, Paul (2012), *Great War Modernisms and 'The New Age'*. London: Bloomsbury.

James, Henry (1914), 'The Younger Generation'. *Times Literary Supplement*, 635, 133–4.

James, Henry (1986), Preface to *The Portrait of a Lady*. Harmondsworth: Penguin, 41–55.

James, Jamie (2019), *Pagan Light: Dreams of Freedom and Beauty in Capri*. New York: Farrar, Strauss, Giroux.

Jenkins, Lee M. (2020), 'Lawrence in Biofiction', in *D.H. Lawrence and the Arts*, ed. Catherine Brown and Susan Reid. Edinburgh: Edinburgh University Press, 385–97.

Jones, Peter, ed. (1972), *Imagist Poetry*. Harmondsworth: Penguin.

Kaplan, Sydney Janet (2010), *Circulating Genius: John Middleton Murry, Katherine Mansfield and D.H. Lawrence*. Edinburgh: Edinburgh University Press.

Katz-Roy, Ginette (2006), 'The Dialogue with the Avant-Garde in *Women in Love*', in *Women in Love: A Casebook*, ed. David Ellis. Oxford: Oxford University Press, 245–72.

Kelly, Alice (2017), 'Words from Home: Wartime Correspondences', in *The Edinburgh Companion to the First World War and the Arts*, ed. Ann-Marie Einhaus and Katherine Isobel Baxter. Edinburgh: Edinburgh University Press, 77–94.

Kelly, Alice (2020), *Commemorative Modernisms: Women Writers, Death and the First World War*. Edinburgh: Edinburgh University Press.

Kendall, Tim (2013), 'Civilian War Poetry', in *The Cambridge Companion to the Poetry of the First World War*, ed. Santanu Das. Cambridge: Cambridge University Press, 198–209.

Kenner, Hugh (1971), *The Pound Era*. Berkeley: University of California Press.

Kinkead-Weekes, Mark (1996), *D.H. Lawrence. Triumph to Exile, 1912-1922*. Cambridge: Cambridge University Press.

Kozak, Lynn and Miranda Hickman, eds (2019), *The Classics in Modernist Translation*. London: Bloomsbury.

Krockel, Carl (2011), *War Trauma and English Modernism: T.S. Eliot and D.H. Lawrence*. London: Palgrave Macmillan.

Laird, Holly A. (1988), *Self and Sequence: The Poetry of D.H. Lawrence*. Charlottesville: University Press of Virginia.

Laird, Holly A. (2020), 'Practitioner Criticism: Poetry', in *The Edinburgh Companion to D.H. Lawrence and the Arts*, ed. Catherine Brown and Susan Reid. Edinburgh: Edinburgh University Press, 204–18.

Larabee, Mark D. (2011), *Front Lines of Modernism: Remapping the Great War in British Fiction*. London: Palgrave Macmillan.

Larsen, David L. (2000), *The Company of the Creative*. Grand Rapids, MI: Kregel Publications.

Latham, Sean (2009), *The Art of Scandal: Modernism, Libel Law, and the Roman à Clef*. Oxford: Oxford University Press.

Lawrence, Frieda (1983), *Not I, but the Wind …* (1935). London: Granada.

Levinson, Marjorie (2018), *Thinking through Poetry: Field Reports on Romantic Lyric*. Oxford: Oxford University Press.

Lewis, Wyndham (1982), *Blasting and Bombardiering: An Autobiography (1914–1926)*. London: John Calder.

Lowell, Amy (1914), 'The Bombardment'. *Poetry* 5.2, 60–2.

Lowell, Amy (1915), 'Preface', in *Some Imagist Poets: An Anthology*. Boston: Houghton Mifflin, v–viii.

Lowell, Amy (1918), *Can Grande's Castle*. Boston: Houghton Mifflin.

Lowell, Amy (2008), *Tendencies in Modern American Poetry* (1917). Charleston: Bibliolife.

Lowell, Amy, et al., eds (1915), *Some Imagist Poets: An Anthology*. Boston: Houghton Mifflin.

Lowell, Amy, et al., eds (1916), *Some Imagist Poets: An Anthology*. Boston: Houghton Mifflin.

Lowell, Amy, et al., eds (1917), *Some Imagist Poets: An Anthology*. Boston: Houghton Mifflin.

Luhan, Mabel Dodge (1933), *Lorenzo in Taos*. London: Martin Secker.

MacDougall, Sarah (2002), *Mark Gertler*. London: John Murray.

MacDougall, Sarah (2012), *Mark Gertler: Works 1912–28*. London: Piano Nobile.
MacGreevy, Thomas (1931), *Richard Aldington: An Englishman*. London: Chatto and Windus.
MacKay, Marina (2007), *Modernism and World War II*. Cambridge: Cambridge University Press.
Mackenzie, Compton (1941), *The West Wind of Love*. London: The Book Club.
Mackenzie, Compton (1942), *The South Wind of Love*. London: Chatto and Windus.
Mackenzie, Compton (1967), *My Life and Times: Octave Six 1923–1930*. London: Chatto and Windus, 84–5.
Mackenzie, Compton (1985), *Vestal Fire* (1927). London: Hogarth Press.
Maclean, Caroline (2020), *Circles & Squares: The Lives & Art of the Hampstead Modernists*. London: Bloomsbury.
MacLeod, Alison (2021), *Tenderness*. London: Bloomsbury.
McCabe, Susan (2021), *H.D. & Bryher: An Untold Love Story of Modernism*. New York: Oxford University Press.
McDiarmid, Lucy (2014), *Poets and the Peacock Dinner: The Literary History of a Meal*. Oxford: Oxford University Press.
McGann, Jerome J. (1983), *A Theory of Modern Textual Criticism*. Chicago: University of Chicago Press.
McGann, Jerome J. (1991), *The Textual Condition*. Princeton, NJ: Princeton University Press.
McLane, Maureen (2023), review article on H.D. *London Review of Books* (January).
McLoughlin, Kate (2015), '*All of Us*: D. H. Lawrence's War Poems for the People'. *Journal of D. H. Lawrence Studies*, 4.1, 45–66.
Marcus, Laura (2013), 'Modernism and Visual Culture', in *A Handbook of Modernism Studies*, ed. Jean-Michel Rabaté. Oxford: Wiley-Blackwell, 239–54.
Materer, Timothy (1996), 'Make It Sell!: Ezra Pound Advertizes Modernism', in *Marketing Modernisms: Self-Promotion, Canonization, Rereading*, ed. Kevin J.H. Dettmar and Stephen Watts. Ann Arbor: University of Michigan Press, 17–36.
Matthews, Sean (2022), review of Alison MacLeod, *Tenderness. Journal of D.H. Lawrence Studies* 6.2 241–4.
Millett, Kate (1977), *Sexual Politics* (1970). London: Virago.
Milton, John (2007), *Paradise Lost*, 2nd edn, ed. Alastair Fowler. London: Pearson Longman.
Mitchell, W.J.T. (1987), *Iconology: Image, Text, Ideology*. Chicago: University of Chicago Press.
Monroe, Harriet (1913), 'Notes'. *Poetry* 1.4, 135.
Monroe, Harriet (1917a), 'The New Era'. *Poetry* 9.4, 195–7.
Monroe, Harriet (1917b), 'Will Art Happen?' *Poetry* 10.4, 203–5.
Monroe, Harriet (1918), 'The War and the Artist'. *Poetry* 11.6, 320–2.
Monroe, Harriet (1919), 'Other Poets of the War'. *Poetry* 14.4, 223.
Monroe, Harriet (1929), 'An Imagist at War'. *Poetry* 34.1, 42–6.

Moody, A. David (2007), *Ezra Pound: A Portrait of the Man and His Work. Vol. I: The Young Genius 1885–1920*. Oxford: Oxford University Press.
Moore, Alison (2018), *Missing*. Cromer: Salt Publishing.
Moore, Harry T. (1954), *The Intelligent Heart: The Life of D.H. Lawrence*. New York: Farrar, Straus and Young.
Morrisson, Mark S. (2000), *The Public Face of Modernism: Little Magazines, Audiences, and Reception, 1905–1920*. Madison: University of Wisconsin Press.
Munday, Jeremy (2008), *Introducing Translation Studies: Theories and Applications*. London: Routledge.
Munton, Alan (2006), 'Abstraction, Archaism and the Future: T.E. Hulme, Jacob Epstein and Wyndham Lewis', in *T.E. Hulme and the Question of Modernism*, ed. Edward P. Comentale and Andrzej Gasiorek. Aldershot: Ashgate, 73–91.
Murry, John Middleton (1935), *Between Two Worlds: An Autobiography*. London: Jonathan Cape.
Nehls, Edward (1958), *D.H. Lawrence: A Composite Biography. Vol. 2: 1919–1925*. Madison: University of Wisconsin Press.
Nicholson, Virginia (2008), *Singled Out: How Two Million Women Survived without Men after the First World War*. Harmondsworth: Penguin.
Nilsson, Ingela, ed. (2009), *Plotting with Eros: Essays in the Poetics of Love and the Erotics of Reading*. Copenhagen: Museum Tusculanum Press.
Nin, Anaïs (1964), *D.H. Lawrence: An Unprofessional Study*. Denver, CO: Alan Swallow.
Nisbet, Gideon, ed. and trans. (2000), *Epigrams from the Greek Anthology*. Oxford: Oxford University Press.
Norris, Nanette, ed. (2015a), *Great War Modernism: Artistic Response in the Context of War, 1914–1918*. Madison: Fairleigh Dickinson University Press.
Norris, Nanette (2015b), 'H.D. and the Secrets of Redemption', in *Great War Modernism*, ed. Nanette Norris. Madison: Fairleigh Dickinson University Press, 103–18.
Norris, Nanette (2015c), 'Introduction: Great War Modernism', in *Great War Modernism*, ed. Nanette Norris. Madison: Fairleigh Dickinson University Press, 1–12.
Olusoga, David (2014), *The World's War: Forgotten Soldiers of Empire*. London: Head of Zeus.
Ostriker, Alicia Suskin (1986), *Stealing the Language: The Emergence of Women's Poetry in America*. Boston: Beacon Press.
Palmer, Andrew and Sally Minogue (2015), 'Modernism and First World War Poetry: Alternative Lines', in *The Cambridge History of Modernist Poetry*, ed. Alex and Davis Lee M. Jenkins. Cambridge: Cambridge University Press, 227–51.
Parker, Sarah (2013), *The Lesbian Muse and Poetic Identity, 1889–1930*. London: Routledge.
Pater, Walter (2005), *The Renaissance: Studies in Art and Poetry* (1893). Mineola: Dover Fine Art.

Pearson, Norman Holmes (1969), 'A Selection of Poetry and Prose Introduction'. *Contemporary Literature* 10, 587.

Pederson, Joshua (2014), 'Speak, Trauma: Toward a Revised Understanding of Literary Trauma Theory'. *Narrative* 22.3, 333–53.

Peppis, Paul (1997), '"Surrounded by a Multitude of Other Blasts": Vorticism and the Great War'. *Modernism/Modernity* 4.2, 39–66.

Peterson, Houston (1928), *Havelock Ellis: The Philosopher of Love*. London: G. Allen and Unwin.

Pinkney, Tony (1990), *D.H. Lawrence and Modernism*. Iowa City: University of Iowa Press.

Poggi, Christine (2009), *Inventing Futurism: The Art and Politics of Artificial Optimism*. Princeton, NJ: Princeton University Press.

Pollnitz, Christopher (1986), 'Raptus Virginis: The Dark God in the Poetry of D.H. Lawrence', in *D.H. Lawrence: Centenary Essays*, ed. Mara Kalnins. Bristol: Classical Press, 111–38.

Pondrom, Cyrena N. (2012), 'H.D. and the "little magazines"', in *The Cambridge Companion to H.D.*, ed. Nephie J. Christodoulides and Polina Mackay. Cambridge: Cambridge University Press, 37–50.

Pound, Ezra (1913a), 'A Few Don'ts by an Imagiste'. *Poetry* 1.6, 200–6.

Pound, Ezra (1913b), 'In a Station of the Metro'. *Poetry* 2.1, 12.

Pound, Ezra, ed. (1914a), *Des Imagistes: An Anthology*. New York: Albert and Charles Boni.

Pound, Ezra (1914b), 'Vortex'. *Blast: Review of the Great English Vortex* I, 153–4.

Pound, Ezra (1932), 'Harold Monro'. *The Criterion* 11.45, 581–92.

Pound, Ezra (1964), *The Cantos*. London: Faber and Faber.

Pound, Ezra (1971), *Selected Letters of Ezra Pound, 1907–1941*, ed. D.D. Paige. New York: New Directions.

Pound, Ezra (1973), *Selected Prose 1909–1965*, ed. William Cookson. New York: New Directions.

Pound, Ezra (1990), *Personae: The Shorter Poems*, ed. Lea Baechler and A. Walton Litz. New York: New Directions.

Pound, Ezra (2011), *Selected Poems and Translations*, ed. Richard Sieburth. London: Faber and Faber.

Prins, Yopie (1995), 'Sappho Doubled: Michael Field'. *Yale Journal of Criticism* 8.1, 165–86.

Rabaté, Jean-Michel, ed. (2013), *A Handbook of Modernism Studies*. Oxford: Wiley-Blackwell.

Ramazani, Jahan (2009), *A Transnational Poetics*. Chicago: University of Chicago Press.

Ramazani, Jahan (2012), 'Poetry, Modernity, and Globalization', in *The Oxford Handbook of Global Modernisms*, ed. Mark Wollaeger with Matt Eatough. Oxford: Oxford University Press, 288–309.

Ramazani, Jahan (2020), '"Cosmopolitan Sympathies": Poetry of the First Global War', in *Poetry in a Global Age*. Chicago: University of Chicago Press, 25–50.

Read, Forrest, ed. (1967), *Pound/Joyce: The Letters of Ezra Pound to James Joyce, with Pound's Critical Essays and Articles about Joyce*. New York: New Directions.
Ridgway, Christopher (1984), Introduction to Richard Aldington, *Death of a Hero*. London: Hogarth Press.
Robinson, Janice S. (1982), *H.D.: The Life and Work of an American Poet*. Boston: Houghton Mifflin.
Rogan, Eugene Rogan (2014), 'Egyptian Labour Corps on the Western Front', in *Forgotten Heroes: North Africans and the Great War*, 14–15. http://www.forgottenheroes.eu (accessed 1 October 2016).
Rohrbach, Erika (1996), 'H.D. and Sappho: A Precious Inch of Palimpsest', in *Re-Reading Sappho: Reception and Transmission*, ed. Ellen Greene. Berkeley: University of California Press, 184–98.
Ross, Charles L. (1979), *The Composition of 'The Rainbow' and 'Women in Love'*. Charlottesville: University Press of Virginia.
Ross, Charles L. (1991), *Women in Love: A Novel of Mythic Realism*. Woodbridge: Twayne.
Ruderman, Judith (2014), *Race and Identity in D.H. Lawrence: Indians, Gypsies, and Jews*. London: Palgrave Macmillan.
Rudnick, Lois Palken (1984), *Mabel Dodge Luhan: New Woman, New Worlds*. Albuquerque: University of New Mexico Press.
Sagar, Keith (2011), *'Art for Life's Sake': Essays on D.H. Lawrence*. Nottingham: Critical, Cultural and Communications Press.
Said, Edward (1994), *Orientalism*. New York: Vintage.
Sassoon, Siegfried (1988), *Memoirs of a Fox-Hunting Man* (1928). London: Faber and Faber.
Sassoon, Siegfried (2022), *Counter-Attack and Other Poems* (1918). Charleston, SC: Legare Street Press.
Saunders, Max (2010), *Self-Impression: Life-Writing, Autobiografiction, & the Forms of Modern Literature*. Oxford: Oxford University Press.
Schäfer, Heinrich (2010), *The Songs of an Egyptian Peasant: Collected and Translated into German*, trans. Frances Hart Breasted (1904). Whitefish, MT: Kissinger Legacy Reprints.
Schaffner, Perdita (1984), 'A Profound Animal'. Afterword to H.D., *Bid Me to Live*, ed. Helen McNeil. London: Virago, 185–94.
Schwartz, Selby Wynn (2022), *After Sappho*. Norwich: Galley Beggar Press.
Scott, Bonnie Kime, ed. (1990), *The Gender of Modernism: A Critical Anthology*. Bloomington: Indiana University Press.
Seaton, Beverly (1995), *The Language of Flowers: A History*. Charlottesville: University Press of Virginia.
Seward, Barbara (1960), *The Symbolic Rose*. New York: Columbia University Press.
Shail, Andrew (2012), *The Cinema and the Origins of Literary Modernism*. London: Routledge.

Sherry, Vincent (2013), *The Great War and the Language of Modernism*. Oxford: Oxford University Press.

Shorter, Clement (1970), review of *The Rainbow* (1915), in *D.H. Lawrence: The Critical Heritage*, ed. R.P. Draper. London: Routledge, 96–7.

Sillars, Stuart (1999), '"Terrible and Dreadful": Lawrence, Gertler and the Visual Imagination', in *D.H. Lawrence in England and Italy*, ed. George Donaldson and Mara Kalnins. London: Palgrave Macmillan, 193–210.

Sinclair, May (1921), 'Aldington'. *English Review* (May), 397–410.

Smith, Angela K. (2004), *Gender and Warfare in the Twentieth Century: Textual Representations*. Manchester: Manchester University Press.

Smith, Barry (1994), *Peter Warlock: The Life of Philip Heseltine*. Oxford: Oxford University Press.

Spivak, Gayatri Chakravorty (1993), 'The Politics of Translation', in *Outside in the Teaching Machine*. London: Routledge, 179–200.

Stevens, Wallace (1997), 'The Noble Rider and the Sound of Words', in *Wallace Stevens: Collected Poetry and Prose*, ed. Frank Kermode and Joan Richardson. New York: Library of America, 643–65.

Stewart, Jack (1999), *The Vital Art of D.H. Lawrence: Vision and Expression*. Carbondale: Southern Illinois University Press.

Stillinger, Jack (1991), *Multiple Authorship and the Myth of Solitary Genius*. Oxford: Oxford University Press.

Sword, Helen (1989), 'Orpheus and Eurydice in the Twentieth Century: Lawrence, H.D., and the Poetics of the Turn'. *Twentieth Century Literature* 35.4, 407–28.

Tate, Trudi (1998), *Modernism, History and the First World War*. Manchester: Manchester University Press.

Tedlock, E.W. (1952), 'A Forgotten War Poem by D.H. Lawrence'. *Modern Language Notes* xvii, 410–13.

Tickner, Lisa (1997), 'The Popular Culture of Kermesse: Lewis, Painting, and Performance'. *Modernism/Modernity* 4.2, 67–120.

Torgovnick, Marianna (1990), *Gone Primitive: Savage Intellects, Modern Lives*. Chicago: University of Chicago Press.

Turner, John and John Worthen (1999), 'Ideas of Community: Lawrence and "Rananim"'. *D.H. Lawrence Studies [Korea]* 8 July, 135–71.

Tylee, Claire (1990), *The Great War and Women's Consciousness*. Iowa City: University of Iowa Press.

Vandiver, Elizabeth (2010), *Stand in the Trench, Achilles: Classical Receptions in British Poetry of the Great War*. Oxford: Oxford University Press.

Vandiver, Elizabeth (2019), '"Seeking Buried Beauty": The Poets' Translation Series', in *The Classics in Modernist Translation*, ed. Lynn Kozak and Miranda Hickman. London: Bloomsbury, 7–20.

Venuti, Lawrence (1995), *The Translator's Invisibility: A History of Translation*. London: Routledge.

Venuti, Lawrence, ed. (2004), *The Translation Studies Reader*. London: Routledge.
Venuti, Lawrence (2013), *Translation Changes Everything: Theory and Practice*. London: Routledge.
Verner, Miroslav (1994), *Forgotten Pharaohs, Lost Pyramids*. Praha: Academia Skodaexpocrt.
Vine, Steven (1995), Introduction to D.H. Lawrence, *Aaron's Rod*. Harmondsworth: Penguin, xv–xxxvi.
von Glinski, Marie Louise (2012), *Simile and Identity in Ovid's Metamorphoses*. Cambridge: Cambridge University Press.
Wade, Francesca (2020), *Square Haunting: Five Women, Freedom and London between the Wars*. London: Faber and Faber.
Walker, James (2022), 'Shelfie: Alison Moore's "Missing" – D.H. Lawrence: A Digital Pilgrimage'. *wordpress.com*, 6 June. Available online: https://thedigitalpilgrimage.wordpress.com/2022/06/06/shelfie-alison-moore-missing/ (accessed 13 December 2023).
Whalan, Mark (2018), *World War One, American Literature, and the Federal State*. Cambridge: Cambridge University Press.
Wharton, H.T. (1908), *Sappho: Memoir, Text, Selected Renderings and a Literal Translation*. London: John Lane.
Whelpton, Vivien (2013), *Richard Aldington: Poet Soldier and Lover, 1911–1929*. Cambridge: Lutterworth Press.
Whelpton, Vivien (2019), *Richard Aldington: Novelist, Biographer and Exile, 1930–1962*. Cambridge: Lutterworth Press.
Whelpton, Vivien (2021), 'Vivien Whelpton on Richard Aldington in Frances Wilson's Burning Man'. *wordpress.com*, 12 August. Available online: https://nclsn.wordpress.com/2021/08/ (accessed 13 December 2023).
Williams, Ellen (1977), *Harriet Monroe and the Poetry Renaissance: The First Ten Years of Poetry, 1912–1922*. Urbana: University of Illinois Press.
Wilson, Frances (2021a), *Burning Man: The Ascent of D.H. Lawrence*. London: Bloomsbury.
Wilson, Frances (2021b), 'D.H. Lawrence Predicted Cancel Culture – And then Became Its First Victim'. *The Telegraph*, 29 May 2021, online edition.
Wollaeger, Mark and Matt Eatough, ed. (2012), *The Oxford Handbook of Global Modernisms*. Oxford: Oxford University Press.
Wood, Ritchie (2017), *Miners at War 1914–1919: South Wales Miners in the Tunnelling Companies on the Western Front*. Warwick: Helion.
Woodeson, John (1972), *Mark Gertler*. London: Sidgwick and Jackson.
Woolf, Virginia (1976), *The Question of Things Happening: The Letters of Virginia Woolf, Vol. II: 1912–1922*, ed. Nigel Nicolson. London: Hogarth Press.
Woolf, Virginia (1988), 'Character in Fiction', in *The Essays of Virginia Woolf. Vol. 3: 1919 to 1924*, ed. Andrew McNeillie. London: Hogarth Press, 420–38.

Woolf, Virginia (1992a), *'A Room of One's Own' and 'Three Guineas'*. Oxford: Oxford University Press.

Woolf, Virginia (1992b), *Orlando*. Oxford: Oxford World's Classics.

Worthen, John (2002), 'Lawrence or Not? The Letter Fragments of H.D. and E.T.'. *D.H. Lawrence Review* 30.3, 43–53.

Wright, T.R. (2000), *D.H. Lawrence and the Bible*. Cambridge: Cambridge University Press.

Yao, Steven (2002), *Translation and the Languages of Modernism: Gender, Politics, Language*. London: Palgrave Macmillan.

Yeats, W.B. (1994), '"Introduction" to *The Oxford Book of Modern Verse* (1936)', in *The Collected Works of W. B. Yeats. Vol. 5: Later Essays*, ed. William H. O'Donnell. New York: Charles Scribner's Sons, 199.

Zilboorg, Caroline (1990), 'H.D.'s Influence on Richard Aldington', in *Richard Aldington: Reappraisals*, ed. Charles Doyle. English Literary Studies Monograph Series. Victoria: University of Victoria Press, 26–44.

Zilboorg, Caroline (1991), 'Joint Venture: The Poets' Translation Series'. *Philological Quarterly* 70.1, 67–98.

Index

Note: page references to Notes will be followed by the letter 'n' and number of the Note.

Aaron's Rod (Lawrence) 1, 3, 7, 8, 25, 46, 47, 49–55, 57, 60, 64, 70, 144
   and the Bloomsbury Group 46
   characters
      Aaron Sisson 46
      Algy Constable 50
      Captain Herbertson 55
      Cyril Scott 46
      James Argyle 50
      Julia Cunningham 46, 60
      Josephine Ford 46, 59
      Louis Mee 50
      Rawdon Lily 64
      Robert Cunningham 46, 57, 58, 60
      Tanny Lily 60
      Walter Rosen 50
   compared with *Death of a Hero* 57–8
   early chapters 61
   musical motif 56
   PTSD theme 55
Albright, Daniel 23
Aldington, Richard 3, 7, 9, 45, 75
   affair with Dorothy Yorke 4, 9, 45, 63
   break-up of marriage to H.D. 1, 4, 47, 114
   collaboration with H.D. 12, 61
   correspondence with Lowell 56
   in Devon 4
   and Eliot 92
   and First World War 85–9
      army, entering (1916) 12
      as a Great War modernist 2
      war poems 10
      wartime verse translations 11
   literary editor of *The Egoist* 11
   at Mecklenburgh Square 4
   original 'Imagist' 87
   prose poetry *see* prose poetry
   translations by 12, 109, 112, 113, 116, 120
   on 'verse revolutionaries' 4, 14n9
   works of
      'Captive' 90, 106n19
      Collected Poems 90
      Complete Poems 90
      'Daughter of Zeus' 100, 101
      Death of a Hero see Death of a Hero (DH), Aldington
      'Discouragement' 93
      'Eumenides' 86, 87
      'The Faun Captive' 90, 106n19, 119
      Images of Desire 87, 106n25
      Images of War 10, 87, 91–5, 100, 106n25, 118–19, 132, 134n26
      'Lemures' 78, 87
      'Letters to Unknown Women' 12, 119
      'In the Library' 118
      Life for Life's Sake 56, 71n1
      The Love of Myrrhine and Konallis 12, 93, 94, 116–17
      'Madrigal' 62
      Meleager of Gadara 116
      'Penultimate Poetry: Xenophilometropolitana' 88
      'Resentment' 89
      Reverie: A Little Book of Poems for H.D. 101, 117, 118
      Roads to Glory 119
      Soft Answers 72n10
      'Sorcery of Words' 117–19
      Stepping Heavenward: A Record 91
      'Sunsets' 90, 106n19
      'Trench Idyll' 94
      'In the Tube' 87, 88, 89
      'A Village' 94, 118–19
      War and Love 10, 14n12, 62, 89, 95, 106n25, 107n35

Index

'All of Us' (Lawrence) 12–13, 85, 109–10, 120–2, 126–32, 135n36, 137n50, 137n54
   'Drill on Salisbury Plain in Summer Time' 126
   First World War, response to 124
   'Foreign Sunset' 124–5
   'Fragile Jewels' 127
   'The Grey Nurse' 131
   'Munitions Factory' 126
   'The Prophet in the Rose-Garden' 130–1
   'The Saint' 131
   'Star Sentinel' 128, 132
   'Straying Thoughts' 126
   'The Well of Kilossa' 126
Allinson, Adrian Paul 42n5
'Amaranth' poems (H.D.) 96–8, 99, 102, 113, 114
Amis, Martin 19, 142
Amygism (wartime Imagism) 76, 77
anti-imperialism 127
Antipater of Sidon 109
Anyte of Tegea 11, 109
AR see *Aaron's Rod* (*AR*), ed. Mara Kalnins
architectural expressionism 25
Arendt, Hannah 123–4
Arlen, Michael
   The Green Hat 7
The Art of Scandal (Latham) 19
Asphodel (H.D.) 6
Asquith, Cynthia 49, 78, 83–5
Asquith, Herbert Henry 83, 85
autobiofiction 46, 56, 72n22, 144
autobiografiction 3, 8, 46
autobiography 3, 19, 71n1
   impersonal 146n5
   straight 65
autofiction 3, 8, 13, 48, 142
   see also autobiofiction; autobiography; biofiction
avant-garde 20, 23
   in the *avant-guerre* 29, 69, 76, 89
   colour 22
   experimentalism 76
   interior design 68
   Lawrence's involvement with 26
   metropolitan 26
   Parisian 67
   platforms 87
   print circuits and friendship circles 1, 65
   writers and artists 3

Babel (Cournos) 9, 48, 65, 66, 68–9, 73n26
   African statue in 66–9, 73n26
   see also *Miranda Masters* (Cournos); *Women in Love* (Lawrence)
Badenhausen, Richard 80
Baudelaire, Charles 92
Beardsley, Aubrey 117
Beasley, Rebecca 129
Beauman, Sally 52
Beaumont, Cyril 94, 132
Beebe, Maurice 73n24
Bell, Clive 17, 40, 68
   Art 33
Benjamin, Walter
   'The Task of the Translator' 123, 127
Bennett, Arnold 20
Berkeley Hotel, London 3
Bhabha, Homi 98–9
Bid Me to Live (H.D.) 1, 5, 7–8, 13, 11, 25, 45, 47, 49, 56, 59–65, 66, 70, 71, 76, 79, 95, 97, 102, 143
   Bloomsbury setting 47, 70
   characters
      Bella 59, 95, 97
      Cyril Vane 60
      Elsa 62
      Julia Ashton 48, 59, 60, 62, 63, 68, 97, 102
      Rafe Ashton 59, 63, 64, 95, 97, 101
      Rico 61, 62, 64, 101, 102
   collaboration with Lawrence, Aldington and Cournos 61
   compared with works of Lawrence 143
   critique of *Aaron's Rod*, *Death of a Hero* and *Miranda Masters* 61
   and 'Eurydice' 101
   intertextuality 62
   rewriting as feminist revision 61
   wartime London, images of 79
biofiction 3, 18, 19, 22
   see also autofiction
biography 3, 8, 72n19, 97, 101, 104, 114, 133n9, 142, 146, 146n4
   'satirical portrait-biographies' 72n10
Birds, Beasts and Flowers (Lawrence) 11, 103

Blast (Vorticist journal) 10, 22, 41n1, 43n22
Blau DuPlessis, Rachel 101, 116, 134n21
Bleyl, Fritz 25
Bloch, Ernst 123
Bloomsbury/Bloomsbury Group 3, 18, 24, 29, 46, 53, 75
  aestheticians 33
  appearing in *Bid Me to Live* 47, 70
  appearing in *Miranda Masters* 70
  Significant Form doctrine 33
  see also H.D. (Hilda Doolittle); Mecklenburgh Square, Bloomsbury; Morrell, Lady Ottoline
BML see Bid Me to Live (*BML*), Zilboorg
Boldrini, Lucia 14n13
Bollus, Christopher 64
'The Bombardment' (Lowell) 10, 82
Bomberg, David 28, 43n22
Boulton, James T. *see Late Essays and Articles* (*LEA*), ed. Boulton; *Letters of D.H. Lawrence. Volume I, September 1901–May 1913* (*L1*), ed. Boulton; *Letters of D.H. Lawrence. Volume V, March 1924–March 1927* (*L5*), ed. Boulton and Vasey; *Letters of D.H. Lawrence. Volume VI, March 1927–November 1928* (*L6*), ed. Boulton, Boulton and Lacy; *Letters of D.H. Lawrence. Volume VIII, Previously Uncollected Letters and General Index* (*L8*), ed. Boulton
Boulton, Margaret *see Letters of D.H. Lawrence. Volume VI, March 1927–November 1928* (*L6*), ed. Boulton, Boulton and Lacy
Breasted, Frances Hart 121
Brooke, Rupert 90
Brooker, Peter 26, 69
  Bohemia in London 14n17
Browning, Robert 79
Bubb, Reverend Charles C. 117
Bullen, J.B. 32, 43n28
Burke, Joan A. 145
Burnet, John
  Early Greek Philosophy 80
Burrows, Louie 120, 121, 122

Café Royal, London 22, 30, 38, 42n5
Caffe Morgano, Capri 50
The Cambridge Biography of D.H. Lawrence (Kinkead-Weekes) 18
Cambridge Companion to Modernist Poetry 14n7
Cambridge Companion to the Poetry of the First World War 13n2
Cannan, Gilbert 3, 6, 9, 22, 24, 26, 40
  Cholesbury circle 5, 35
  works of
    Mendel: A Story of Youth 5, 25, 38, 39, 73n24
    Miles Dixon 23
    Peter Homunculus 37
    Windmills: A Book of Fables 35, 36
Cannan, Mary 22, 24, 64
canonical war poetry 128
'Captive' (Aldington) 90, 106n19
Carco, Francis 24
Carr, Helen 76, 80
Carrington, Dora 24, 29–30, 38, 44n42
Carswell, Catherine 6, 18, 51
Chambers, Jessie 141
Channing, Minnie Lucy ('Puma'), later Heseltine 6
Chesham, Buckinghamshire 22
Cholesbury Mill, Buckinghamshire 24, 26, 37
  as a Greater London Vortex 22
Choruses from Iphigeneia in Aulis (H.D.) 109, 132
Churchill, Winston 29, 76
civilian poetry 128
Cole, Sarah 82–3
Collecott, Diana 48, 101
Collected Poems 1912–1944 (*CPHD*), ed. Martz 11–13, 96–8, 100, 101, 104, 110, 112–16, 144–6
Collected Poems (Aldington) 90
Collected Poems (H.D.) 101
Collected Poems (Lawrence) 120
combatant literature 2
Complete Poems of D.H. Lawrence (1964) 121
Complete Poems of Richard Aldington (*CPRA*), Aldington 14n9, 78, 86–95, 100, 114, 117–19
Cournos, John 3, 4, 7, 14n19, 45, 75
  Babel 9, 48, 51, 65, 66, 68–9, 73n26
  collaboration with H.D. 61, 65, 96

'The Death of Futurism' 100, 101
and Imagism 68
The Mask 9, 48, 70
Miranda Masters see Miranda Masters (Cournos)
as a prose poet 119
The Wall 9
Cowley, Abraham 68
CPHD see Collected Poems 1912–1944 (CPHD), ed. Martz
CPRA see Complete Poems of Richard Aldington (CPRA), Aldington
Craig, Gordon 50
Cram, David 121, 130
'Craving for Spring' (Lawrence) 78
Crawford, Fred 47, 59
The Criterion 92
Cubism 21
culture, utopian theory 123
Cunard, Nancy 72n10
Currie, John 38
Cusk, Rachel 13
  Outline 141
  Second Place 39, 139, 140, 142

d'Adelswärd-Fersen, Count Jacques 51
Dante Alighieri
  Inferno 79, 84, 91
  Paradiso 98
Das, Santanu 14n7, 129
'Daughter of Zeus' (Aldington) 100, 101
David Eder Farm, Kent 49, 71n2
de Beauvoir, Simone 103
Death of a Hero (*DH*), Aldington 1, 2, 7–9, 46, 48, 56–60, 63, 71n1, 85–6, 90, 94, 119, 137n53
  characters
    Comrade Bobbe 57
    Elizabeth Paston 58, 63, 72n10
    Evans 94
    Fanny Welford 58–9, 72n10
    George Winterbourne 58, 59, 63, 94, 119
    Mark Rampion 57
    Shobbe 57
    Tubbe 57
    unnamed narrator 57, 58, 59, 86, 88
  compared with *Aaron's Rod* 57–8
  completion (1928) 56

'drama of the double' 58
introduction to 1950 Penguin edition 56
tragedy born from satire, as 58
trilogy with *Aaron's Rod* and *Bid Me to Live* 60
Defence of the Realm Act 4
Delany, Paul 48, 83
Depero, Fortunato 50
DH see Death of a Hero (*DH*), Aldington
Diaghilev, Sergei 22, 23
The Dial 12, 52, 119
dialect ballads 125
Die Brücke group 25
Dillon, Sarah 61
  The Palimpsest 72n11
'Discouragement' (Aldington) 93
Dobrée, Valentine 72n10
Doolittle, Hilda (H.D.) *see* H.D. (Hilda Doolittle)
Dorset Trio (H.D.) 96–7, 113, 115
  see also 'Amaranth' poems (H.D.); 'Envy' (H.D.); 'Eros' (H.D.)
Douglas, Norman 46, 50
  Florentine café-society clique 55
  Looking Back: An Autobiographical Excursion 54
  Siren Land 51
  South Wind 50–1
du Bellay, Joachim 117, 118, 119, 134n27
  'Jeux Rustiques' 135n31
Duncan, Robert 144

Eatough, Matt
  translational aesthetic 11
'Ecce Homo' (Lawrence) 81, 82–3, 84, 86–7
écriture feminine 142
Eder, David 49
The Egoist (magazine) 10, 77, 80, 83, 88, 98, 100, 101, 109
  Aldington as literary editor 11, 99
Egyptian Labour Corps 124
Eliot, T.S. 57, 88
  Four Quartets 2
  'The Love Song of J. Alfred Prufrock' 90, 91
  'Tradition and the Individual Talent' 80
  '*Ulysses*, Order, and Myth' 91, 106n24
  The Waste Land 78, 79, 91, 92

'Eloi, Eloi, lama sabachthani?' (Lawrence) 9, 10, 76–7, 83–6, 132
'England, My England' (Lawrence) 14n15
English Review 50
'Envy' (H.D.) 96–8, 107n30, 113
'Epigram' (H.D.) 87
Epstein, Jacob 31, 68
   Female Figure in Flenite 66, 67*f*
'Eros' (H.D.) 96–8, 107n30, 113, 115
'Errinyes' (Lawrence) 76–7, 84, 85, 105n12
ethnocentrism 125
'Eumenides' (Aldington) 86, 87
Euripides
   Choruses from the Iphigeneia in Aulis 12
   Orestes 83
'Eurydice' (H.D.) 11, 97–104, 107n39, 107n42, 145
   and *Bid Me to Live* 101
   in *The Egoist* 99
   manifesto-poem 98
   Orpheus-and-Eurydice leitmotif from 'Amaranth' and 'Eros' 97, 99, 102
   reverse myth in 102
Experiments in Life-Writing (Boldrini and Novak) 14n13
expressionism
   architectural 25
   'creaturely' 26
   Northern 25–6

Fallas, Carl 4, 96
Fallas, Florence ('Flo') 4, 96, 97, 99
Farmer, David *see Women in Love* (*WL*), ed. Farmer, Worthen and Vasey
'The Faun Captive' (Aldington) 90, 106n19, 119
Feigel, Lara 13, 140
   Look! We Have Come Through! Living with Lawrence 139
Feininger, Lyonel 25
fellaheen songs 121, 122, 126, 129, 130, 132, 136n39
Felski, Rita 99
feminism 11, 61, 103, 139
Fergusson, J.D. 23
Fernihough, Anne 88, 123, 127
Ferri, Jessica 142
Firchow, Peter 47, 72n18

First Post-Impressionist Exhibition 19
First 'Woman in Love' (*FWL*), ed. Worthen and Vasey 3, 18
First World War 6, 10
   consequences 77
   effect on H.D. 77
   Gertler's opposition to 28–9
   Great War modernists 2
   killing fields of Flanders 89
   literature studies 2
   poetry 13
   Second Battle of Ypres 89
   soldier-poetry 84, 119
   war art 86
   war poetry 14n7, 86
   Women in Love unpublishable during 18, 49
   see also Great War modernism; Second World War; trench verse
Fletcher, John Gould 10
Flint, F. S. 10, 80, 100, 105n1
'flower poems' (H.D.) 11, 77, 78, 95, 97, 112
folk songs 23, 130
   see also fellaheen songs
Ford Madox Ford 57
   The Good Soldier 17
   Parade's End 8, 56
'Fragment' poems (H.D.) 12, 113, 114
Frayn, Andrew 13n2, 118
Frazer, J.G.
   The Golden Bough 78
   Totemism and Exogamy 78
Freer, Scott 78
Freud, Sigmund 63, 98
Friedman, Susan Stanford 60, 62, 77, 101
   'Who Buried H.D.?' 143
Froula, Christine 129
Fry, Roger 19, 33
Fussell, Paul 84, 90, 118
   The Great War and Modern Memory 2, 128
Futurism 20, 21, 50
FWL see First 'Woman in Love' (*FWL*), ed. Worthen and Vasey

Garnett, Edward 20
Gaskell, Elizabeth
   Cranford 52

Gates, Norman T. 100
Gaudier-Brzeska, Henri 21, 106n23, 129
gender and poetry 130
gender inequality 131–2
Genesis, book of 26
Genette, Gérard 58, 66
    Palimpsests 61
Gertler, Mark 5–6, 22–4, 27, 30, 43n25, 73n24, 89
    The Creation of Eve painting 26, 27f, 34
        Blake-like quality 27
        hostile reception of 27–8
    Gilbert Cannan at his Mill portrait 36, 37f, 38
    and Lawrence 26–33
    The Merry-Go-Round painting 26, 30, 89
        cyclical rotation of 29–30
        inspiration for 28
        seen as a war machine 29
        on 'whirligig of London' 29, 31, 38
        opposition to war 28–9
Gibson, Wilfred
    'The Going' 90
Goldman, Jane 89
Goodman, Nelson
    Ways of Worldmaking 21
Gray, Cecil 11, 45, 62, 73n24, 75, 114, 142
    correspondence with Lawrence 49, 77–8, 86, 103, 104
    father of H.D's daughter 5, 8
    liaison with H.D. 4–5, 60, 64, 104
    views on male superiority 103, 107n41
    womanizing tendencies 5, 60, 103
Great War *see* First World War
Great War modernism 2, 13n1, 146
    global 13
    'literary work' 142
    and translation 130
    see also Aldington, Richard; Eliot, T.S.; First World War; H.D. (Hilda Doolittle); Lawrence, D.H.; Pound, Ezra
Greek Anthology (Meleager) 12, 111, 112, 115, 116
Greek tragedies 58
Greenspan, Ezra *see Studies in Classic American Literature* (*SCAL*), ed. Greenspan, Vasey and Worthen

Gropius, Walter 25, 31
group studies 13n1
Guest, Stephen 144
Guillaume, Paul 67

Harding, Jason 113
Harrison, Andrew 20, 35
Harrison, Jane 7
Hart, Matthew 125
H.D. (Hilda Doolittle) 3, 5, 10
    autofiction 8, 13
    at Bloomsbury *see* at Mecklenburgh Square *below*
    break-up of marriage to Aldington 1, 4, 47, 114
    collaboration with Cournos 60, 65, 70, 96
    in Cornwall 4–5, 104
    D.H. and Frieda Lawrence staying with 4, 7, 45, 77
    in Devon 4
    engagement to Ezra Pound 4
    experimental life-writing 70
    feminist turn in works 11
    'flower poems' 11, 77, 78, 95, 97, 112
    'Fragment' poems 12, 113, 114
    giving sanctuary to Lawrence and Frieda 4
    as a Great War modernist 2
    Imagism, prewar figurehead for 87, 105n7
    liaison with Cecil Gray 4–5, 60
    at Mecklenburgh Square, Bloomsbury 4, 6, 7, 45
    mother of Perdita 5, 65, 104, 114
    personality theory 70
    postwar poetry 114
    stillborn daughter 4, 59
    translations by 11, 12, 109, 112, 114, 133n9, 134n26
    works of
        'Amaranth' poems 96–8, 99, 102, 113, 114
        Asphodel 6
        Bid Me to Live see Bid Me to Live (H.D.)
        Choruses from Iphigeneia in Aulis 109, 132
        Collected Poems 101
        Dorset Trio (1916) 96–7, 113, 115

'Envy' 96–8, 107n30, 113
'Epigram' 87
'Eros' 96–8, 107n30, 113, 115
'Eurydice' see 'Eurydice' (H.D.)
Heliodora 97, 114
'Hermes of the Ways' 87
Magic Mirror 144
'Orchard' 104
'Oread' 9–10
Palimpsest 60, 61
Pilate's Wife 144
'The Poet' 144
'Priapus' 87
Sea Garden 96, 97
Tribute to Freud 5
Trilogy 2, 13, 145–6
Heckel, Erich 25
Heliodora (H.D.) 114
Hellenism 92, 93
Hemingway, Ernest 119
Henderson, Alice Corbin 81–2, 105n4
'Hermes of the Ways' (H.D.) 87
Herrick, Robert
   'To Anthea' 63
Heseltine, Philip 6, 18, 20, 30, 41, 41n3, 42n5, 65–6, 68, 73n23, 73n24, 75
Heydt, Erich 63
Hickman, Miranda 96
Homer
   Odyssey 50
Hopkin, Willie 34
Hulme, T.E. 66, 67–8, 88, 106n23
Huxley, Aldous 64
   Point Counter Point 39, 56–7
Hynes, Samuel 92
hypertextuality 61, 66
hypotext 61

Images of Desire (Aldington) 87, 106n25
Images of War (Aldington) 87, 91–5, 100, 106n25, 118–19, 132, 134n26
   'Epilogue' 91
   'Proem' 92–3, 94
   prose poetry 93
   trench verse 10
Imagist Anthology 1930 87
Imagist school of poetry 9–11, 12, 68, 75–107
   Aldington as original Imagist 87
   Amygism (wartime Imagism) 76, 77

anthologies 3, 4, 10, 11, 15n19, 87, 99, 105n3, 107n40
compression criterion 10, 83, 94
cooperative venture 76
early Imagism, of Aldington and H.D. 9–10, 77
The Egoist, Imagist issues 83
experimentalism 95–6
H.D. prewar figurehead for 87, 105n7
and Lawrence 77
and Lowell 11, 76, 99
networks 80
post-Poundian Imagists 76, 87
Poundian 76, 88
prewar phase 87
print circuits 9
protocols 11
School of Images 87, 88, 105n15, 111
see also Pound, Ezra
imperialism 126–7
'In the Library' (Aldington) 118
'In the Tube' (Aldington) 87, 88, 89
industrialism 126–7
intertextuality 62, 66
Introductions and Reviews (*IR*), ed. Reeve and Worthen 50
IR see Introductions and Reviews (*IR*), ed. Reeve and Worthen

Jaffe, Else 28
James, Henry 40, 52
   The Portrait of a Lady 71n6
James, Jamie 50
Jansohn, Christa *see Woman Who Rose Away and Other Stories* (*WWRA*), ed. Mehl and Jansohn
Jazz Age 56
Jenner, Kitty Lee
   Christian Symbolism 34

K see Kangaroo (*K*), ed. Steele
Kalnins, Mara *see Aaron's Rod* (*AR*), ed. Mara Kalnins
Kangaroo (Lawrence) 46, 55, 57, 75, 86, 104, 126
Kaplan, Sydney Janet 62
Kelly, Alice 62, 72n15, 119
Kennedy, Jackie 141
Kenner, Hugh
   The Pound Era 129

Kinkead-Weekes, Mark 18–19, 46, 64
    see also *The Rainbow* (*R*), ed. Kinkead-Weekes
Kipling, Rudyard 125
Kirchner, Ernst 25
Koteliansky, S.S. ('Kot') 5, 24, 34, 39
Krenkow, Fritz 121

L1 see Letters of D.H. Lawrence, Volume I, September 1901–May 1913 (L1), ed. Boulton
L2 see Letters of D.H. Lawrence. Volume II, June 1913–October 1916 (L2), ed. Zytaruk and Boulton
L3 see Letters of D.H. Lawrence, Volume III, October 1916–June 1921 (L3), ed. Boulton and Robertson
L4 see Letters of D.H. Lawrence. Volume IV, June 1921–March 1924 (L4), ed. Roberts, Boulton and Mansfield
L5 see Letters of D.H. Lawrence. Volume V, March 1924–March 1927 (L5), ed. Boulton and Vasey
L6 see Letters of D.H. Lawrence. Volume VI, March 1927–November 1928 (L6), ed. Boulton, Boulton and Lacy
L8 see Letters of D.H. Lawrence. Volume VIII, Previously Uncollected Letters and General Index (L8), ed. Boulton
Lacy, Gerald M. *see Letters of D.H. Lawrence. Volume VI, March 1927–November 1928 (L6)*, ed. Boulton, Boulton and Lacy
Lady Chatterley's Lover (Lawrence) 7, 43n35, 141, 143
Laird, Holly A. 81
Landor, Walter Savage 135n34
Last Poems (Lawrence) 79
Late Essays and Articles (LEA), ed. Boulton 33
Latham, Sean, *The Art of Scandal* 7, 19, 63–4
Lawrence, D.H. 10, 23, 24, 38–9, 40, 41, 47
    antagonism to war and protests against it 82
    in Capri 50–1
    in Chesham, Buckinghamshire 22
    collaboration with H.D. 61
    correspondence with Gertler 30, 31
    dialect ballads 125
    disaffection with Bloomsbury Group 46
    expulsion from Cornwall 4, 45, 75
    first meeting with H.D. and Aldington 75–6
    and Gertler 26–33
    as a Great War modernist 2
    and Imagism 76–7
    introduction to H.D. and Aldington (1914) 3
    on journalism 5
    'Leadership' novels 55
    leaving Capri 51
    marriage to Frieda (1914) 4
    at Mecklenburgh Square 4, 7, 45
    and modernism 26
    objections to war literature 128
    perceived as serious life writer 19
    phoenix emblem 34, 43n34, 43n35, 48
    relationship with H.D. and Aldington 1
    satirical sketches of Mecklenburgh Square 56
    status as a modernist 2–3
    translation by 109, 110, 125, 126, 127, 131, 132, 136n38
    wartime verse translations 11
    white consciousness, critique of 127
    works of
        Aaron's Rod see Aaron's Rod (Lawrence)
        'All of Us' 12–13, 85, 109–10, 120–2, 124, 126–32, 135n36, 137n50, 137n54
        Amores 30
        Birds, Beasts and Flowers 11, 103
        Collected Poems 120
        'Craving for Spring' 78
        'Ecce Homo' 81, 82–3, 84, 86–7
        'Eloi, Eloi, lama sabachthani?' 9, 10, 76–7, 83–6, 132
        'England, My England' 14n15
        'Errinyes' 76–7, 84, 85, 105n12
        'Gipsy' 127
        'Gloire de Dijon' 72n22
        'The Grey Nurse' 131
        'Introduction to These Paintings' 33
        Kangaroo 46, 55, 57, 75, 86, 104, 126
        Lady Chatterley's Lover 7, 43n35, 141, 143

Last Poems 79
Look! We Have Come Through! 78, 81, 96, 106n27, 131, 142, 146
'The Man Who Died' 139, 144
'The Man Who Loved Islands' 52, 141
'Medlars and Sorb-Apples' 103, 104, 107n43
Memoir of Maurice Magnus 140, 142
The Plumed Serpent 46, 55
The Rainbow see The Rainbow (Lawrence)
'Resurrection' 9, 76–7, 78–81, 83, 85, 102
'The Sisters' 24
Studies in Classic American Literature 46
'The Turning Back' (*later* 'Errinyes') 84, 85
'Why the Novel Matters' 19
Women in Love see Women in Love (Lawrence)
Lawrence, Frieda (neé von Richthofen) 3, 4, 23, 24, 28, 38–9, 75
  in Capri 50
  in Chesham, Buckinghamshire 22
  expulsion from Cornwall 4, 45, 75
  first husband (Ernest Weekley) 60
  at Mecklenburgh Square 4, 7, 45
  in Sicily 50
League of Nations 35
'Lemures' (Aldington) 78, 87
Lessing, Doris 140
Letters of D.H. Lawrence. Volume I, September 1901–May 1913 (*L1*), ed. Boulton 122, 127, 136n38
Letters of D.H. Lawrence. Volume II, June 1913–October 1916 (*L2*), ed. Zytaruk and Boulton 5, 10, 20, 25, 29–31, 33–5, 37, 41, 43n33, 49, 73n23, 78, 82, 83, 85, 132, 136n45
Letters of D.H. Lawrence, Volume III, October 1916–June 1921 (*L3*), ed. Boulton and Robertson 6, 13, 31, 39, 43n26, 43n30, 45, 49, 51, 52, 54, 77–8, 86, 96, 103, 104, 105n8, 109, 110, 128, 129, 132
Letters of D.H. Lawrence. Volume IV, June 1921–March 1924 (*L4*), ed. Roberts, Boulton and Mansfield 46, 64

Letters of D.H. Lawrence. Volume V, March 1924–March 1927 (*L5*), ed. Boulton and Vasey 42n6, 71n3
Letters of D.H. Lawrence. Volume VI, March 1927–November 1928 (*L6*), ed. Boulton, Boulton and Lacy 42n6, 52, 53
Letters of D.H. Lawrence. Volume VIII, Previously Uncollected Letters and General Index (*L8*), ed. Boulton 11, 80, 102, 107n39, 132
'Letters to Unknown Women' (Aldington) 119
Lewis, Wyndham 9, 10, 22, 100
  A Canadian Gun Pit (painting) 125
  Design for a Programme Cover – Kermesse 31–2, 38, 43n27
  Tarr 17, 19
life-writing 3
  modernist 5, 6
Look! We Have Come Through! (Lawrence) 78, 81, 96, 106n27, 131, 142, 146
Louÿs, Pierre
  The Songs of Bilitis 117
  The Love of Myrrhine and Konallis (Aldington) 12, 93, 94, 116–17
Lowell, Amy 3, 4, 9, 76, 93, 94
  correspondence with Aldington 56
  and Imagism 11, 76, 99
  prose poetry 134n29
  works of
    'The Bombardment' 10, 82
    Some Imagist Poets see Some Imagist Poets (Lowell)
    Tendencies in Modern American Poetry 95
LP1 see The Poems. Volume I. Poems (*LP1*), ed. Pollnitz
LP2 see The Poems. Volume II. Notes and Apparatus (*LP2*), ed. Pollnitz
LP3 see The Poems. Volume III. Uncollected Poems and Early Versions (*LP3*), ed. Pollnitz
Luhan, Mabel Dodge 140

McCabe, Susan 114
MacDiarmid, Hugh 125
MacDougall, Sarah 28, 43n25
McGann, Jerome 95, 99, 142
MacGreevy, Thomas 90, 91, 94

Mackenzie, Compton 23, 37, 40, 52, 71n5, 141
  Extraordinary Women 51
  Four Winds of Love 53
  The South Wind of Love 22, 36, 40, 50–1, 54
    character of Daniel Rayner based on Lawrence 53, 54
  Vestal Fire 51, 52
  The West Wind of Love 53
Mackenzie, Faith 51, 52–3
McLane, Maureen 8
MacLeod, Alison 13
  Tenderness 7, 139, 141
MacLeod, Arthur 20
Magic Mirror (H.D.) 144
Magnus, Maurice
  Memoirs of the Foreign Legion 50
'The Man Who Died' (Lawrence) 139, 144
'The Man Who Loved Islands' (Lawrence) 52, 141
Mann, David 139
Mansfield, Katherine 5, 21, 23, 24, 30, 41, 62
  'Brave Love' 24
  'Tales of a Courtyard' 23
Marcks, Gerhard 31
Marcus, Laura 19
Marinetti, F.T. 43n22, 51–2, 58
  'Manifesto tecnico' 20
  'masculomaniac' movement 100
Marsh, Edward 29
  Georgian Poetry 76
Martz, Louis L. 96, 144
  see also Collected Poems 1912–1944 (CPHD), ed. Martz
The Mask (Cournos) 9, 48, 70
Mechau, Frank 117
Mecklenburgh Square, Bloomsbury 1
  Aldington at 4
  H.D. at 4, 6, 7
  novels 3, 5–9, 13, 25, 45–73
    autobiofictional 'spider-web' 56, 62
    intertextuality 62
  as a radical address 6
  see also Bloomsbury/Bloomsbury Group
'Medlars and Sorb-Apples' (Lawrence) 103, 104, 107n43

Mehl, Dieter see *The Woman Who Rose Away and Other Stories (WWRA)*, ed. Mehl and Jansohn
Meleager of Gadara (Aldington) 116, 120
Memoir of Maurice Magnus (Lawrence) 140, 142
Millett, Kate 41n2, 139
  Sexual Politics 140
Milton, John
  Paradise Lost 98
Miranda Masters (Cournos) 1, 9, 25, 46–8, 65–71, 102–3, 119
  Bloomsbury rooms 70
  characters
    John Gombarov 9, 48, 65, 68–71
    Winifred Gwynne 48, 69
    Arnold Masters 48, 69, 70, 71
    Miranda Masters 48, 69
    Richard Ramsden 48
  satyr play 9, 48
  threading and weaving metaphors 70
Mitchell, W.J.T. 20
modernism 11, 68
  collective life of modernist experiment 26
  high 2, 26, 87, 130
  inter-arts, of the 1910s 17
  language of 2
  and Lawrence 26
  life-writing 5, 6
  Northern 25–6
  pre-war and postwar high 2, 92
  and translation 130, 133n1
    'age of translations' 129
  visual turn 19
  'World War II' 2
  see also Great War modernism
Moest, Josef
  Godiva figurine in *Women in Love* 32, 33
Monroe, Harriet 76, 80–1, 82, 105n4, 121
Moore, Alison 13
  Missing 141
  The Retreat 141
Moore, Harry T. 54
Morrell, Lady Ottoline 6, 17–18, 21, 24, 30, 34–5, 46, 63, 64, 66, 68, 73n25
  Bloomsbury *salonnière* 6, 17–18
  at Garsington Manor, Oxfordshire 22, 35
Morrell, Philip 41n3, 68

'munitionettes' (young women working in munitions families) 4
Munton, Alan 67
Murray, Gilbert 111
Murry, John Middleton 23, 24, 35, 41, 62
   Still Life 5, 25

Nash, John 113
Nash, Paul 94–5
Nehls, Edward 54
Nevinson, C.R.W. 28, 38, 43n22
The New Age avant-garde magazine 67, 88, 105n15, 147n10
New Modernist Studies 2
New Poems 127, 128
Nichols, Robert
   Ardours and Endurances 75, 84
Nin, Anaïs 102
Nisbet, Gideon
   Select Epigrams from the Greek Anthology 111, 115
Norris, Nanette 2, 3, 14n5
Novak, Julia 14n13

Olusoga, David 128
   The World's War: Forgotten Soldiers of Empire 124
Orage, A.R. 88, 91, 92
'Orchard' (H.D.) 104
'Oread' (H.D.) 9–10
Oresteia (Aeschylus) 58
Orientalism 122, 130
Ostriker, Alicia 98
Owen, Wilfred 128

Palazzo Ferraro, Capri 44n44, 50, 51
Parker, Sarah 114
parody 66
pastiche 66
Pater, Walter 117–19, 135n31
'Penultimate Poetry' (Aldington) 88
Peppis, Paul 29
Persephone poems 77, 78, 96, 104
Picasso, Pablo
   Portrait of Gertrude Stein 21
Pilate's Wife (H.D.) 144
Pinker, J.B. 41n3, 128
Pinkney, Tony 25–6
plagiarism 66
The Plumed Serpent (Lawrence) 46, 55

poem-letters 84
The Poems. Volume I. Poems (*LP1*), ed. Pollnitz 9, 57, 81, 96, 103, 104, 124–7, 131, 132, 135n35, 136n41, 137n54
The Poems. Volume II. Notes and Apparatus (*LP2*), ed. Pollnitz 121, 128, 132
The Poems. Volume III. Uncollected Poems and Early Versions (*LP3*), ed. Pollnitz 80, 81, 82, 84–7, 105n12
'The Poet' (H.D.) 144
Poetry (magazine) 9, 76–7, 79, 80–1, 87, 90
   'War Films' 121
   War Poems Prize Award 81, 83, 128
Poetry Review of America 99
Poets' Translation Series (PTS) 11–13, 109, 116, 117
Pollnitz, Christopher 81, 85, 121, 130
   'D.H. Lawrence as Verse Translator' 121
   see also The Poems. Volume I. Poems (*LP1*), ed. Pollnitz; *The Poems. Volume II. Notes and Apparatus* (*LP2*), ed. Pollnitz; *The Poems. Volume III. Uncollected Poems and Early Versions* (*LP3*), ed. Pollnitz
Polunin, Vladimir 22
Pondrom, Cynthia 99
Portrait of Mabel Dodge at the Villa Curonia (Stein) 21
Post-Impressionism 19
postwar high modernism 2
Pound, Ezra 2, 3–4, 10, 77, 81, 87, 133n4
   Cathay 128, 129, 130
   Des Imagistes 9, 10, 73n27, 75, 76, 93, 100, 105n2, 110, 133n4
   engagement to H.D. 4
   Homage to Sextus Propertius 128
   objections to war literature 128
   as *Poetry* magazine's 'Foreign Correspondent' 87
   School of Images 87, 88, 105n15, 111
   'In a Station of the Metro' 88
   'Three Cantos' 79, 106n23
   see also Imagist school of poetry
Power, Eileen 7
'Priapus' (H.D.) 87
'primitive' peoples 127

prose poetry 12, 14n19, 15n19, 93, 101, 116–18, 135n32
  'The Bombardment' (Lowell) 10, 82
  Cournos as a prose poet 119
  'Discouragement' (Aldington) 93
  'Eurydice' *see* 'Eurydice' (H.D.)
  French tradition 116
  and Landor 135n34
  'In the Library' 118
  of Lowell 134n29
  see also Aldington, Richard; *The Love of Myrrhine and Konallis* (Aldington)
pseudo-translation 12, 117

R see The Rainbow (*R*), ed. Kinkead-Weekes
The Rainbow (Lawrence) 25, 46, 88
  architectonics 25
  The Creation of Eve painting depicted in 26, 27f, 34
  generational narrative 5
  Gothic modernism 25
  Northern modernism 25–6
  prosecuted for obscenity 4
  revision of 5
  suppression of 49, 77, 140
  and *Women in Love* 17, 25
The Rainbow (*R*), ed. Kinkead-Weekes 25, 26, 34
Ramazani, Jahan 127, 130
'Rananim' (community of like-minded friends) 5, 34, 35, 49
Read, Herbert 92
'real-life' fiction 5
Reeve, N.H. 50
'Resentment' (Aldington) 89
'Resurrection' (Lawrence) 9, 76–7, 78–81, 83, 85, 102
Reverie: A Little Book of Poems for H.D. (Aldington) 101, 117
Reynolds, Stephen 3
Rhythm (modernist magazine) 23, 24, 37
Rice, Anne Estelle 23
Ridgway, Christopher 59
Roads to Glory (Aldington) 119
Robinson, Janice 8
  'The Sacrifice of Iphigeneia ' 133n9
romans à clef 7, 19, 51, 71
Romantics 130
Russell, Bertrand 34, 78

Sa'di
  Gulistān 130–1
Sadler, Sir Michael 23
Said, Edward 122, 123, 125
Sappho 11, 12, 69, 109, 111, 113–16, 119, 120, 133, 134n16
  mask of 97, 114
Saqqāra excavation 123
Sassoon, Siegfried 128
  Sherston trilogy 59
Saunders, Max 3, 6, 19
Sayers, Dorothy L. 7
SCAL see Studies in Classic American Literature (*SCAL*), ed. Greenspan, Vasey and Worthen
Schäfer, Heinrich 122
  Die Lieder Eines Ägyptischen Bauern (*Songs of an Egyptian Peasant*) 121, 124, 137n50
  'Gipsy' 121, 124, 126, 127, 137n50
Schaffner, Perdita (H.D.'s daughter) 5, 65, 104, 114
School of Images
Scott, Bonnie Kime
  The Gender of Modernism 14n8
Sea Garden (H.D.) 96, 97
Secker, Martin 22–3, 41n3, 43n35
Second World War 2, 13, 90, 128
  see also First World War
second-wave feminism 103, 139
Selkirk, Alexander 35
Shelley, Percy Bysshe 81
  'Ode to the West Wind' 79
'shell-shock' 56
Sherry, Vincent
  The Great War and the Language of Modernism 2
Shone, Richard 44n43
Shorter, Clement 91
The Signature (anti-war journal) 35
Sillars, Stuart 26–7
Slade School of Fine Art 28, 29, 38
Soft Answers (Aldington) 72n10
soldier-poetry 84, 119
Some Imagist Poets (Lowell) 4, 76, 78, 82, 83, 98, 101, 106n19, 106n27, 107n39, 114
  editorial oversight by H.D. 11
  see also Lowell, Amy
'Sorcery of Words' (Aldington) 117–19
Steele, Bruce *see Kangaroo* (*K*), ed. Steele

Stein, Gertrude 50
   'Pablo Picasso' 21
Stein, Leo 50
Stepping Heavenward: A Record (Aldington) 91
Stevens, Wallace 90–1
STH *see Study of Thomas Hardy and Other Essays* (*STH*), ed. Steele
Storer, Edward 109
   translation by 134n14
Strachey, Lytton 29, 30, 38
Study of Thomas Hardy and Other Essays (*STH*), ed. Steele 19, 53, 55, 123, 124
'Sunsets' (Aldington) 90, 106n19
Sword, Helen 98, 99, 101, 144
Synge, J.M. 125

tabloid journalism 5
Tedlock, E.W. 83
The Triangle (cottage near Chesham, Bucks) 22, 25, 34, 40
Tickner, Lisa 43n30
Torgovnick, Marianna 125, 128
'Tradition and the Individual Talent' (Eliot) 80
translation
   by Aldington 12, 109, 112, 113, 116, 120
   as asymmetrical communication 122–3
   classical 112
   English-language 127
   equivalence a contested subject for 125
   ethnocentrism 125
   faux translation 93, 116
   as 'flowering' 123
   free 122
   of German 121
   of Greek and Latin poetry and prose 111, 115, 116
   by H.D. 11, 12, 109, 112, 114, 133n9, 134n26
   as ideological 122
   and immediacy principle 128
   joint translations 117
   key task 127
   by Lawrence 109, 110, 125, 126, 127, 131, 132, 136n38
   between mediums 40
   mistranslation 110, 133n3
   and modernism 129, 130, 133n1
   modernist 'non-translation' 113

   of Murray 111
   Poets' Translation Series (PTS) 11–13, 109, 116, 117
   politics of 122
   process of 112, 123, 132
   prose 113, 116
   pseudo-translation 12, 117
   pure 122
   quasi-translations 110
   re-translation 113, 115, 124
   Schäfer's Lieder no. 68 137n50
   Schäfer's Lieder nos. 34 and 36 124
   scholars 125
   source and target text 122, 127
   by Storer 134n14
   translation theory 12–13, 110
   of translations 122
   and translocation 129
   utopian 123
   verse-translations 11, 12, 109, 120, 121
   of war poetry 129
   by Wharton 115
transtextuality 66, 79
'Trench Idyll' (Aldington) 94
Trench verse 10, 86, 94
Tribute to Freud (H.D.) 5
Trilogy (H.D.) 2, 13, 145–6
'The Turning Back,' later 'Errinyes' (Lawrence) 84, 85

Upward, Allen 93

Vasey, Lindeth *see The First 'Women in Love'* (*FWL*), ed. Worthen and Vasey; *Letters of D.H. Lawrence. Volume V, March 1924–March 1927* (*L5*), ed. Boulton and Vasey; *Women in Love* (*WL*), ed. Farmer, Worthen and Vasey
Venuti, Lawrence 122–3, 127
vernacular language 125
'verse revolutionaries' 4, 14n9
verse-translations 11, 12, 109, 120, 121
'A Village' (Aldington) 94, 118–19
von Richthofen, Frieda *see* Lawrence, Frieda (neé von Richthofen)
Vortex 10, 22, 29, 38
Vorticism 9, 10, 21, 22, 28, 29, 31, 32, 43n22

Wade, Francesca
   Square Haunting 6

Wadsworth, Edward
   War-Engine 29
The Wall (Cournos) 48
Walpole, Hugh 40
War and Love (Aldington) 14n12, 62, 89, 95, 106n25, 107n35
   Trench verse 10
war neurosis/trauma 55, 63
war poetry 13
   dominant definitions 129
   First World War 14n7
   postwar poetry 114
'war-time hysteria' 9, 28, 29, 69, 88
Weekley, Ernest 60
Whalan, Mark 80
Wharton, H.T. 112–13, 115, 133n10, 134n17
Whelpton, Vivien 14n2
white consciousness, Lawrence's critique of 127
Whitman, Walt
   Leaves of Grass 121
Wilde, Oscar 50, 67
Wilson, Frances 13, 14n10, 72n19
   Burning Man 18, 139, 140, 142, 146
WL see Women in Love (*WL*), ed. Farmer, Worthen and Vasey
Woman Who Rose Away and Other Stories (*WWRA*), ed. Mehl and Jansohn 52, 53, 71n5
Women in Love (Lawrence) 3, 13, 17, 20, 21, 23, 29–35, 63, 66, 69, 73n23, 73n24
   'art-speech' 31
   and *Babel* 66
   biofictionality 18, 19
   chapters
      'Death and Love' 30
      'Gudrun in the Pompadour' 30
      'Snow' 30
   characters
      Rupert Birkin 18, 30, 33–5, 46, 64, 83
      Gudrun Brangwen 21
      Ursula Brangwen 23, 32
      Gudrun Brangwen 23, 33
      Gerald Crich 32, 46, 66, 83
      Minette Darrington 6

      Julius Halliday 6, 18, 30, 65–6, 68
      Loerke 24, 30, 31, 32, 33, 38, 43n26, 43n28
      Hermione Roddice 17, 35, 41n3, 63–4, 66, 68
   English edition 25
   'fetish' episode 68
   granite frieze, Loerke's design for 30, 31, 32, 38, 43n28, 43n30
   H.D. on 6
   London chapters 38
   The Merry-Go-Round painting depicted in 26, 28
   mythico-symbolic form 46
   origins of 5
   premodern Egypt evoked in 130
   and *The Rainbow* 17, 25
   triangular relationships 30
   unpublishable during the First World War 18, 49
   visual and verbal arts 6
Woolf, Virginia 2, 7, 17–18, 20, 49, 65, 72n22, 98
   'Character in Fiction' 19
   A Room of One's Own 8
word paintings 21, 42n6, 46, 132
Worthen, John *see The First 'Woman in Love'* (*FWL*), ed. Worthen and Vasey; *Women in Love* (*WL*), ed. Farmer, Worthen and Vasey
WWRA see Woman Who Rose Away and Other Stories (*WWRA*), ed. Mehl and Jansohn

Yao, Steven 129, 130
Yeats, W.B. 58, 132
   The Wind Among the Reeds 90
Yorke, Dorothy ('Arabella') 46, 48, 49, 58, 59, 69, 72n10, 75, 95, 106n25
   affair with Richard Aldington 4, 9, 45, 63
   fiancé of Cournos 4, 45

Zamzam well, Masjid al-Haram 126
Zilboorg, Caroline 11, 120
   see also Bid Me to Live (*BML*), Zilboorg

www.ingramcontent.com/pod-product-compliance
Lightning Source LLC
Chambersburg PA
CBHW052121300426
44116CB00010B/1755